PATTERN GRAMMAR

SCL

Studies in Corpus Linguistics

Studies in Corpus Linguistics aims to provide insights into the way a corpus can be used, the type of findings that can be obtained, the possible applications of these findings as well as the theoretical changes that corpus work can bring into linguistics and language engineering. The main concern of SCL is to present findings based on, or related to, the cumulative effect of naturally occuring language and on the interpretation of frequency and distributional data.

Volume 4

Susan Hunston and Gill Francis

Pattern Grammar
A corpus-driven approach to the lexical grammar of English

Pattern Grammar

A corpus-driven approach
to the lexical grammar of English

SUSAN HUNSTON
GILL FRANCIS
The University of Birmingham

JOHN BENJAMINS PUBLISHING COMPANY
AMSTERDAM / PHILADELPHIA

The paper used in this publication meets the minimum requirements of
the American National Standard for Information Sciences – Permanence
of Paper for Printed Library Materials, ANSI z39.48-1984.

Cover design: Françoise Berserik
Cover illustration from original painting *Random Order*
by Lorenzo Pezzatini, Florence, 1996.

Library of Congress Cataloging-in-Publication Data

Hunston, Susan, 1953-
Pattern Grammar : A corpus-driven approach to the lexical grammar of English / Susan
    Hunston and Gill Francis.
p. cm. (Studies in Corpus Linguistics, ISSN 1388-0373 ; v. 4)
Includes bibliographical references and index.
1. English language--Grammar, Generative. 2. English language--Discourse analysis.
    I. Francis, Gill. II. Title. III. Series.
PE1106.H453   1999
425--dc21   99-043483
ISBN 978 90 272 2273 2 (EUR) / 978 1 55619 398 9 (US) (Hb ; alk. paper)
ISBN 978 90 272 2274 9 (EUR) / 978 1 55619 399 6 (US) (Pb ; alk. paper)
ISBN 978 90 272 9889 8 (Eb)

John Benjamins Publishing Co. · P.O. Box 36224 · 1020 ME Amsterdam · The Netherlands
John Benjamins North America · P.O. Box 27519 · Philadelphia PA 19118-0519 · USA

For Sam and Vivek

and for Elliott, Laura, Matthew and Toby

Table of Contents

Acknowledgements

Much of the research for this book was undertaken as part of the project to publish the two 'pattern grammars': Collins COBUILD Grammar Patterns 1: Verbs; and Collins COBUILD Grammar Patterns 2: Nouns and Adjectives. The authors wish to acknowledge the outstanding contribution of Elizabeth Manning, co-author of those books, and of Professor John Sinclair, their instigator. Corpus examples in this book are taken from the Bank of English. The authors would like to thank HarperCollins publishers and The University of Birmingham for permission to use and quote from this corpus.

CHAPTER 1

A Short History of Patterns

1.1 About this book

This book is about the patterns that are associated with particular lexical items and that are observable from investigation of an electronically-stored corpus of written and spoken texts. The concept can be illustrated by this short extract from an article written by a lecturer in Philosophy on the subject of how Philosophy should be taught:

(1)   *[1] Philosophy is different from many other disciplines [2] in that learning about it is as much a matter of developing skills (in reasoning and argument) as it is a matter of learning a body of information. [3] In this sense there are no definitive 'answers' to many philosophical problems: [4] becoming a philosopher is a matter of becoming able to reason coherently and relevantly about philosophical issues. [5] Consequently, valuable contact time with lecturers is best spent actually 'doing philosophy', [6] and that means actively thinking and talking about it.*

There are several aspects of the grammar of this extract that a linguist may wish to draw attention to. For example, clauses 3, 5 and 6 each begin with something that summarises or 'encapsulates' (Sinclair 1995) the preceding clause or clauses: *In this sense; Consequently; that*, and that the grammar of each clause is therefore heavily dependent on the organisation of meaning in the text as a whole. Alternatively, we might make the observation that many of the processes indicated by this extract — learning about philosophy, becoming a philosopher, students interacting with lecturers — are expressed in the text as nouns (the Subjects of clauses) rather than as verbs, and that the relation of the grammar to the world is therefore metaphoric rather than congruent (Halliday 1994).

  The aspect of the extract that this book focuses on, however, is the interaction between the particular lexical items in it and the grammatical patterns that they form a part of. A clear example is the noun *matter*, which appears three times in the extract. Each time it follows the indefinite article *a* and is followed by *of* and a clause beginning with an '-ing' form: *a matter of developing skills; a matter of learning a body of information; a matter of becoming able to reason coherently and relevantly about philosophical issues.* It is clear that there is little point in treating *matter*, in the sense in which it is used here, as a single lexical item that can be slotted into a general grammar of English. Rather, the word comes, as it were, with its attendant phraseology, which in this case consists of '*a ___ of* -ing'. This phraseology is the grammar pattern belonging to the word *matter*.

The noun *matter* is far from unusual in having particular patterns or phraseologies associated with it. All words, in fact, can be described in this way. Let us take the verbs in the extract above:

[1]	is	different from many other disciplines
[2]	is	… a matter of…
[3]	are	no definitive answers…
[4]	is	a matter of…
[5]	is spent	actually doing philosophy
[6]	means	actively thinking and talking about it

From this we may note that the verb *to be* is followed by a noun group (*a matter of, no definitive answers*) or by an adjective group (*different from...*); the passive verb *be spent* is followed by an '-ing' clause; as is the verb *to mean*. Investigation of a corpus will tell us whether these uses are typical or not. For example, here are ten concordance lines illustrating a typical use of *be spent*:

```
of this man whose early career was spent teaching at Harvard Business
evening many valuable minutes were spent recounting the non-story of the
is hard to find and empty days are spent wandering the streets or riding
much of her time at the college is spent sifting through paperwork, Carolin
job properly. 'Much of my time is spent making copious notes on what actio
iles of border. Most of the day is spent riding along the riverbank. This
out, son — a third of your life is spent sleeping, a third in daily
early ancestors' waking lives was spent chasing or being chased by various
Much of the next 12 months will be spent celebrating or decrying the Spanis
nd the rest of Bradford's life was spent restoring it. He planted well over
```

In each case, the verb is followed by an '-ing' clause, and is preceded by a noun group indicating a period of time.

A grammatical description of the verbs in this extract, then, needs to take into account their complementation patterns, that is, the kind of group or clause that may follow them, just as a description of *matter* needs to take into account its phraseology. The same could be said for the adjectives in the extract (*different from, able to*) — in fact, all words can be described in terms of their patterns. Patterns can be observed, intuitively, in a single text. This intuition is based on our previous experience of language: we know that we say *a matter of learning a body of information* rather than *the matter of learning a body of information* and that, therefore, the article *a* is important to the pattern associated with *matter*. Intuition is not always a reliable guide, however, and it is advantageous to have a corpus to reveal what is typical patterning and what is unusual. The corpus is a concrete replacement for the rather vague 'previous experience of language'.

Briefly, then, a pattern is a phraseology frequently associated with (a sense of) a word, particularly in terms of the prepositions, groups, and clauses that follow the word. Patterns and lexis are mutually dependent, in that each pattern occurs with a restricted set of lexical items, and each lexical item occurs with a restricted set of patterns. In addition, patterns are closely associated with meaning, firstly because in many cases different senses of words are distinguished by their typical occurrence in different patterns; and secondly because words which share a given pattern tend also to share an aspect of meaning. The purpose of this book is to describe patterns and their association with meaning in more detail, and to discuss some of the theoretical issues arising out of this approach to grammar.

Chapter 1 sets the work in context, starting with the work by Hornby on patterns and usage and the growing interest in 'fixed phrases' by both lexicographers and language teachers. The immediate inspirations for corpus-driven grammar — Sinclair (1991) and Francis (1993) — are then discussed. In Chapters 2 and 3 we discuss the concept of 'pattern' in detail, and in Chapters 4 and 5 we give several examples of the association between pattern and meaning.

The second part of the book discusses various issues that arise in relation to a pattern-based approach to grammar. Chapter 6 takes a theoretical perspective and considers the relationship between patterns and the traditional structural analysis of clauses. Another comparison between patterns and traditional grammar is found in Chapter 7, which considers the notion of 'word class' in the light of our work on patterns. Chapter 8 takes the work in yet another direction by applying patterns to the analysis of running text. In Chapter 9 we consider some of the implications of this work for theories of grammar and for language teaching.

1.2 Hornby: A Guide to Patterns and Usage in English

1.2.1 *Introduction*

The closest forerunner (in concept, though not in time) of the work to be described in this book is Hornby's *A Guide to Patterns and Usage in English*, published in 1954. In the preface to this book, Hornby sets out his agenda: to give practical guidance to the language learner on usage rather than to expound analysis:

Analysis is helpful, but the learner is, or should be, more concerned with sentence-building. For this he needs to know the patterns of English sentences and to be told which words enter into which patterns. (Hornby 1954: v)

He points out that analogy is not an infallible guide to sentence patterns, especially with regard to verbs:

[The learner] may suppose that because he has heard and seen 'I intend (want, propose) to come', he may say or write 'I suggest to come', that because he has heard or seen 'Please tell me the meaning', 'Please show me the way', he can say or write 'Please explain me this sentence'. (Hornby 1954: v)

Hornby's book is not restricted to verbs, however, and he advocates learning pattern along with meaning for nouns and adjectives as well: "When [the learner] learns the meanings of the adjective *anxious*, he should also learn its patterns: 'anxious about his son's health', 'anxious for news', 'anxious (= eager) to start'." (Hornby 1954: vi).

Although he appears to make a sharp distinction between pattern and meaning — "A knowledge of how to put words together is as important as, perhaps more important than, a knowledge of their meanings" (Hornby 1954: v) — the description of *anxious* quoted above implicitly links the two.

The bulk of *A Guide to Patterns and Usage in English* is devoted to the description of 25 verb patterns, 4 noun patterns and 3 adjective patterns, as well as sections on adverbs, 'time and tense', indefinite pronouns and determinatives. A long final section details the way that various concepts can be expressed. The approach to grammar detailed in the book also informed the first three editions of the *Oxford Advanced Learner's Dictionary* (1948, 1963, 1974).

1.2.2   *Verb patterns*

Hornby's radical attention to usage rather than to analysis — to encoding rather than to decoding — leads him to describe pattern rather than structure. He does distinguish between transitive and intransitive verbs, and comments on which part(s) of the pattern constitute(s) the Object, but makes no further attempt at analysis. The headings to his tables, therefore, indicate the pattern (e.g. *Subject + Verb + to-infinitive*) rather than the elements of structure. In some cases, however, he distinguishes between examples of a single pattern that have different structures. For example, he comments with respect to *He likes his coffee strong* (verb followed by noun and adjective) that "[t]he combination of (pro)noun and adjective is the object of the verb" (Hornby 1954: 33). This is contrasted with *Can you push the door open*, which has the comment "...the adjective denotes a state or condition that results from the action indicated by the verb". Although an analysis of this is not given, the implication is that the noun and the adjective comprise separate elements of the clause rather than a single element. Hornby's sparse use of functional categories occasionally leads to some curious analyses. In examples of a verb followed by two noun groups, as in *They made Newton President of the Royal Society*, the second noun group is termed a 'predicative adjunct' rather than an Object Complement. However, Hornby's stated aim is to describe usage, not to enter into the complexities of analysis: our discussion in Chapter 6 indicates our reasons for sympathising with this aim.

Hornby's descriptions of patterns are not entirely based on surface realisation, however. Possible transformations also play a role. For example, we have seen above how he deals with the pattern 'verb+noun+adjective'. In that pattern, however, he considers only those examples where the alternative 'verb+noun+to-be+adjective' (as in *Most people suppose him (to be) innocent*) is not possible. Another pattern (Verb Pattern 4, Hornby 1954: 22–25) deals with examples such as *They proved him wrong* (verb+noun+adjective) and *I have always found Smith to be friendly* (verb+noun+to-be+adjective), as well as *They knew the man to have been a spy* (verb+noun+to-be+noun). The same pattern accounts for examples such as *We all consider it wrong to cheat in examinations*, which could be considered a transformation of *We all consider [the act of] cheating in examinations to be wrong*. Arguably, Hornby groups together these particular patterns because he identifies a common meaning in the verbs with these patterns (verbs such as *believe, consider, declare, feel, find, guess, know, judge, prove, suppose* and *think*) and wishes to deal with them together.

As noted above, Hornby advocates that learners be told "which words enter into which patterns", and he attempts to do that by giving lists of the most common verbs used in each pattern. For example, for Verb Pattern 3 (verb followed by a noun and a to-infinitive, as in *We can't allow them to do that* and *They warned me not to be late*) he provides the following list:

> *advise, allow, ask, (can't) bear, beg, cause, challenge, choose, command, compel, dare* (=challenge), *decide, determine, encourage, entreat, expect, force, get, give (someone to understand...), hate, help, implore, instruct, intend, invite, lead* (=cause), *leave, like, love, mean* (=intend), *oblige, order, permit, persuade, prefer, prepare, press* (=urge), *promise, remind, request, teach, tell, tempt, trouble, urge, want, warn, wish* (Hornby 1954: 21).

Using a corpus of course allows such a list to be made much more comprehensive (Francis et al. 1996 lists no fewer than 219 verbs and phrasal verbs with this pattern). However, it is more pertinent to note Hornby's concern with meaning and pattern in this list, shown by his indication that some of the verbs in it occur with this pattern only when they have a particular meaning. In some cases, this concern is made more central. Verb Pattern 5, for instance (verb followed by noun and bare infinitive) is divided into verbs of perception (*feel, hear, listen to, look at, notice, observe, perceive, see, watch*) and others indicating permission, obligation and awareness: (*bid, help, know, let, make*).

The main omission in Hornby's work is that he does not deal with the large numbers of verbs that are associated with particular prepositions (although the item-by-item coding in the *Oxford Advanced Learner's Dictionary* does show the prepositions used with each verb). Instead of dealing with the prepositions separately, he puts them all together in Verb Pattern 18 (*We congratulated him on his success; They accused her of taking the money; What prevented you from coming earlier; I must remind him about it; Compare the copy with the original*) and Verb Pattern 24 (*You can rely upon that man; He succeeded in solving the problem; They all longed for the holidays; He consented to the proposal; She complained of the heat.*) In some cases, he gives a prepositional phrase as a variant of another pattern. For example, in describing the pattern 'verb followed by two noun groups', as in *They elected Mr Grey chairman*, he notes that *choose* and *elect* often have *as* or *for* before the second noun group, as in *They elected Mr Grey as chairman*.

1.2.3   *Noun and adjective patterns*

Hornby identifies only a handful of noun and adjective patterns, as follows:

Noun patterns

noun + to-infinitive e.g. *Anne's desire to please her mother-in-law*
noun + preposition + noun e.g. *a specialist in chest diseases; our anxiety for news*
noun + that-clause e.g. *a hope that you would soon be well again*
noun (+ preposition) + conjunctive + phrase or clause e.g. *the knowledge of how it should be done*

Adjective patterns

adjective + to-infinitive e.g. *You were unwise to accept his offer*
adjective + preposition + noun e.g. *Are you afraid of the dog?*
adjective (+preposition) + clause or phrase e.g. *She was not aware that her husband earned £10 a week.*

Each of these patterns covers quite a range of examples. For instance, 'adjective + to-infinitive' includes patterns with introductory *it* and a prepositional phrase, such as *It's kind of you to say so.*

Hornby explicitly relates these patterns to the similar or contrasting verb patterns. For example, he points out that *another attempt to climb the mountain* can be seen an analogous to *They will attempt to climb the mountain*, but that whereas the noun *discussion* is followed by a preposition such as *on*, its cognate verb *discuss* is followed by a noun without an intervening preposition. Thus, learners can be encouraged to link together patterns that show similarities, but need to be warned against making false analogies.

1.2.4   *Conclusion*

It would be difficult to overestimate Hornby's achievement in *A Guide to Patterns and Usage in English*. The amount of detailed observation in the book is impressive, and the priority given to pattern over structure represents a radical reinterpretation of grammar from the point of view of the learner rather than the academic. It is perhaps an indication of the unusual quality of Hornby's work that it could be superseded only when technology gave us electronic corpora that allow the details missing from Hornby's classifications to be fleshed out.

1.3   Lexical phrases

Perhaps one reason for the comparative neglect of Hornby's work in language description is that he deliberately blurred the distinction between lexis and grammar, whereas theories since the fifties have tended to prioritise either one or the other. Both structuralism and Chomsky's work (largely) treated grammar as a system independent of lexis. On the other side of the coin, since the 1970s there has been an increasing emphasis, in both theoretical and applied linguistics, on lexis rather than grammar as the central principle of language. In this section we look at work in the area of lexis which has added to the perception of the phraseological nature of language.

It is by now a truism that a large amount of language encountered is not constructed from 'basic' structures and a lexicon, but occurs in sequences of morphemes that are more or less fixed in form. These sequences are called, variously, "lexical phrases" (Nattinger and DeCarrico 1989, 1992), "composites" (Cowie, following Mitchell in Cowie 1988), "gambits" (Keller in Cowie 1988), "routine formulae" (Coulmas in Cowie 1988), "phrasemes" (Melčuk 1988, 1995), "prefabricated routines and patterns" (Krashen 1981), "sentence stems" (Pawley and Syder 1983), "formulae" (Peters 1983), and "formulaic language" (Weinert 1995; Wray 1999). The research in this aspect of language comes from three areas: lexicography, language teaching, and psycholinguistics. Common concerns are: the frequency and therefore importance of lexical phrases, the varying degrees to which lexical phrases are open to variation in wording, the functions of lexical phrases, and the importance of lexical phrases to a model of language that gives lexis and grammar equal priority.

1.3.1 *The lexicographical perspective*

Phrases of any kind pose a problem for the lexicographer in that they do not fit comfortably into the alphabetical headword list of the traditional dictionary. There is a time-honoured concern with 'idioms', that is, phrases which cannot be analysed or transformed according to normal syntactic rules (e.g. *He kicked the bucket* but not *They kicked the buckets* or *The bucket was kicked (by him)*), and whose meaning cannot be derived from their component parts (the meaning of *kick the bucket* cannot be derived from a knowledge of the meaning of *kick* and of *bucket*). However, as Melčuk (1995: 167) points out, idioms are only one small part of the total set of phrases which are, to some extent, 'fixed'. Moon (1992), for example, distinguishes between three types of so-called 'fixed expressions':

a. 'anomalous collocations', which include examples such as *by and large* or *through thick and thin*, which cannot be analysed according to the normal rules governing English, in that a preposition (*by*) and an adjective (*large*) are not normally able to be coordinated, and adjectives such as *thick* and *thin* cannot normally occur as the completive of a preposition. Also included in this category are examples such as *kith and kin* in which one of the components 'is fossilised within that particular collocation': *kith*, for example, is found only in this phrase.
b. 'formulae' such as proverbs, slogans, quotations, gambits, and closed-set turns, as in *You've never had it so good* and *Shut your mouth*. These items are in no way anomalous with respect to the language as a whole.
c. 'fossilised or frozen metaphors': the 'pure idioms' such as *skate on thin ice* or *spill the beans*. These items are anomalous only in the sense that they cannot be manipulated grammatically, thus each part of the idiom (*skate, thin, ice, spill, beans*) is not treated by speakers as a separate lexical item, but as part of a phrase.

Melčuk (1988, 1995) proposes a complex set of what he calls 'non-free phrases' or 'phrasemes', each of which is 'fixed' in a particular way. According to Melčuk, a phrase is free "if and only if all its semantic and syntactic properties are completely determined by the respective properties of its constituent lexemes (and by the general rules of syntax)" (1988: 169). All other phrases are non-free.

He distinguishes between types of phraseme using formulae based on how transparent the meaning of the phrase is. In true idioms such as *shoot the breeze*, the meaning is not derivable from the constituents of the phrase; in collocations, or 'semiphrasemes' such as *crack a joke*, the meaning of one constituent (*joke*) is derivable from the general lexicon, but the meaning of the other constituent (*crack*) is determined by this particular collocation; in 'quasi-phrasemes' such as *start a family*, the meaning of the whole includes the meaning of both *start* and *family*, but includes also a further meaning: 'have one's first child'. In addition, he notes the existence of what he calls 'pragmatemes', that is, phrases which are transparent in meaning, but which are fixed in the sense that by convention one wording is consistently chosen over other possible alternatives in any given situation. He cites as an example the conventional phrase *Best before [date]*, used on food containers, which is consistently chosen in preference to, say, *To be consumed before...* or *Don't use after...*, each of which would be roughly equivalent in meaning.

For lexicographers, then, there appear to be two main questions with respect to lexical phrases: how fixed are they? and what is their relation to the grammar and lexicon of the language? This presupposes what Melčuk, with his distinction between 'free' and 'non-free' phrases, makes explicit: that lexical phrases compose only a part of the language as a whole, leaving the rest of the language to be described in other ways. The oddness of this becomes apparent when we consider Melčuk's category of 'collocation'. Collocation is to be accounted for in terms of non-free phrases only when the meaning of one of the items is tied to its co-occurrence with the other item. Thus *crack a joke* is a non-free phrase but *tell a joke* and *make a joke*, presumably, are free phrases. Yet *crack, tell* and *make* all collocate with *joke*. Among the significant collocates of the noun *joke(s)* in the Bank of English, for example, are the following (figures show the t-score which indicates how significant this collocate is for the node-word *joke*; see p. 231):

telling	14.6
make	13.9
tell	13.6
making	13.1
told	12.2
made	12.1
cracking	10.5
cracked	7.9
crack	7.8
makes	7.2

For the speaker wishing to talk about jokes, there is a limited set of verbs available. Neither *crack, make* nor *tell* represents a free choice: all are constrained by collocation, and in each case the precise meaning of the verb is determined by that collocation.

1.3.2   *Language teaching*

The second perspective from which lexical phrases have been investigated is that of language teaching and learning. Writers in this field include Pawley and Syder (1983), Nattinger and DeCarrico (1989, 1992), and more recently, Lewis (1993) and Willis (1990).

Researchers who are interested in language teaching place importance upon lexical phrases because of their frequency and their importance to a 'nativelike' production of the language. Pawley and Syder (1983: 191) argue that "fluent and idiomatic control of a language rests to a considerable extent on knowledge of a body of 'sentence stems' which are 'institutionalized' or 'lexicalized'". The relative fixedness of the phrases, they suggest, allows speakers to concentrate on other aspects of discourse, and thus to achieve the fluency that we associate with native speakers. They define lexicalised sentence stems thus:

> A lexicalized sentence stem is a unit of clause length or longer whose grammatical form and lexical content is wholly or largely fixed; its fixed elements form a standard label for a culturally recognized concept, a term in the language (Pawley and Syder 1983: 191).

Nattinger and DeCarrico (1989: 118) offer a similar definition of what they call lexical phrases: "These phrases are patterned sequences, usually consisting of a syntactic frame that contains slots for various fillers, and run the gamut from completely fixed, unvarying phrases to phrases that are highly variable". In a later work they add that lexical phrases are fixed in their functional application, as well as in their form (Nattinger and DeCarrico 1992: 11).

For researchers in the field of language teaching, then, lexical phrases are important because they should allow language learners to produce language that is phraseologically similar to that of native speakers and to produce language without undue hesitation or disfluency. (This assumes, of course, that learners *wish* to sound similar to native speakers: this will be discussed further in Chapter 9.) Cowie (1992: 10) comments that

> It is impossible to perform at a level acceptable to native users, in writing or speech, without controlling an appropriate range of multiword units. Moreover, the demands of creative expression in the foreign language rests, as it does for

native speakers and writers, on prior knowledge of a repertoire of such expressions.

Lexical phrases are typically said to occupy a position 'between' lexis and syntax. Nattinger and DeCarrico (1989: 118) assert:

> multi-word lexical phenomena ... exist somewhere between the traditional poles of lexicon and syntax. They are similar to lexicon in being treated as a unit, yet most of them consist of more than one word, and many of them can at the same time be derived from the regular rules of syntax, just like other sentences.

Pawley and Syder (1983: 217) suggest that they need to be described both as individual items (as lexical items) and as if they were created from rules of grammar:

> If the native speaker knows certain linguistic forms in two ways, both as lexical units and as products of syntactic rules, then the grammarian is obliged to describe *both* kinds of knowledge; anything less would be incomplete.

We will return to the relationship between lexis and grammar in the discussion of the work of psycholinguists below.

1.3.3 *Psycholinguistics*

The concern of psycholinguists is how expert speakers of a language store and retrieve the language system, and how learners (of a first or second language) acquire the language. It is argued that lexical phrases play an important role in both processes, though there is substantial disagreement about this (see Weinert 1995; Wray 1999 for comprehensive reviews). Nattinger and DeCarrico (1989: 132) speculate that second language learners may acquire phrases which then provide the evidence for the learners' analysis of the language:

> Lexical phrases may also provide the raw material itself for language acquisition... Later, on analogy with many similar phrases, they [learners] break these chunks down into sentence frames that contain slots for various fillers...

Krashen, on the other hand, suggests that the acquisition of prefabricated routines (such as *how are you*) and prefabricated patterns (such as *down with* _____ or *that's a* _____) proceeds independently of what he calls the 'creative construction process', and that routines and patterns do not necessarily feed into the more important creative language. He concludes that "[t]he use of routines and patterns is certainly a part of language, but it is probably not a large part" (Krashen 1981: 98) and that "[t]he available evidence indicates that routines and patterns are essentially and fundamentally different from creative language" (Krashen 1981: 99).

Peters, from the point of view of first language development, disagrees (and

see Nattinger and DeCarrico 1992: 24–29 for a review of work in this area).
Contrasting her own work with that of Krashen, she proposes "that formulaic
speech ... is merely a facet of creative language" (Peters 1983: 4). She argues
that children begin by acquiring phrases, rather than words or structure, and that
these are then analysed into a system. She points out that, for the child, phrases
constitute more meaningful data than words or syntactic systems:

> It is not a dictionary of morphemes that the child is exposed to, but rather an
> intermittent stream of speech sounds containing chunks, often longer than a
> single word, that recur with varying frequency. It is out of this stream of
> unknown meaning and structure that the child must attempt to capture some
> pieces in order to determine their meaning and to preserve them for future use
> (Peters 1983: 5).

For some writers (e.g. Langacker 1987 cited in Weinert 1995) the distinction
between formula and creativity is not a dichotomy but a continuum. Weinert
(1995: 198) points out that this view leads to a theory of language production as
comprising several distinct components, in place of the more conventional view
that a single explanation may be found for it: "The view of language as a
formulaic-creative continuum suggests that the units of knowledge and production may vary, including fixed formulas, mini-grammars, and general rules".

The issue relates to language storage as well as to language acquisition.
Peters argues that adult speakers of a language store the language in phrases, as
well as in the form of words and syntactic rules. Becker (1975: 72, cited in
Nattinger and DeCarrico 1989: 119) concurs, in a passage that is similar in
essence to Francis' suggestion for how language is encoded (see Section 1.5):

> [the frequency of lexical phrases in performed speech implies] that the process
> of speaking is *Compositional*: We start with the information we wish to
> express or evoke, and we haul out of our phrasal lexicon some patterns that
> can provide the major elements of this expression. Then the problem is to
> stitch these phrases together into something roughly grammatical, to fill in the
> blanks with the particulars of the case at hand, to modify the phrases if need
> be, and if all else fails to generate phrases from scratch to smooth over the
> transitions and fill in any remaining conceptual holes.

Nattinger (1988: 75; see also Wray and Perkins 2000) refers to this approach as
a more general theory of language performance:

> Many theories of language performance suggest that vocabulary is stored
> redundantly, not only as individual morphemes, but also as parts of phrases, or
> even as longer memorized chunks of speech, and that it is oftentimes retrieved
> from memory as these preassembled chunks (Bolinger 1975).

Peters (1983: 90) concurs that 'dual storage', that is, having phrases available in memory as single (lexical) items, as well as the syntactic rules that allow them to be created, leads to redundancy in language knowledge. This in turn, she suggests, implies a fluidity between lexis and syntax:

> ...[T]here is considerable redundancy in the storage of both lexical and syntactic information. The relation between syntax and lexicon may therefore be more fluid than is usually supposed: Under some circumstances an expression may be retrieved from the lexicon as a single unit; under others it may be constructed from partially assembled pieces in the lexicon, requiring somewhat more syntactic processing; under yet other circumstances it may be constructed de novo from morphemes. Syntax and lexicon are thus seen to be complementary in a dynamic and redundant way. The same information may be present in both, in different forms...

This argument sounds somewhat similar to Sinclair's assertion that "[t]he evidence now becoming available casts grave doubts on the wisdom of postulating separate domains of lexis and syntax" (Sinclair 1991: 104; see Section 1.4 for full discussion). It is worth pointing out, however, that the two positions are different. Peters does not disagree with the distinction between syntactic rules, which offer an abstract, very productive, system for the production of all possible sentences in a language, and the lexicon of that language. She simply argues that the speaker's mind may store certain items both lexically (as single items) and syntactically (as the product of the operation of rules). The 'fluidity' she identifies refers to how the speaker encodes on different occasions, rather than to the description of the language itself. Sinclair's position is more radical, and relates to the description of the language rather than to how speakers might encode. He argues that syntactic rules account for only a minimal part of the grammar of a language, and that the more important part is composed of the phraseological constraints upon individual lexical items. Thus, syntax is not a system independent of lexis: lexis and syntax must, ultimately, be described together.

1.3.4   *Lexical phrases and a pattern grammar*

It may seem that this discussion of lexical phrases has strayed a long way from the central concern of a pattern approach to grammar. There are two reasons for this digression. Firstly, the work on lexical phrases, much of which took place before language corpora were commonplace, in a sense prefigures Sinclair's work on collocation and the 'idiom principle' (see Section 1.4). The availability of corpora allows us to identify with some certainty the frequently-occurring sequences of items that the lexicographers, language teachers, and psycholinguists discussed in this section could identify only through intuition (see J. Willis 1997 for a discussion of the unreliability of intuition in this respect). In addition, placing the lexical item and its patterning centre-stage, as it were, breaks down the distinction which the concern for lexical phrases maintained: the distinction between what Melčuk called free and non-free phrases. The work of Sinclair and other corpus linguists suggests that *all* language is patterned, that there is no such thing as a free phrase, and that ultimately, the study of lexical phrases can simply be subsumed into a more general description of language.

Secondly, and more specifically, it is important to note that the grammar patterns discussed in the rest of this book are in a sense examples of lexical phrases. Although none of the writers we have discussed here mention phrases that we would call the product of grammar patterns, phrases such as *it is hard to believe that..., be interested in..., the fact that...* or *apologise to ____ for ____ing* surely come within the remit of lexical phrases. Writers on lexical phrases and on grammar patterns, it might be argued, seek to account for the some of the same evidence in different ways.

It would be wrong to suppose, however, that grammar patterns are simply a special case of lexical phrases. Collections of lexical phrases are, ultimately, fairly random lists of phrases, organised either according to their relative fixedness, or to their function (discourse organising, opinion-giving and so on), or to one of their core words (see Pawley and Syder 1983 for examples of phrases with *think*). They are an attempt to account for a portion only of the lexicon. Grammar patterns, on the other hand, constitute an attempt to describe the whole of the language (or rather, all the frequently-occurring items in the language) in a principled way, and the lists of words collected in a given pattern are not random. The two approaches are far apart theoretically and in terms of language description in general.

1.4 Sinclair: Corpus Concordance Collocation

1.4.1 *Corpus-driven language description*

This section reviews the work of Sinclair, largely as it appears in the book *Corpus Concordance Collocation* (1991). This book is about more than it seems; from a handful of deceptively simple examples Sinclair sets out an agenda for a radical departure in the description of English.

Sinclair's work differs from that of other linguists in that he prioritises a method, or group of methods, and a kind of data rather than a theory. This approach is what has come to be known as corpus linguistics: a way of investigating language by observing large amounts of naturally-occurring, electronically-stored discourse, using software which selects, sorts, matches, counts and calculates. The data that is the basis for this differs from that used with other methods of linguistic investigation in five respects:

The data is authentic;
The data is not selected on linguistic grounds;
There is a lot of data;
The data is systematically organised;
The data is not annotated in terms of existing theories.

Each of these features may be stated as a principle, and is discussed in turn below.

The data is authentic. The observation of actually-occurring language may be contrasted with introspection and intuition as ways of obtaining information about how language works. As Sinclair points out (1991: 39): "It has been fashionable among grammarians for many years now to introspect and to trust their intuitions about structure...". He is, however, critical of the reliability of such intuition as an accurate reflection of language in use:

> ...the contrast exposed between the impressions of language detail noted by people, and the evidence compiled objectively from texts is huge and systematic. It leads one to suppose that human intuition about language is highly specific, and not at all a good guide to what actually happens when the same people actually use the language (Sinclair 1991: 4).

As a result of this, Sinclair (1991: 4) argues that "Their [intuition-led grammarians] study has ... been more about intuition than about language" and states what has become a commonplace: to find out about the language that people actually use, one must observe the language that people actually use.

Francis and Sinclair (1994: 197) quote the identification of ergative verbs as an example of the superiority of authentic data over intuition. They argue that it is not possible to tell whether a given verb is used ergatively or not simply by consulting intuition, and they cite the verb *clarify* as an instance: the authors could not determine through intuition whether this was an ergative verb or not. Consultation of a corpus of authentic English solved the problem, as *clarify* was found being used transitively in examples such as *She clarified the situation* and intransitively in examples such as *The situation clarified,* and could thus be classified as an ergative verb.

The data is not selected on linguistic grounds. Sinclair is by no means unique in advocating a reliance on authentic language as data. Halliday and other proponents of Systemic-Functional Grammar, for example, typically derive their analytical categories from instances of actually-occurring discourse. Indeed, it would scarcely be possible to propose a grammar as social-semiotic (Halliday 1978) without taking as its starting-point language in actual use.

For most grammarians and other linguists, however, data is selected because it illustrates a particular language point. The grammarian cites observed instances of language in use that have caught his/her eye or ear. Sinclair (1991:100) comments that: "This method is likely to highlight the unusual in English and perhaps miss some of the regular, humdrum patterns."

In other words, where instances of language are selected for analysis precisely because they strike the linguist as interesting, they are likely to exemplify the unusual rather than the mundane. Of course all language data is selected, but the texts that go into a corpus are chosen because they play a particular social role, rather than because they demonstrate a peculiarity of usage (see, for example, Renouf 1987).

There is a lot of data. Perhaps what is most striking about the data that Sinclair, and other corpus linguists, uses is its quantity. Even the earliest corpora consisted of around 1 million words of running text (Leech 1991:10), far more than most linguists use as data. The corpus that Sinclair describes in *Corpus Concordance Collocation* consisted of just over seven million words; the current (1997) Bank of English corpus consists of over 300 million words. As a corpus gets bigger, it is possible to describe more and more accurately items of less and less frequency. For this reason, no corpus is really big enough, and no corpus could be too big (provided that other issues, such as spread of sources, are also taken into account; see Leech 1991). Limitations of size are imposed by storage considerations, and by the problems of devising software that can search, sort and count very large number of items quickly, but these are problems of hardware and software, not problems of language description.

Sinclair's argument that 'bigger is always better' relies on the assertion that in this case quantity is also quality. He says (1991:4): "... the ability to examine large text corpora in a systematic manner allows access to a quality of evidence that has not been available before", and observes dryly that "[t]he language looks rather different when you look at a lot of it at once" (1991:100). But why should quantity be quality? The difference between looking at a lot of data and a little, is that when a lot of data is examined, conclusions as to frequency can be drawn. Sinclair (1991:4) draws attention to two observations about language which cannot be made without recourse to frequency information: firstly that some sequences of words co-occur surprisingly often, given that every utterance or written sentence spontaneously produced is unique; secondly, and in contrast, that even so-called fixed expressions demonstrate surprising amounts of variability (cf. Moon 1994; 1998).

These observations are not peripheral to the serious business of grammatical description but challenge its very heart. Sinclair contradicts the 'received wisdom' that a small corpus is sufficient for doing grammar (an argument later propounded by Carter and McCarthy 1995: 143) by arguing that "[t]he new evidence suggests that grammatical generalizations do not rest on a rigid foundation, but are the accumulation of the patterns of hundreds of individual words and phrases" (1991: 100).

Sinclair's choice of the word 'generalizations' is significant here, in that it contrasts with those approaches to grammar that expound an abstract 'langue' or system that in some way underlies actual instances of language use. For Sinclair, it appears, there is no system setting the parameters of what may be said or written, only a set of generalisations capturing the essence of what has been said or written. Systemic-Functional terminology might be borrowed to rephrase this: language is not a system that is realised in actual instances, but a set of actual instances that may be regarded as construing an approximate and ever-changing system. Such a construal stems from the interpretation of hundreds of observations, made possible by the sheer amount of data available.

One of the outcomes of using large quantities of data is that some of it may be discarded, in the sense that instances of word-play or language that is strange because it is being used in strange circumstances, are deliberately ignored in terms of the general description of the language (Sinclair 1991: 99), though they may form the focus of studies of a different kind (e.g. Louw 1993, 1997). This is a different approach from that of many grammars, which concentrates on what is possible, not on what is frequent. Obviously, the view of what is of minor importance changes as the corpus gets bigger, and might differ according to the perceived audience for the description, but the point about a very large corpus is that it enables the observer to see what is 'central and typical' (Hanks 1987) and distinguish that from the less frequent usage. Sinclair (1987: 108) distinguishes between the typical and the possible thus:

> For example, it is significant if, in several hundred instances of the base form of a verb, none signal the imperative. This is not to say that in the ethereal world of theoretical, school or traditional grammar the imperative of that verb is 'impossible'.

The data is systematically organised. Data alone is not enough, however. The greater the amount of data, the greater the need for organisation. Faced with a corpus containing hundreds of millions of words and no systematic organisation, a researcher would be in the same position as a person walking into a library of volumes written in English to find out how the verb 'to be' is used. Clearly, observations about frequency, and all that follows, can only be made if the data is organised in such a way as to allow this to happen.

Although Sinclair eschews an *a priori* categorisation of items (see below), some decision has to be taken about how the data is to be presented to the researcher. Essentially, in the approach suggested by Sinclair, the word-form (a series of characters separated from other series by a space) is the unit. Software is designed which will search the corpus for all instances of a given word-form, and which will present those instances together with a limited amount of the preceding and following text (concordance lines). Further software can sort these concordance lines so that they are arranged alphabetically, thereby encouraging the observation of pattern.

It would be naïve to suppose that this presentation of data has no effect upon the resulting observation and the theories built upon them. We should perhaps view phrases like "evidence compiled objectively" (Sinclair 1991: 4) with some caution. Put simply, a method that takes the word-form as the focal point in the presentation of data is bound to result in a theory of language that prioritises the word-form and its behaviour. This point in no way invalidates a theory of that kind: it merely makes the obvious caveat that *no* observation is 'theory-free'.

The data is not annotated in terms of existing theories. An alternative to the approach outlined above is to annotate a corpus so that, instead of searching for a particular word-form, the software searches for a particular category: passives, or to-infinitive clauses, or complements, or adverbs of manner, for example. The development of such software reflects a position vis-à-vis corpus studies that McEnery and Wilson (1996: 56) call 'problem-oriented': researchers seek to find a corpus-based solution to a problem which has not arisen as an outcome of corpus research, but from language research based on other methods. Tognini-Bonelli (1996) uses the term 'corpus-based' to describe this kind of research, and contrasts it with the 'corpus-driven' research that is the focus of this book. There are numerous examples of research based on annotated corpora. For example, Biber et al. 1994 calculate the frequency of categories such as '*that* relative clause restrictive'; '*wh* relative clause restrictive'; and '*wh* relative clause non-restrictive', work which is presumably based on an annotated corpus. By contrast, Halliday 1993b describes a way of calculating the relative frequency of positive and negative clauses in a large corpus without recourse to annotation of negativity (see also Halliday and James 1993). Kettermann (1997) uses an annotated corpus to answer questions relating to language acquisition. Wichmann (1997) suggests a corpus annotated for prosodic features to teach aspects of prosody.

Annotation software involves several practical problems: automatic taggers and parsers have limited accuracy; if the alternative — manual annotation — is used, the size of the corpus that can be annotated is limited by the person-time available. Greenbaum et al. (1996), for example, describe a study of complement clauses which is based on the manual annotation of a 2,000 words corpus. Short et al. (1996) report on a study of speech and thought presentation based on a corpus of just under 89,000 words. One of their aims was to develop an automatic parser which would enable to processing of larger corpora, an aim which was unfulfilled at the time that their paper was written.

Conrad and Biber (2000) describe an interactive programme for labelling all the adverbials in a corpus. The software selects words and phrases which might have an adverbial function, and asks the human researcher to confirm the function and to assign a semantic label from a set of choices. McEnery and Wilson (1996: 53; see also Garside et al. 1997; Garside and Rayson 1997) describe a similar system, this time for coding anaphora, in which interactive software again assists the human analyst to make and record choices. The objective is 'bootstrapping', that is, the human analyst trains the computer programme to undertake more and more of the analysis itself. Whether such techniques will lead to fully automated systems remains to be seen. The important point is that for many people, corpus annotation is the basis of corpus linguistics (see, for example, Leech 1991: 20–25; Garside et al. eds. 1997).

Sinclair, however, notes the problems associated with an over-reliance on annotation. If a corpus is annotated in any way, the annotation will reflect a particular theory of grammar, and the results will naturally be cast in terms of that theory. Leech (1991: 24) comments that "...all schemes are likely to be biased in some way or another — however minor — towards a particular theoretical or descriptive position." The main disadvantage of this bias lies in the fact that, with a detailed annotation system, the likelihood of discovering facts about the language that have not been previously hypothesised is severely curtailed. Sinclair (1987: 107) comments:

> If ... the objective is to observe and record behaviour and make generalisations based on the observations, a means of recording structure must be devised which depends as little as possible on a theory. The more superficial the better.

Searching by word-form and sorting by the superficial similarity of one instance to another is the 'means of recording structure' that Sinclair advocates. The next section will examine some of the findings that emerge. First, however, it is worth noting that the question of method — *how* to investigate the large amounts of data available in a corpus — is a crucial one to corpus linguistics, and one that no-one as yet is in a position to answer fully. What is more surprising, perhaps, is that the literature reveals very little in the way of methodological debate. In the sections below we will refer to dilemmas of method as and when the issue arises.

1.4.2   *Sense and structure*

One of the main points that is made in *Corpus Concordance Collocation* is that sense and what Sinclair calls 'structure' are associated. Sinclair uses the term 'structure' to indicate a lexical item and its patterns and collocations. He defines it as "any privileges of occurrence of morphemes", whether those morphemes are lexical (as in the collocation of *yield* and *profit*), or grammatical (as in the collocation of *yield* and *up*) (1991: 104). 'Structure' therefore encompasses both what we refer to as 'pattern' and further collocational regularities.

Sinclair makes the point about sense and structure, or pattern, largely in the context of distinguishing between senses of polysemous words. If a word has several senses, and is used in several patterns, each pattern will occur more frequently with one of the senses than the others, such that the patterning of an individual example will indicate the most likely sense of the word in that example. This is demonstrated with respect to three verbs: *decline, yield* and *set*. Sinclair (1987: 109–110) summarises his argument by referring to his experience when working with compilers of the 1987 COBUILD dictionary, when compilers were asked to identify the most typical examples of a (sense of a) word and to describe their structure:

> In nearly every case, a structural pattern seemed to be associated with a sense... In the vast majority of cases, the compiler, in choosing typical instances, had little doubt about the kind of syntactic pattern that would have to be featured.

and more briefly: "It seems that there is a strong tendency for sense and syntax to be associated" (Sinclair 1991: 65).

He points out, however, that the association of sense and pattern (or syntax, or structure) is not one-to-one. It is rare that a sense of a word is found only in one pattern, or that one pattern is found only with one sense of a word. Referring again to the compiling process, Sinclair (1987: 109) notes that a given pattern "was rarely if ever found in every instance [of a given sense] unless it was a marginal sense with a very few citations." If there was a one-to-one association, ambiguity would not be possible. In fact, ambiguity is possible (many jokes, for example, rely on it) but it is rare in normal interaction. In ordinary discourse, structure does satisfactorily distinguish sense.

Sinclair raises the inevitable question: if sense and pattern are associated, is this link a causal one, and if so, in which direction is the causality? In other words, does a pattern necessitate the selection of a particular sense of a word, or does the selection of a particular sense necessitate the use of a particular pattern? Phrasing the question in this way underlines the implausibility of either process being part of the process of composition (speaking or writing). Instead, Sinclair postulates that "the underlying unit of composition is an integrated sense-structure complex" (1991: 105) and argues that "[t]here is ultimately no distinction between form and meaning" (1991: 7). In other words, it is not patterns and words that are selected, but phrases, or phraseologies, that have both a single form and a single meaning. The outcome of this view is the idiom principle, which we discuss next.

1.4.3   *The idiom principle*

The observation that meanings are made in chunks of language that are more-or-less predictable, though not fixed, sequences of morphemes leads Sinclair to an articulation of the 'idiom principle'. He states the principle thus:

> The principle of idiom is that a language user has available to him or her a large number of semi-preconstructed phrases that constitute single choices, even though they might appear to be analysable into segments (Sinclair 1991: 110).

The study of fixed phrases has a fairly long tradition (see Section 1.3), but phrases are normally seen as outside the normal organising principle of language. Here, Sinclair extends the notion of phraseology to encompass a great deal more of language than it is commonly considered to encompass. At its strongest, we might say that all senses of all words exist in and are identified by the sequences of morphemes in which they typically occur. If, then, these semi-preconstructed phrases are the general rule in language rather than the exception, they are able to be incorporated into the normal organising principle of language as the idiom principle.

The idiom principle is, however, insufficient to account for all instances of language use. Sinclair (1991: 109–110) contrasts it with the 'open-choice principle', defined as follows:

> This is a way of seeing language as the result of a very large number of complex choices. At each point where a unit is completed (a word or a phrase or a clause), a large range of choice opens up and the only restraint is grammaticalness... Virtually all grammars are constructed on the open-choice principle.

Both the idiom principle and the open-choice principle are described as 'ways of seeing' or of interpreting language. In other words, a language user, faced with an instance of language use, has to decide whether to interpret this as a chunk, or as a series of individual items. For example, suppose a language user hears the words *I must confess*. Using the idiom principle, the meaning of this sequence of words may be paraphrased as 'I am going to tell you something you may find unpleasant, or something I find embarrassing' (as in *I must confess I rather like Jeffrey Archer*). There is evidence that the sequence *I must confess* acts as a single item here, in that the various parts are not freely substituted with other words. *He must confess*, or *I must not confess* are not frequently found in this sense. If, on the other hand, the sequence *I must confess* is interpreted according to the open-choice principle, the meaning may be paraphrased as 'I am under an obligation (possibly self-imposed) to admit to a wrong-doing' (as in *The police have found my fingerprints on the gun. I must confess*). In this case, other words may be substituted (*He must confess; I must not confess; I must run away*). The point is that the hearer, on hearing *I must confess* in any circumstances, must decide which meaning is appropriate, in other words, must decide whether to take the words as constituting a phrase or not. Both interpretations are not simultaneously possible, although two hearers may activate different interpretations (Sinclair 1991: 114).

This last observation precludes what seems an attractive possibility: that any stretch of language can at any one time be interpreted according to the idiom principle *and* according to the open-choice principle. Such an option is not, however, open to us. Sinclair instead posits a situation in which a hearer interprets a stretch of text according to one principle and then switches to the other principle to interpret another stretch, when the first principle no longer works. He suggests that the idiom principle takes priority:

> For normal texts, we can put forward the proposal that the first mode to be applied is the idiom principle, since most of the text will be interpretable by this principle. Whenever there is good reason, the interpretive process switches to the open-choice principle, and quickly back again. Lexical choices which are unexpected in their environment will presumably occasion a switch; choices which, if grammatically interpreted, would be unusual are an affirmation of the operation of the idiom principle (Sinclair 1991: 114).

It is possible to demonstrate the only-one-at-a-time relationship between the idiom and the open-choice principles with relation to the following extract from *The Hitchhiker's Guide to the Galaxy* (Adams 1979: 92). The hero of the novel, Arthur Dent, is in a spaceship and is having difficulty following the conversation of the other characters.

(2)   Arthur blinked at the screens and felt <u>he was missing something</u> <u>important</u>. Suddenly he realized what it was.
       'Is there any tea on this spaceship?' he asked. [emphasis added]

The verb *miss* has two senses that are exploited in this extract: 'not understand' and 'be without'. At first reading, the phrase *he was missing something important* is interpreted with *missing* in the first of these senses, but the subsequent question *Is there any tea on this spaceship?* necessitates a re-interpretation of the verb *missing* in the second sense. An explanation of this can be offered in terms of the two principles: the reader first interprets *he was missing something important* according to the idiom principle, and only later re-interprets it in terms of the open-choice principle. We can see how this works if we look for instances of *missing something* in the Bank of English corpus.

The phrase normally means 'not understanding', as in *Am I missing something here?* or 'not having an experience', as in *If you have never had fresh tongue, you are really missing something special.* The word *something* is sometimes followed by an adjective, either an adjective such as *obvious* or *important* for the first of these senses or one such as *wonderful* or *pleasant* for the second. More rarely, the phrase is part of a more general phraseology, in which *missing* is followed by a noun group and means 'be without', as in these examples: *your rooms are missing something extra in the way of decoration... my sister was missing a hank of hair... her jacket is missing a button... they were missing some key players... the Daimler is missing its head lamps and bumper.* In these examples, the relation between the noun group realising the Subject (e.g. *her jacket*) and the noun group realising the Object (e.g. *a button*) is one of whole-part (a button is part of a jacket).

Returning to the *Hitchhiker* example, then, we can observe that the phrase *he was missing something important* is likely to be interpreted according to the idiom principle as meaning 'there was something important he did not understand'. Only when we meet the unexpected lexical item *tea* do we reject that meaning and re-interpret the phrase according to the open-choice principle: 'there was something important that he did not have', even though *Arthur* and *tea* do not really form a whole-part relationship.

This example illustrates Sinclair's point that the idiom principle and the open-choice principle cannot be operated simultaneously as principles of interpretation. The joke works only because, on first reading, *he was missing something important* has only one meaning: it is in no way ambiguous because it is interpreted only in line with the idiom principle. The subsequent re-interpretation is the linguistic equivalent of a double-take: clever grammatical punning that occurs only in comedy of this kind, and which Adams uses with particular skill.

1.4.4   *Units of meaning*

The idiom principle raises issues concerning units of language description. When discussing the association between sense and structure, Sinclair (1987: 110) comments that, in particular with relation to recurring phraseologies associated with common words, we find "a distribution of meaning across a number of words". This phenomenon is particularly associated with what Sinclair (1991: 113) calls "a progressive delexicalization". A simple example is the phrase *have a bath*, where the frequent verb *have* has lost much of its meaning, and where the meaning is spread across the whole phrase rather than being restricted to one word or another.

A more complex example discussed by Sinclair (1994) is based on the two-word combination *naked eye*. Below are nearly 30 randomly-selected lines from the 1997 Bank of English corpus:

```
ouble Cluster. Easily visible to the naked eye, these two clusters lie more
ther and are actually visible to the naked eye. It should be pointed out
mear and missing one or two with the naked eye is possible but the computer
      its effects cannot be seen by the naked eye. For a better understandi
   the base you can't see it with the naked eye but you know it's there
            anything you can see with your naked eye, probably has adequate amino
iewers that Lammtarra would win. The naked eye instantly caught the sudden
arc, 30 000 times as accurate as the naked eye. The less accurate Tycho
till 15 to 20 times fainter than the naked eye can see. During August,
      in the night sky visible to the naked eye in his book Sky Phenomena: A
   the star might be visible to the naked eye. The star's true colour is
      and it is clearly visible to the naked eye. The next problem at the
So it's kind of a fight because the naked eye and the viewer sees things
as a transformation invisible to the naked eye, and certainly unbeknown to
it. The worms cannot be seen by the naked eye. Horses grazing the paddock
   the first supernova visible to the naked eye since 1604 erupted in the La
   Double and Multiple Stars To the naked eye, stars appear as solitary,
   at the top, as it appears to the naked eye and in binoculars. Through a
at times it is just visible to the naked eye. Vesta is the third-largest
   its twisted roots visible to the naked eye as they snaked right down th
they were specks too small for the naked eye. The mass that was the audie
so happily and who looked to the naked eye as right as rain, be about t
hotoaging changes are visible to the naked eye. And even more disturbing
on a level that is invisible to the naked eye. Shields. Your circle might
   interactions imperceptible to the naked eye. Among these interpersonal
passage among them, visible to the naked eye. Time to settle down for a
         the new Pele's point all the naked eye could see was a sea of
accurate form of scoring than by the naked eye. It will never be possible
```

As Sinclair points out, and as these lines illustrate, *naked eye* typically appears in a context that is restricted yet not fixed. Typically, *naked eye* occurs at the end of a clause and is preceded by *the*. Furthermore, *the naked eye* is preceded by *to*, or, less frequently, *with*. The prepositional phrase *to/with the naked eye* follows a range of words related to sight, most frequently *visible* or a form of the verb *see*. Prior to that is an indication of something that might be too small to be seen. About half the instances of this typical usage are negative (as against a general figure of 10% of all clauses being negative, see Halliday 1993b); in other words, something is described as being _invisible to the naked eye_. Of the positive instances, over half include modification, such as _easily, actually, might be_ or _the first_.

Sinclair's conclusion is that there is a unit of which _naked eye_ is a part, which has a specific meaning but a range of lexical realisations. This unit does not correspond to any syntactic unit, and the variation in lexis precludes simply calling it a 'fixed phrase'. Instead, Sinclair calls this a 'meaning unit'. If language is to be analysed according to the idiom principle, the meaning unit would be the primary unit of analysis.

1.4.5   _Frames_

Many discussions of collocation, and of the idiom principle, take as their starting point lexical, as opposed to grammatical, words. Common sense suggests that phrases, or units of meaning, will be centred around items with lexical meaning. To look for collocates of _of_ or _the_ or _be_ seems intuitively to be less useful, in that the information given will be too general, applicable to a word-class in general rather than to the specific lexical item (but see Sinclair 1999). Sinclair and Renouf (1991: 128), however, point out that "co-occurrences in the language most commonly occur among grammatical words". They propose the notion of 'collocational frameworks'; these frameworks "consist of a discontinuous sequence of two words, positioned at one word remove from each other". They give as examples '_a_ + ? + _of_', '_an_ + ? + _of_', '_be_ + ? + _to_', '_too_ + ? + _to_', '_for_ + ? + _of_' '_had_ + ? + _of_ and '_many_ + ? + _of_. In each case, "the frameworks are highly selective of their collocates" (Sinclair and Renouf 1991: 130), and the framework accounts for a significant proportion of the occurrence of the collocate in the corpus used. For example, the triplet _a series of_ is the seventh most frequent exponent of the framework '_a_ + ? + _of_', yet of all the words that sometimes occur in that framework, _series_ is only the seventeenth most frequent in terms of overall frequency in the corpus. Furthermore, the triplet _a series of_ accounts for no fewer than 57% of all the occurrences of _series_ in the corpus. In short, _series_ is important to the framework '_a_ + ? + _of_', and, conversely, that framework is important to the word.

Sinclair and Renouf pick up the point made above about the association of sense and syntax by demonstrating that the words that occur in a particular framework are not a random selection but belong to particular groupings. Nouns occurring with particular frequency in the framework '_an_ + ? + _of_', for example, belong to the following groups:

1. Measurement and quantifiers (e.g. *army, average, inch, ounce*)
2. Indicating part of something (e.g. *edge, end, evening, hour, part*)
3. Specification of an attribute (e.g. *array, index*)
4. Support for the noun following *of* (e.g. *act, example, expression, inkling, object*)
5. Indicating an activity (e.g. *extension, explanation, invasion, upsurge*)
6. Indicating a quality or circumstance (e.g. *absence, awareness*)
7. Indicating a relationship (e.g. *enemy, officer*)
(based on Sinclair and Renouf 1991: 136–7)

Sinclair and Renouf (1991: 143) are modest about the extent to which their concept of frameworks should be used in the description of a language, in that they claim simply a consciousness-raising agenda:

> Linguists are accustomed to seeing the language as divisible into coherent units such as phrase, group or clause. The simple frameworks proposed here are intended to raise consciousness of the many different and eminently sensible ways we might develop to present and explain language patterning.

The notion of there being many different ways of describing the same phenomenon in language is both intriguing and unsettling: intriguing because it suggests a description of, say, English, which the user can access from a number of perspectives, unsettling because it implies that a description can never be complete, in that there would always be another perspective that had not been considered. More radically, perhaps, it raises the question of whom a description of English is for, and how it may be used.

Consider for example the triplet *an examination of*, which Sinclair and Renouf cite as an example of the framework '*an + ? + of*'. The observation that *examination* often (significantly often) occurs in that framework clearly does not give us complete information about the word *examination*. Indeed, in the current (1997) Bank of English corpus, of 7327 occurrences of *examination*, only 408 (less than 6%) are in the triplet *an examination of*, even though *an* is the most significant item immediately to the left of *examination* and *of* is the most significant item immediately to the right. From a total of 2031 instances of *examination of*, there are approximately 400 instances of another determiner being used (e.g. *his/its/the examination of*), another 400 instances of the triplet *an examination of* being interrupted by an adjective, as in *a detailed examination of* and a total of 704 lines of *ADJECTIVE examination of*, with or without a determiner. From the point of view of the word *examination*, then, the important information is that it is often followed by a prepositional phrase beginning with *of*. Less important is that the noun group of which *examination* is head may begin with a determiner, most usually *a* or *an*, and that it may or may not include another modifier.

For a user of language descriptions, such as a learner, the information about *examination* seems to be more useful than that about the framework. For the learner to gain knowledge of a pattern represented by:

(a)   (something)   examination   (of)

where brackets indicate 'often' as opposed to 'always' seems to be the useful way forward. The establishment of frameworks themselves might be of more use to the theoretical linguist. As a description, it represents a statistical working of actual language occurrences and is perhaps the strongest demonstration to date of a description of language that is independent of traditional notions of abstract language categories. It has been shown to be particularly useful when describing relatively small, specialised corpora, where the co-occurrence of high-frequency items can give larger amounts of data than information about less frequently-occurring items (e.g. Gledhill 1996).

In a description of English in general, though, it is not yet clear to us how an analysis in terms of frameworks would fit with an analysis in terms of units of meaning, or with other measurements of collocation. What is clear, however, is that a data-driven grammar of English would need to be multi-faceted, approaching the description from many perspectives. A practical consequence might be that it would also need to be unrestricted as to length, implying an electronic resource rather than a traditional book. As it would be almost impossible for such a grammar to be comprehensive — there would always be other ways of cutting the cake — we might learn a sobering lesson about the very limited range of current grammars.

An important implication of Sinclair and Renouf's work on frameworks lies in the area of method. Going through a corpus and making generalisations about each lexical item in turn is an extremely time-consuming business, and this possibly puts a limit on the size of corpus that can usefully be used, or on the accuracy of the observations that can be made. The advantage of Sinclair and Renouf's method is that it is wholly automatic: the computer carries out a relatively simple matching and counting exercise and arrives at a list of frequent frameworks. The disadvantage, as we have seen, is that it omits information that cannot be found by this method. Potentially, then, we have two competing (or complementary) sets of generalisations arising from a corpus, one that depends entirely on frequency of co-occurrence and is able to be generated by computer software alone, and one that is more interpretative and demands the input of a human researcher. How these sets of generalisations might differ from each other, and the implications of such difference, are topics that have yet to be explored.

1.4.6 *Towards a lexico-grammar*

Traditional descriptions of English make a clear separation between lexis and grammar. Arguments in favour of this separation include the possibility of making a judgement of grammatical well-formedness about a clause whose lexical items are clearly nonsensical, as in *Colourless green ideas sleep furiously*, and the possibility of processing nonsense poetry, such as the *Jabberwocky*. The unity of lexis and grammar has also, however, been recognised. Halliday calls his description of English 'lexicogrammar', involving both lexis and grammar, and Hasan (1987/1996) discusses how lexis and grammar are related, suggesting that the end-point of bundles of system choices is not a range of lexical options but a single lexical option. In this sense, lexis represents grammatical choices at their most delicate. The disadvantage of this view is that it does not explicitly take into account the kind of phraseology that Sinclair has noted. If words have their typical phraseologies, such that words are not selected in isolation but in variable phrases, then it is unsatisfactory to propose that each lexical item is the end-point of an individual bundle of system choices. The best compromise that could be reached would be to propose that each bundle of system choices should end, not in a lexical item *per se* but in a 'unit of meaning'. As units of meaning are, by their nature, indeterminate in extent, however, such an interpretation would involve system-choices leading to fuzzy-edged and overlapping units, at best.

Sinclair insists that the evidence of corpus-linguistics points to the falsity of the distinction between lexis and grammar. He argues that these aspects of language are separate only in those cases where the open-choice principle operates (1991: 114). If they are taken to be the central organising feature of language, then all instances of idiomaticity, collocation etc must be seen as anomalous. But if it is true that the idiom principle is all-pervading, then it would follow that most English discourse is itself anomalous. If a system of description makes it necessary for most of the data it is designed to describe to be dismissed as anomaly, there is clearly something wrong with the system of description. Sinclair (1991: 103–4) puts this argument thus:

> The decoupling of lexis and syntax leads to the creation of a rubbish dump that is called 'idiom', 'phraseology', 'collocation', and the like. If two systems are held to vary independently of each other, then any instances of one constraining the other will be consigned to a limbo for odd features, occasional observations, usage notes, etc. But if evidence accumulates to suggest that a substantial proportion of the language description is of this mixed nature, then the original decoupling must be called into question. The evidence now becoming available casts grave doubts on the wisdom of postulating separate domains of lexis and syntax.

The starting point for the observations that lead to this conclusion is the experience of doing lexicography. Describing how compilers of the 1987 Cobuild dictionary worked, Sinclair (1987: 110) notes:

> There was in practice no clear distinction between grammar and lexis, and grammatical rules merged with restrictions in particular instances, and those restrictions ranged from the obviously grammatical to the obviously lexical.

In other words, the world of the lexicographer is of necessity invaded by the grammarian. Sinclair (1991: 65) suggests that the opposite must also happen: "the traditional domain of syntax will be invaded by lexical hordes." In practical terms, this means that the learner's reference collection will no longer be divided into 'dictionary', 'grammar' and 'usage book' (Sinclair 1987: 107). The theoretical implications for the description of language have only just begun to be understood.

1.5   Francis: A corpus-driven grammar

Many of Sinclair's ideas regarding the association of meaning and pattern are taken up and further developed by Francis (1993, 1995).

1.5.1   *Meaning and pattern revisited*

Francis develops further Sinclair's observation that there is a close association between meaning and pattern, or between sense and syntax. While Sinclair concentrates on the fact that different senses of polysemous words are distinguished by differences in typical pattern use, Francis concentrates on the other side of the coin, that certain patterns 'select' words of particular meanings.

For example, she notes (Francis 1995) that in the pattern '*it* + link verb + adjective + clause' (e.g. *It is interesting/likely/clear/important/true that* or *It is useful/sensible/possible to*), the only adjectives that occur fall into a limited number of meaning groups, which she lists as "modality, ability, importance, predictability, obviousness, value and appropriacy, rationality, truth". Furthermore, each adjective co-occurs with a particular kind of clause, such as a 'that-clause' or a 'to-infinitive clause' (although some adjectives, such as *possible,* occur with both kinds). In addition, more precise observations can be made. The phrase *it is surprising that,* for example, is less frequent than its negative counterpart *it is not/hardly surprising that.* Phrases such as *it is hard to* are most typically followed by mental process verbs, as in *it is hard to believe.*

Francis (1993) offers another example of the same kind. Nouns which are followed by appositive that-clauses (*argument that, decision that, fact that, problem that, sorrow that*) can again be divided into a limited number of meaning groups: illocutionary processes; language activity of some kind; mental states vis-a-vis particular issues; thought processes or their results; feelings and attitudes; and general nouns. Furthermore, examination of each noun used with such a clause reveals different sub-types within that clause (Francis 1993: 150). Some nouns are used with genuinely appositive that-clauses, as in *idea that, hypothesis that*, where the that-clause indicates what the idea or the hypothesis is. In the case of nouns that refer to feelings, such as *annoyance that, fear that*, the that-clause indicates the cause of the feeling. A few nouns, such as *hint that, reminder that*, interpret what is in the that-clause as, for example, a hint or a reminder. As with the adjective example mentioned above, further phraseological restrictions can be observed. The noun *reason*, for example, is followed by an appositive that-clause only when it is both in a prepositional phrase beginning with *for* and modified by a definite article and an adjective such as *simple*. In other words, whereas it would be true to say that *reason* may be followed by an appositive that-clause, it would be more accurate to say that *reason* often occurs in the phrase *for the simple reason that*, where *that* begins an appositive that-clause. Phrases such as *for the simple reason that* and *it is hard to believe that* represent good candidates for the 'units of meaning' proposed by Sinclair.

1.5.2   *Lexis and grammar revisited*

When discussing the limitations on adjective choice in patterns with introductory *it*, Francis (1995) argues that these limitations are not a simple necessary consequence of the nature of that-clauses and to-infinitive clauses, but that it is rather "a fact about the grammar of these adjectives (or these adjective-senses)". In other words, the observations about the adjectives fall as much into the category of lexical description as into the category of grammatical description. Francis joins with Sinclair in proposing that lexis and grammar should not be treated as separate categories, but as a single category. She argues as follows:

> Particular syntactic structures tend to co-occur with particular lexical items, and — the other side of the coin — lexical items seem to occur in a particular range of structures. In short, syntax and lexis are co-selected, and we cannot look at either of them in isolation (Francis 1995).

She also follows Sinclair in proposing a hypothesis of how language is encoded which prioritises meaning and lexis instead of grammatical choices. Sinclair (1991: 8) argues that speakers have meanings which they want to make and that these meanings naturally attract to themselves phraseologies which incorporate lexis and grammar:

> ...decisions about meaning are made initially at a very abstract level, and also in very broad and general terms. At that point there is no distinction between meaning and strategy. A new-born communicative intent passes through various stages of realization, during which decisions about expression begin to be taken. These have lexical and grammatical ramifications, and are moved towards final form through a series of default options, unless a specific effect is specified in the design.

Francis (1995) echoes this in somewhat simpler terms:

> ...lexis is communicatively prior to syntax. As communicators we do not proceed by selecting syntactic structures and independently choosing lexical items to slot into them. Instead, we have concepts to convey and communicative choices to make which require central lexical items, and these choices find themselves syntactic structures in which they can be said comfortably and grammatically.

1.5.3   *Towards a methodology*

As we saw above (Section 1.4), Sinclair's work is based on two possibly contradictory methodologies. One involves the researcher painstakingly investigating the phraseology of one lexical item after another. The other involves the use of a computer to list the most frequently-occurring word sequences. Francis faces the same problem of whether to take the lexical item as the starting point or whether to take the patterns as the starting point. She investigates the adjective *possible*, for example, and notes that it occurs with an unusually wide range of patterns, each of which it shares with other adjectives. On the other hand, she investigates patterns such as the appositive that-clause, exemplified above, and lists the nouns which share that pattern.

For her study, Francis advocates "moving from environment to item and back to environment again" (Francis 1993: 146). For example, her study of the pattern (environment) '*it* + link verb + adjective + that-clause' leads to an interest in an item, *possible*, and then to an investigation of the other patterns (environments) in which that adjective occurs. Similarly, she suggests that the investigation of appositive that-clauses "could profitably lead to an exploration of the grammar of some of the more frequent noun-heads, of which *fact* and *reason*, for example, promise rich findings" (Francis 1993: 155).

If a study is to be limited to the most frequent words and patterns of

English, a method which, as Francis (1993: 155) suggests, "[allows] the compiler considerable freedom of movement" is probably highly satisfactory. Once the aim is to compile a comprehensive lexical grammar of English, however, greater restrictions are needed, to ensure complete coverage. In the next section we describe how the two 'grammar pattern' volumes (Francis et al. 1996; Francis et al. 1998) were compiled.

1.6   COBUILD: the grammar pattern series

1.6.1   *Introduction*

The proposal that Francis made in her 1993 paper for a comprehensive lexical grammar of English came to partial fruition in the two-volume 'pattern grammar' series published by COBUILD (Francis et al. 1996, 1998). In this section we describe briefly how the research that led to that series was done.

The original methodology of the research was to examine the English language lexical item by lexical item. This research was carried out by lexicographers working on the Collins COBUILD English Dictionary (1995), who as a matter of course worked through the list of items to be included in the dictionary, and who allocated grammar coding as part of the data they collected on each item. The dictionary includes the 75,000 most frequent words and phrases found in the Bank of English corpus.

As Sinclair notes (1987: 114), the compilation of a word-by-word grammar database allows exploitation along many lines. The two volumes in the grammar patterns series took the dictionary codings as the starting point, supplementing that information where necessary with further investigation of particular patterns. Using Francis' (1993) terminology, then, the methodology was in most cases to move from the item (the lexical item being investigated for the dictionary entry) to the environment (the pattern), and where necessary to supplement this with movement from the environment to the item. The aim was to produce lists of items that have each pattern, each list being as complete as the sample of English consulted (the 300 million word Bank of English corpus) would allow.

1.6.2   *Grammar in the Collins COBUILD English Dictionary*

From the early days of the COBUILD project, the identification of grammar patterns was seen as an integral part of the lexicographer's task. This was partly because of Sinclair's (1987: 106) concern that the dictionary should "give specific help in composition". Learners who wished to use a word, rather than simply to understand it, needed explicit instruction as to how the word is typically used (and compare Hornby's aims, Section 1.2). In addition, however, the acknowledgement of the association of meaning and grammar, as discussed above in sections 1.4 and 1.5, meant that meaning could not in fact be explained without an indication of the patterns of use of each word sense. Hanks (1987) explains how the COBUILD definitions (or 'explanations') and examples themselves provide an indication of these patterns of use. The grammar codings give more explicit information.

The principles behind the design of the grammar codes have been described in Clear et al. (1996). The codes are a radical departure from those traditionally used in dictionaries, even learners' dictionaries, in that they do not employ the usual metalanguage such as 'transitive verb' or 'verb + object'. Instead a string of elements is given, each element representing an actual word (usually prepositions such as *for* or *with*, but sometimes other items such as *way* or *the*) or a type of clause or group. The element that represents the word being exemplified is shown in capital letters, other elements are in lower-case letters. Actual words are shown in italics, group and clause types are shown in roman script. No plus signs are used: the sequence of elements is shown by the sequence of the codes in the string. Thus **N that** means 'noun followed by a that-clause'; **V *for* n** means 'verb followed by *for* and a noun group i.e. a prepositional phrase beginning with *for*'; **ADV adj** means 'adverb occurring before an adjective'; and **v-link ADJ** means 'adjective following a link verb'. (Several examples of patterns are given in Chapter 2.)

The rationale behind this coding is that it fulfills three requirements. It is designed to be flexible, transparent, and consistent.

The coding is *flexible* because, with no categories used apart from the surface ones of clause and group type and actual words, there is no limit to the kind of phraseology that can be represented in the coding. No pattern is too long to be coded in detail. For example, the sense of *face* that is exemplified in *the unacceptable face of capitalism* always occurs in this kind of phrase, with a definite article, an adjective, and a prepositional phrase beginning with *of*. This information is economically captured in the coding ***the* adj N *of* n**.

The coding is *transparent* rather than simple: it is not possible to provide simple coding for the behaviour of words in English, because they do not behave in simple ways. A simple coding would, then, be a partial coding. However, because there is only a limited set of elements that make up the codes, and because the codes relate only to surface manifestations and not to syntactic abstractions, the metalanguage is such that, we hope, learners can quickly come to understand it. A learner, or, more likely, a teacher, may initially object to seeing **V n** (verb followed by noun group) rather than the more familiar 'transitive verb' or 'verb + object', but our codes have the advantage of representing iconically the patterns they describe. For example, a learner may have difficulty remembering the distinction between attributive and predicative adjectives, but the patterns **ADJ n** and **v-link ADJ** actually show in their own form how the adjectives behave. For this reason the Collins COBUILD English Dictionary does not need a comprehensive list of codes; a simple list and explanation of the code elements is sufficient.

Finally, the coding is *consistent* in that it does not mix types of meta-language. It is possible, of course, to code something such as *make her happy* as 'verb + object + adjective'. Such a coding might be quite comprehensible, but it would not be consistent, as it mixes a functional label ('object') and a word-class one ('adjective'). This consideration would be of only theoretical interest, but given that the surface coding has other advantages, it is an additional benefit.

For various reasons, verbs in the dictionary were coded a little differently from other word-classes. For verbs, lexicographers were asked to list every pattern that each sense of the verb has, exemplifying the most frequent ones. The result is a complete profile of the behaviour of each sense of the verb. For example, sense 1 of the verb *fantasize* has the following coding:

VERB
V *about* **n/-ing**
V that
also V -ing

This means that most frequently this verb is followed by a prepositional phrase beginning with *about* (the example given is *I fantasized about writing music*) or by a that-clause (e.g. *Her husband died in 1967, although she fantasised that he was still alive*). Another pattern, where the verb is followed by an '-ing' clause, is less frequent and is not exemplified in the dictionary (this is indicated by ***also***).

For nouns and adjectives, however, only the most frequent or noticeable behaviour is coded and exemplified. For example, the noun *implication*, for its first sense, is coded thus:

N-COUNT
usu pl
oft N *of/for* **n**

This indicates a count noun, usually plural (but the singular is also found), often followed by a prepositional phrase beginning with *of* or *for*. The examples given are ...*the political implications of his decision... serious implications for future economic growth.* No information is given, however, about the behaviour of the noun when it is not followed by these prepositions.

The second sense of the noun (which indicates a specific logical consequence of something) is given no coding other than **N-COUNT**. One of the examples (*The implication that marital infidelity enhances a leader's credibility is preposterous*) shows the noun followed by an appositive that-clause, yet this is not frequent enough to be reflected in the coding.

This difference in coding has implications for the methodology of exploiting the database for pattern information. For verbs, the database is almost complete, the only omissions being errors on the part of the dictionary compilers, which were easily rectified. For nouns and adjectives, however, the database is less complete, and further searching of 'environments' had to be done in order to ensure that all words with a given pattern had been found.

1.6.3   *The grammar patterns series*

The COBUILD grammar patterns series consists of two volumes: Collins COBUILD Grammar Patterns 1: Verbs (referred to in this book as Francis et al. 1996) and Collins COBUILD Grammar Patterns 2: Nouns and Adjectives (referred to in this book as Francis et al. 1998). A simplified version of volume 1, with exercises, was published under the title Verbs: Patterns and Practice (Francis et al. 1997).

The aim of the series was simple but ambitious: to show all the patterns of all the lexical items in the Collins COBUILD English Dictionary, and within each to show all the lexical items that have that pattern. For convenience, each of the word-classes is dealt with separately, resulting in a volume covering patterns of verbs, and another volume with two sections dealing with nouns and adjectives respectively. (At the time of writing no other volumes are planned, although it would be feasible to bring out volumes covering all word-classes.) The division into word-classes has the benefit of showing, for example, all verb patterns together, but it has the disadvantage of obscuring relations between patterns. For example, the following patterns with introductory *it* all perform similar functions, yet they are not grouped together in the 'grammar patterns' books:

it **V n to-inf**	e.g. *It hurts me to think of that*	verb pattern
it **v-link N to-inf**	e.g. *It would be a shame to lose touch*	noun pattern
it **v-link ADJ to-inf**	e.g. *It was terrible to see his face*	adjective pattern

Each volume is arranged pattern by pattern, each pattern occupying a section. Within each section, with a few exceptions that will be described below, lists of all the words with that pattern are given, grouped according to meaning. The sections, then, give a complete profile of each pattern; inevitably, this means that in each section only a partial description of the behaviour of each sense of each word is given. This complements the information in the dictionary, where complete information of each word is given, but the information about patterns is not easily retrievable.

The aim in the grammar patterns volumes is to be comprehensive, to list all the words that have a particular pattern. There are some places, however, where this is not possible. Listing all the verbs that have the patterns **V** or **V n**, or all the nouns with the pattern **N** *of* **n**, or all graded adjectives, would result in books of an unmanageable size, although it would be possible for an electronic resource to list all these verbs and nouns. In cases such as this, therefore, the books list only the frequent words in each category.

A more radical problem arises, which reflects a difference between verbs on the one hand and nouns and adjectives on the other. In the case of verbs there tends to be a sharp distinction between the patterns that a verb has and the patterns that it does not. For example, *suggest* clearly does have the pattern **V that** (*He suggested that we should leave*) and equally clearly does not have the pattern **V to-inf** (**He suggested to leave*). In the case of many nouns and adjectives, however, there is no such sharp distinction. Chapter 3 gives some examples of doubtful patterns, such as *jealousy*, which is sometimes, but rarely, followed by an appositive that-clause, that is, has the pattern **N that**.

1.7   Conclusion to Chapter 1

This chapter has traced the history of an approach to the description of English, from its early manifestation in a reference book in the 1950s to its appearance in a series forty years later. This approach:

is based on phraseology, as observed in large corpora;
avoids a distinction between lexis and grammar;
represents a meeting-point between the concerns of pedagogy — what it is that learners need to know — and those of theory — how the English language can most satisfactorily be described.

CHAPTER 2

What a pattern is

2.1 A word and its patterns

In this chapter we will look in more detail at what a pattern actually is, and show how concordance lines can be used to illustrate the patterning of language.

The patterns of a word can be defined as all the words and structures which are regularly associated with the word and which contribute to its meaning. A pattern can be identified if a combination of words occurs relatively frequently, if it is dependent on a particular word choice, and if there is a clear meaning associated with it.

The procedure for investigating the patterns of a word involves selecting at random a number of concordance lines and sorting them into alphabetical order. They may be right-sorted or left-sorted according to the word one is examining. In the case of a verb, it is more revealing to sort to the right, since most verbs have complementation patterns which follow them (*he decided to leave, he hated leaving*). Though complementation patterns are usually the most interesting facts about verbs, there may be reasons for sorting them to the left, as this would show how often a verb occurs in the passive or infinitive, which modals it is often used with, what are its typical Subjects, whether it is frequently negative and so on.

In the case of nouns, too, sorting to the right reveals their complementation patterns (*his decision to leave, the theory of evolution*). Sorting to the left shows the various ways in which the noun is modified. In the case of adjectives, too, sorting to the right shows both the kind of noun they modify, and their complementation patterns, while sorting to the left will show, for example, whether or not they are often preceded by link verbs. It will also reveal the kinds of modifier that commonly collocates with the adjective.

Below are examples of words taken from each of the four major open classes (verb, noun, adjective and adverb), showing how their patterns can be revealed by concordance lines. The verb is *explain*. There are 54,300 occurrences of this verb in the Bank of English corpus; the following is a random selection of 50 lines whose node is a form of the verb *explain* (slightly edited to exclude the more complex patterns, which will be discussed later in this chapter). These lines have been sorted alphabetically to the right, because we are mainly interested in the complementation patterns of this verb:

```
 1 rs and mash for tea,' he explained. A few years later it's
 2 cam said then went on to explain about the barman at the sta
 3 notherapist Paul McKenna explains: 'After discussing what you
 4 attempt to categorize or explain all the different types. I
 5 hree centuries ago,' she explained: as casually as a girl dis
 6 erwards he was trying to explain Britain's thinking on the is
 7 se of the brain'. No one explained exactly to the parents wha
 8 hotographer Monte Fresco explains: 'He's so consistent, for
 9 nchez: When Cavazos did explain his personal views, they usu
10 e that problem. Can you explain how a baby boom in the Sixti
11 task of immobilizing it explained how it worked: 'Any child
12 original price. 'Let me explain,' I offered. The label, I s
13  an interfaith marriage explains in part the humanitarian
14  you I would be glad to explain in some detail my reasons f
15  knew he was there, she explained 'In the dark, when someon
16 s, she lied to you. She explained it to you on the basis th
17 of view and he tried to explain it to his daughter as he to
18 rate a theory, and thus explain it to someone, by telling a
19 ne of them, Jon Knight, explained on arrival in London that
20 d is included but never explained. Probably because it is of
21 as, paint etc). The fax explained that Newton had the right
22  John, who seemed to be explaining that he had a nappy and
23  TEC Head of Marketing, explained that these were real
24 ical Journal, 23/6/90), explains that a single dose of antib
25 ve to at all. Could you explain that, please? Dominquez: Sur
26 other. He would have to explain that to her when the time
27 t my husband can't. She explained that she never paid
28  Commerce and Industry, explains that Switzerland has a spl
29 at I was doing and so I explained that a copy of the documen
30 headed sensei (teacher) explained the complex rituals of o-c
31 ong blacks could partly explain the fact that they account f
32 ter) Jochen von Maydell ·explained the city's recession-beati
33 es from school. When he explains the problem to her she gene
34 erences Methods Section Explain the method you used to gathe
35 voice said, still calm, explaining the hard facts of life to
36 The upcoming discussion explains the previewing process and
37 that's the reason, they explained, the city has offered to
38 s produced a leaflet to explain the new system. Available fr
39 onths. Dentists have to explain to their patients that they
40 undred yards long. Alex explained to me,' said Barry, how
41 ident Lennart Johansson explains 'We are disappointed that t
42 ven their big chance to explain what they're about, unencumb
43 ng cover prices without explaining what they are for. The Bi
44 ouse and blue jeans, was explaining why she thought that nea
45 pective employer, which explains why the tone of media inter
46 eactions. This helps to explain why a charcoal-grilled steak
47  region. All this might explain why the Thai baht was under
48 ic flavour, which might explain why he was not better known
49 for red burgundy, which explains why six of the best from
50 f clapped-out Chrysler. Explain your itinerary to the driver
```

This set of concordances reveals all the significant patterns of the verb. In lines 1, 3 and 5, for example, it is found with direct speech. In line 2, it is followed by a prepositional phrase introduced by *about*. In lines 4, 6 and 9, the verb is followed by a noun group. In lines 44–49, it is followed by a clause introduced by *why*, and in lines 10 and 11 by a clause introduced by *how*. In lines 42 and

43 it is followed by a clause introduced by *what*. In lines 16 and 17, the verb is followed by a noun group (realised by the pronoun *it*) and a prepositional phrase introduced by *to*, and in line 40 by just the *to* prepositional phrase. Finally, in lines 21–24 and 27–29, it is followed by a that-clause. All the other lines in this sample can be accounted for by these few patterns, which will be explored in more detail in the next section.

A similar procedure can be undertaken for a noun: *decision*. Again the sample of 50 lines is alphabetically sorted to the right, since it this is a noun which has clear complementation patterns:

```
 1 ecause of the commission decision. CFMEU united mineworkers
 2 lso attacked yesterday's decision. Michael Meacher, shadow
 3 of the last to make this decision. Alegria: California is one
 4 are very annoyed at this decision and many people who are at
 5 the reasoning behind the decision, announced yesterday at th
 6 inery to ensure that his decisions are obeyed. Without a new
 7 y not desirable that the decision as to the right electoral
 8 stars. It is no longer a decision as to whether or not to cha
 9 ce Sachs stated that the decision as to what was an immoral p
10 e following Wednesday's decision by the two main nationalist
11 it seems to me that the decision by the administration, havi
12 ote on the result. Most decisions by three-judge panels on
13 ounced. Ironically, the decision comes a year after he relea
14 ament insisted that the decision did not imply recognition o
15 g. Let her make her own decisions. Everyone has a right to d
16 ompany song. Even small decisions have to be passed along fr
17  proven to be an astute decision. He's always kept his integ
18 uchess of York took the decision herself to marry into the
19 gone but before a final decision is made about the future of
20 posing such a move. The decision leaves Mr Kinnock's options
21 tice model of strategic decision making, Organisation Scienc
22 have seen the big-cigar decisions modern publishers take, t
23 on of the prosecution's decision on Monday. At the same time
24 ended in July pending a decision on its German business. The
25 rday. How can they make decisions on Waanyi land when they'r
26  ahead of the council's decision on whether to raise key le
27 rganization along which decisions or orders will pass from t
28 Then they reversed that decision, saying the notices of with
29 tions, the seven-to-one decision settled the issue of Title
30 he jurisdiction to make decisions such as Mabo, there is no
31 tly, I have come to the decision that the earring discovery
32 ittees (to counteract a decision that had required a committ
33 n said: 'This is a good decision that gives Victor the chan
34 esterday stuck by shock decision to quit racing for a month.
35 vernment's genuflecting decision to rename Victory over Japa
36 t a major factor in the decision to start smoking. Numerous
37 d The Goss Government's decision to drop the South Coast Mot
38 unsure about Saturday's decision to abandon the scheduled f
39  has welcomed Baghdad's decision to allow more than three-th
40  to get, so we took the decision to ensure that part-time em
41 e's other controversial decision: to appoint his friend Alan
42 c. Asked to justify its decision to release the information,
43  the rather underhanded decision to use the San Andreas Fault
44 reaffirmed its original decision to approve Halcion, but h
45 s no bed available. The decision to release him was taken by
46  galaxy. Wife scared by decision to stand; John Redwood Cons
47 chose to claim that the decision was irrevocable as he had d
48 at I had made the right decision when I was 15. As he looks
49 mum. As a manager, your decisions will be partly based on ha
50 ssibility that clinical decisions will not be made for the r
```

These lines differ from the lines for *explain* in one important respect. Verbs almost always have complementation patterns, except in the case of verbs used intransitively, which have no complementation. (The most frequent type of complementation is a noun group, as in line 9 of *explain* above.) The majority of nouns, however, do not have complementation patterns at all. In the case of *decision*, just over half of the lines show the word 'on its own', with no associated complementation patterns, for example in lines 1–6. Elsewhere, however, there are patterns: in line 7 the noun is followed by a prepositional phrase introduced by the phrasal preposition *as to*. In lines 8 and 9, *as to* is followed by clauses introduced by *whether* and *what* respectively. In lines 24 and 25 the noun is followed by a prepositional phrase introduced by *on*, and in line 26 *on* is followed by a *whether* clause. In line 31 the noun is followed by a that-clause, and in lines 34–46 by a to-infinitive clause, its most frequent pattern. All these words and clauses constitute the patterns of the noun *decision*.

The next example is an adjective: *afraid*. Some adjectives are both attributive and predicative; that is, they occur both before nouns (*a happy man*) and after link verbs (*he is happy*). Some adjectives only occur in one position, either before a noun (*there are countless reasons*), or after a link verb. *Afraid* is one of the latter: it is always predicative. A brief look at the lines will show that it never occurs before a noun, and a glance to the left of the node will show that it usually follows the verb *be*.

The following lines are again sorted to the right, showing the complementation patterns of the adjective:

```
 1  but was still obviously afraid. A week later he was able to
 2  int near Drvar. They are afraid and are panicking. Everything
 3  ed between those who are afraid and do it and those who stand
 4  d Westerners need not be afraid, for we are about to lift the
 5  ance. If I fail 'Are you afraid for yourself? He looked at h
 6  ve overspent by .98p I'm afraid. I've hung your clothes upsta
 7  e was turned on me. 'I'm afraid I've only got three,' I said
 8  if it costs 18 quid. I'm afraid I'm not very interested in th
 9  n't know how, though I'm afraid it may have come from someone
10  n't worry about it. I'm afraid it comes with the territory.
11  by crumb because she is afraid lest the bread will finish an
12  ionship; she is neither afraid nor ashamed. Since the 'white
13  re popular at home? I'm afraid not. But Edward Heath has
14  ss I say something, I'm afraid nothing will be done. But
15  ership is that they are afraid of the people's awakening.
16  hen she says. 'They are afraid of losing their friends. They
17   guy, I was desperately afraid of being alone again and a bi
18  o wipe out. Everyone is afraid of the Khmer Rouge. Myself t
19  e who had not come were afraid of America and had no courage
20   hit me again, I wasn't afraid of his actions but his words
21  r explain to her. She's afraid of your detachment,' Mrs Van
22  ready in love with, and afraid of, her. Girls seem frighteni
23  ht of her Mr Paul being afraid of anything or anyone was qu
24  arly if that someone is afraid of them. Often they hate them
25  way, both because I was afraid of seeming too needy and bec
26  ld in college — but was afraid of disappointing his father.
```

```
27 y weren't just a little afraid of him, too. So he has been g
28 at people are no longer afraid of it,' says Rene Pelletier,
29 nt of all, he was never afraid of emotional controversy, th
30 ered for it. He was not afraid of death and now he's up ther
31 at and scared me. I was afraid one of the balls might hit
32 iences of hers, but I'm afraid our interpretations differ.
33  morning. He was really afraid. So let's eliminate him. The
34  other words. 'Yes, I'm afraid so, sighs Professor Jean-Paul
35 asoned players. And I'm afraid that I just wasn't ready. And
36  y birthday. I had been afraid that he would be hanging abou
37 drained because she was afraid that one of her little darli
38 of food, and you may be afraid that all the food you enjoy m
39  Johnny shook his head, afraid that if he spoke he'd cry aga
40 you, did they?' No, I'm afraid that was stretching the truth
41 edalus. Serman had been afraid that even Croaker knew that h
42 hat women should not be afraid to trumpet their achievemen
43 complications. Don't be afraid to listen to a new point of
44 e had been offended but afraid to speak out. And one youngs
45 any and we are all very afraid to be swallowed. Wertheimer:
46 h sweat. He lay frozen, afraid to close his eyes and fall as
47 in his approach and not afraid to be shocking. We met in San
48 e, to placate them, but afraid to oppose them. Her weakness
49 Family on holiday. I am afraid to say that it looks as thoug
50 me an example, and I am afraid you will earn a certain fame
```

Again, not all the lines for *afraid* have complementation patterns: lines 1–4 show the adjective used 'on its own'. In line 5 there is the pattern *afraid for* which occurs only once in this small sample but is quite frequent for the word overall. In lines 7–10, the adjective is followed by a that-clause without *that*, while in lines 35–41 the *that* is realised. It is possible to treat that-clauses with and without *that* as separate patterns. In this case *I'm afraid that I just wasn't ready* would exemplify **V that**, while *I'm afraid I've only got three* would exemplify another pattern, say **V clause**. For convenience, in the Collins COBUILD English Dictionary (CCED), both types of example were treated as **V that** because most words that occur with a that-clause take either type of clause. This convention is followed here too; thus we consider lines 7–10 to contain that-clauses. Line 11 shows the pattern *afraid lest*, which is extremely rare and occurs only four times after *afraid* in the whole of the corpus. In lines 13 and 34 we have *afraid not* and *afraid so* respectively — these patterns are peculiar to *afraid*, and do not occur with other adjectives (as far as we know). In lines 15–30 *afraid* is followed by *of*; this is its most frequent pattern. Sometimes it is followed by *of* and a noun group, as in lines 15 and 18, and sometimes by *of* and an '-ing' clause, as in lines 16 and 17. Finally, in lines 42–49 the adjective is followed by a to-infinitive clause; this pattern is also very frequent.

It can be seen that there are two main meanings of *afraid* represented in these lines: one is 'frightened' and the other is when you are apologising for something. The second of these is associated with only with the *that* pattern and the to-infinitive pattern mentioned above, while the first is found with all the patterns. There is a strong tendency for meaning to be associated with pattern in this way, as discussed in Chapter 1 and Chapter 4.

The last word-class to be looked at in this section is an adverb: *presumably*. Again there are 50 lines, left-sorted alphabetically. In the case of adverbs it is often difficult to know which method of sorting will reveal their patterns most clearly.

```
 1 rs, more intelligent and  presumably more wise, is slowly begi
 2 out forked tongues — and  presumably with a less acute sense o
 3 roperty in Tehran — and,  presumably, to the decision to send
 4 Auckland on Thursday and  presumably again during the three-d
 5 ancial reasons. Mr Assad  presumably wants to clarify what arm
 6  he would be looking at,  presumably, would be in 1992. So she
 7 welve disciples because  presumably He felt that was a g
 8 chap that he is, Bernie  presumably saw that tobacco sponsor
 9   My brother (by birth,  presumably, though there are some pu
10    is not explained but  presumably they originate from the p
11 ltion of rows of cacti.  Presumably Helen found that being on
12 ht the virus, which can  presumably therefore only be transmi
13 rs are turning up dead,  presumably at the hands of death squ
14 became writer-director,  presumably on the assumption that so
15 rnal religious dissent:  presumably, it was the still wines o
16 helial surface. Durham:  Presumably you would like to find a
17 about my background erm  presumably you want to understand w
18       The returned exiles  presumably restored both altars in t
19 e for an illicit fling,  presumably with their Mimis and Fifi
20 an aboard the frigate —  presumably the captain — used a loud
21 ay the murdered man had  presumably taken the previous Friday
22 th Americans. There has  presumably been some improvement in
23 range comment, since he  presumably means the plateau which b
24 apped artfully over her  presumably withered legs. Now is it
25 was certainly immoral.  Presumably, these two jobs are inc
26  after five years he is  presumably not about to remodel Num
27  information about it'.  Presumably this is because other pot
28 scientist pans out, it  presumably will mean one more site
29 ence to the FAC letter.  Presumably Qantas decided it was not
30 tionary power of money.  Presumably, it stemmed from money's
31 don't do it', an older,  presumably wiser journo friend warne
32 e last two places. One,  presumably, will go to Mark Ilott, w
33 icularly difficult ones  presumably the Diabolical Dingbats
34 eah and a lot of people  presumably that come here have a big
35  the Rev. William Pitt  (presumably known in church as Pitt t
36  of the Brisbane River.  Presumably the police acted to pre-e
37 any different scholars,  presumably of many different politic
38 rnative Christmas show,  presumably on the grounds that you
39 row a mixture. And then  presumably when we've got that firm
40 cargo is on board. This  presumably means that cargo inspect
41 s held for a long time.  Presumably the preference for long h
42 goods. One who sold up,  presumably at a fair profit, was th
43 ly clean out any weeds.  Presumably the plants will already
44 ing; some bastards will  presumably remain in the Cabinet; th
45 ing the play-offs, will  presumably spend big and Forest have
46  quite interesting work  presumably. Well I helped Colonel
47 ist on the Third World,  presumably more gullible than the F
48 visible employee, would  presumably advance loyalty and compa
49  institution that would  presumably read polls, which show t
50 the same price it would  presumably have done so. But such
```

Adverbs differ from the other three major word-classes in that they do not have complementation patterns. An examination of the concordance lines shows, however, that their behaviour is patterned in observable ways. For example, *presumably* is often found at the beginning of a sentence or clause, where it serves to comment on the whole clause — see lines 11, 16 and 25. Or it appears before a phrase or group as in line 13 — *presumably at the hands of the death squads*, and in line 1 — *presumably more wise*. In other lines it modifies a verb as in line 5: *Mr Assad presumably wants to clarify...* On the whole though, the patterns of adverbs are hard to capture. Many adverbs are like *presumably* in that they can appear at different points in the sentence, while others are more restricted: frequency adverbs like *often* and *usually*, for example, generally occur directly before the head of a verb group. 'Degree' adverbs like *very* and *extremely* always modify adjectives or other adverbs. But there is no parallel to complementation patterns: adverbs can be better described in positional terms.

In all the concordance lines given above, the node words can be seen as having patterns which 'belong' to them. There is another way of looking at patterns, however, which will be explored in the next section.

2.2 A pattern and its words

In the previous section patterns were shown which are associated with particular words. We attempted to show that a word can have a large number of patterns. In this section we will look at patterns from a different perspective. Just as a word can have several different patterns, so a pattern can be seen to be associated with a variety of different words. This is the opposite side of the coin.

Let us take, for example, a pattern in which a verb is followed by the preposition *over* and a noun group or wh-clause. There is a range of verbs which share this pattern, of which the following are just a few. Two lines have been chosen to illustrate the use of each verb in this pattern, and the lines have been sorted to the left so that the verbs followed by *over* are in alphabetical order.

```
      heels while critics argue over the niceties of translation st
   ence they managed to argue over the direction of the wind and
     look at each other bicker over the poisoning of a dog. If th
   ve old quarrels and bicker over territory. That is a general r
    be convinced to compromise over the structure of the competiti
   ans refuse to compromise over independence, everything that h
   eek, and now they disagree over the importance of the ruck duel
  and Mr Thornberry disagree over Piccio's weight problems and t
  other interviewer enthuses over nude pictures of the model Hel
  elcome guest. She enthused over his gift of Fortnum and Mason's
     hat in mind, as they fight over whether to support a rescue pac
   rming that she would fight over Europe, and to assure Saddam
  ucoup Franco-American fret over Frenchie jokes, in New England,
   ides to the president fret over this intra-party friction. Mr
   er bridal showers and fuss over her trousseau. That's her busin
    shows in the way you fuss over Everett. You married him for th
   er. Public officials gloat over the employment numbers which do
   y. Hopefully, we can gloat over a successful football season. I
```

```
11, he had already grieved over her once, and so it made no rea
or 23 years he had grieved over his actress-wife Helen Beck, an
1. When they do not haggle over the price of property, sales mu
the countryside. To haggle over prices and engage in sharp
r Powell continues to muse over a presidential run, almost cert
ybe there was time to muse over the suggestion that 'problems o
ng the class, she pondered over her final placings. In a 23-str
ocket cruiser and pondered over some of her cruising and racing
 Gooch is planning to pore over the record book — not to see wh
a Polaroid taken, and pore over the script. At the appointed ti
own from Armagh to preside over the ceremony celebrating the 80
signed rather than preside over shabby official treatment of t
the regulator prevaricated over whether to make the announcemen
s the Germans prevaricated over an attack on Gibraltar, the
 much time procrastinating over situations which only time can
ation for procrastinating over a decision on the Marseille
a-terrestrials also puzzle over what they call 'the anomalous
tters to come in, I puzzle over one fact. Why is it that people
ts when the giants quarrel over its possession. Fafner brutally
so ill-bred as to quarrel over the last cucumber sandwich. 'N
ain had no wish to quibble over precise institutional details
t think they would quibble over one penny. I have never been in
public manager is seething over Bolton's failure to notify him
 has been quietly seething over various fictions Helen had been
d people openly speculated over who would win. The subject beca
y on the water speculating over rumours that Fields has got a
 hope continues to triumph over experience, for it is hard to
which Japan would triumph over Russia and America. However, at
        commanders wavered over whether to support the Emergenc
rect result. As they waver over which way to vote, those same M
r this they didn't wrangle over this at all and once the vote
ts. And let us not wrangle over who won it, who won the cold wa
```

It can be seen that this pattern is associated with a variety of verbs, often with meanings in common, like *bicker, disagree, fight, quarrel,* and *wrangle.* This point will be expanded at length in the next chapter, where we will attempt to show how the words which share a pattern can be grouped according to their meanings.

2.3 The representation of patterns

Up to now patterns have been introduced discursively: no attempt has been made to represent these patterns in any schematic form. It is convenient, however, to have a shorthand coding system to represent patterns. The need for a simple system of representing patterns arose first for us during the compilation of the second edition of the Collins COBUILD English Dictionary (CCED) (1995). A learner's dictionary requires a way of encoding grammar that is comprehensive and yet transparent.

In the first edition of this dictionary (Collins COBUILD English Language Dictionary 1987) patterns were encoded by a mapping of the word-classes involved in a pattern on to functional labels such as Object, Complement, and Adjunct. Thus, to return to the verb *explain,* an example such as *she explained it to me* would be coded as **V + O + A** (Verb + Object + Adjunct). There are two problems here. Firstly, in a sentence like *She walked four miles,* opinions differ as to whether *four miles* is an Object or an Adjunct. Thus the analysis necessary to produce this coding can be unreliable; different people will code differently. Secondly, the labels do not relate clearly to the surface realisation of the pattern. A learner seeing the coding **V + O + A** would not know how to use the verb *explain.*

Instead, for CCED only the simplest and most superficial word-class labels were used. The major ones used in CCED and in Francis et al. (1996; 1998) are as follows:

v:	**verb group**
n:	**noun group**
adj:	**adjective group**
adv:	**adverb group**
that:	**clause introduced by** *that* **(realised or not)**
-ing:	**clause introduced by an '-ing' form**
to-inf:	**clause introduced by a to-infinitive form**
wh:	**clause introduced by a wh-word (including** *how)*
with quote:	**used with direct speech**

Where a preposition, adverb, or other lexical item is part of a pattern, it is given in italics to indicate that it is a lexical item rather than a code, for example **V n** *on* **n**.

If we return to the concordance lines for *explain*, it can be shown that all the patterns described there can be represented using this very small number of symbols.

The upper-case **V** indicates that this is the word-class whose patterns we are focusing on. It will be seen later in this chapter that the same pattern can be described in terms of any one of its major elements. Note too that the plus sign is not used: sequence is indicated by a space.

V n

```
4  attempt to categorize or explain all the different types. I
6  erwards he was trying to explain Britain's thinking on the is
9  nchez: When Cavazos did explain his personal views, they usu
13  an interfaith marriage explains in part the humanitarian
14 r youI would be glad to explain in some detail my reasons f
20 d is included but never explained. Probably because it is of
30 headed sensei (teacher) explained the complex rituals of o-c
31 ong blacks could partly explain the fact that they account f
32 ter) Jochen von Maydell explained the city's recession-beati
33 es from school. When he explains the problem to her she gene
34 erences Methods Section Explain the method you used to gathe
35 voice said, still calm, explaining the hard facts of life to
36 The upcoming discussion explains the previewing process and
25 ve to at all. Could you explain that, please? Dominquez: Sur
26 other. He would have to explain that to her when the time
38 s produced a leaflet to explain the new system. Available fr
50 f clapped-out Chrysler. Explain your itinerary to the driver
```

V with quote

```
1  rs and mash for tea,' he explained. A few years later it's
3  notherapist Paul McKenna explains: 'After discussing what you
5  hree centuries ago,' she explained: as casually as a girl dis
8  hotographer Monte Fresco explains: 'He's so consistent, for
15   knew he was there, she explained 'In the dark, when someon
37 that's the reason, they explained, the city has offered to
41 ident Lennart Johansson explains 'We are disappointed that t
```

V wh

```
10 e that problem. Can you explain how a baby boom in the Sixti
11 task of immobilizing it explained how it worked: 'Any child
42 ven their big chance to explain what they're about, unencumb
43 ng cover prices without explaining what they are for. The Bi
44 use and blue jeans, was explaining why she thought that near
45 pective employer, which explains why the tone of media inter
46 eactions. This helps to explain why a charcoal-grilled steak
47  region. All this might explain why the Thai baht was under
48 ic flavour, which might explain why he was not better known
49 for red burgundy, which explains why six of the best from Al
```

V *about* n

```
2  cam said then went on to explain about the barman at the sta
```

V n *to* n

```
16 s, she lied to you. She explained it to you on the basis th
17 of view and he tried to explain it to his daughter as he to
18 rate a theory, and thus explain it to someone, by telling a
```

V that

```
19 ne of them, Jon Knight, explained on arrival in London that
21 as, paint etc). The fax explained that Newton had the right
22  John, who seemed to be explaining that he had a nappy and
23  TEC Head of Marketing, explained that these were real
24 ical Journal, 23/6/90), explains that a single dose of antib
27 t my husband can't. She explained that she never paid
28  Commerce and Industry, explains that Switzerland has a spl
29 at I was doing and so I explained that a copy of the documen
```

V *to* n

```
40 undred yards long. Alex explained to me,' said Barry,
```

V *to* n that

```
39 onths. Dentists have to explain to their patients that they
```

V

```
12 original price. 'Let me explain,' I offered. The label, I su
```

The pattern **V n** includes examples in which the verb is passive (such as line 20 above). The issue here is whether to treat passives as separate patterns or as variants of one pattern. The first solution is logical, as it avoids transformational practices, but the second is more economical. If a word occurs more frequently in the passive than the active, however, it makes sense to indicate this by expressing the pattern separately as the lexical word *be* with **V-ed** representing the past participle. Thus the verb *rumour* has the pattern **be V-ed that**: *it is rumoured that...*

The patterns shown in the concordance lines for *decision* and *afraid* can both be represented by these same few symbols. The following is the analysis for *decision*. Here the symbol **N** is in upper case as we are focusing on a noun. Only those lines in which *decision* does have a pattern are included in the analysis.

N *as to* n

```
7 y not desirable that the decision as to the right electoral
```

N *as to* wh

```
8 stars. It is no longer a decision as to whether or not to cha
9 ce Sachs stated that the decision as to what was an immoral p
```

N *on* n

```
24 ended in July pending a decision on its German business. The
25 rday. How can they make decisions on Waanyi land when they'r
```

N *on* wh

```
26 ahead of the council's decision on whether to raise key le
```

N that

```
31 tly, I have come to the decision that the earring discovery
```

N to-inf

```
34 esterday stuck by shock decision to quit racing for a month.
35 vernment's genuflecting decision to rename Victory over Japa
36 t a major factor in the decision to start smoking. Numerous
37 d The Goss Government's decision to drop the South Coast Mot
38 unsure about Saturday's decision to abandon the scheduled f
39  has welcomed Baghdad's decision to allow more than three-th
40  to get, so we took the decision to ensure that part-time em
41 e's other controversial decision: to appoint his friend Alan
42 c. Asked to justify its decision to release the information,
43  the rather underhanded decision to use th San Andreas Fault
44 reaffirmed its original decision to approve Halcion, but h
45 s no bed available. The decision to release him was taken by
46  galaxy. Wife scared by decision to stand; John Redwood Cons
```

The following is the analysis for *afraid*. Here the code **ADJ** is in upper case, as we are focusing here on the adjective. Again, only those lines in which *afraid* has a pattern are included in the analysis; here the lines with a pattern are in the majority:

ADJ *for* n

```
5 ance. If I fail 'Are you afraid for yourself? He looked at h
```

ADJ that

```
7 e was turned on me. 'I'm afraid I've only got three,' I said
8 if it costs 18 quid. I'm afraid I'm not very interested in th
```

```
 9 n't know how, though I'm afraid it may have come from someone
10 n't worry about it. I'm afraid it comes with the territory.
14 ss I say something, I'm afraid nothing will be done. But
31 at and scared me. I was afraid one of the balls might hit
32 iences of hers, but I'm afraid our interpretations differ
35 asoned players. And I'm afraid that I just wasn't ready. And
36  y birthday. I had been afraid that he would be hanging abou
37 drained because she was afraid that one of her little darli
38 of food, and you may be afraid that all the food you enjoy m
39  Johnny shook his head, afraid that if he spoke he'd cry aga
40 you, did they?' No, I'm afraid that was stretching the truth
41 edalus. Serman had been afraid that even Croaker knew that h
50 me an example, and I am afraid you will earn a certain fame
```

ADJ lest

```
11 by crumb because she is afraid lest the bread will finish an
```

ADJ *so/not*

```
13 re popular at home? I'm afraid not. But Edward Heath has
34  other words. 'Yes, I'm afraid so, sighs Professor Jean-Paul
```

ADJ *of* n

```
15 ership is that they are afraid of the people's awakening.
18 o wipe out. Everyone is afraid of the Khmer Rouge. Myself t
19 e who had not come were afraid of America and had no courage
20  hit me again, I wasn't afraid of his actions but his words
21 r explain to her. She's afraid of your detachment,' Mrs Van
22 ready in love with, and afraid of, her. Girls seem frighteni
23 ht of her Mr Paul being afraid of anything or anyone was qu
24 arly if that someone is afraid of them. Often they hate them
27 y weren't just a little afraid of him, too. So he has been g
28 at people are no longer afraid of it,' says Rene Pelletier,
29 nt of all, he was never afraid of emotional controversy, th
30 ered for it. He was not afraid of death and now he's up ther
```

ADJ *of* -ing

```
16 hen she says. 'They are afraid of losing their friends. They
17  guy, I was desperately afraid of being alone again and a bi
25 way, both because I was afraid of seeming too needy and bec
26 ld in college — but was afraid of disappointing his father.
```

ADJ to-inf

```
42 hat women should not be afraid to trumpet their achievemen
43 complications. Don't be afraid to listen to a new point of
44 e had been offended but afraid to speak out. And one youngs
45 any and we are all very afraid to be swallowed. Wertheimer:
46 h sweat. He lay frozen, afraid to close his eyes and fall as
47 in his approach and not afraid to be shocking. We met in San
48 e, to placate them, but afraid to oppose them. Her weakness
49 Family on holiday. I am afraid to say that it looks as thoug
```

This then is the way patterns are presented in CCED.

2.4 What's in a pattern?

It is now necessary to consider which elements are and which are not included in the concept of 'pattern'. Certain elements are excluded on the grounds that they can occur with almost any word of the same class. These have to be distinguished from genuine pattern elements. For example, in both the following sentences the noun *decision* is followed by a clause beginning with *that:*

(1)   *I have come to the <u>decision</u> that the earring discovery scene does not work*

and

(2)   *...to counteract a <u>decision</u> that required a committee's questioning of a witness*

The first that-clause is an appositive or defining clause qualifying *decision*, while the second is an ordinary relative clause. A defining that-clause is considered to be part of the complementation pattern of a noun; there are only a few hundred nouns that are typically followed by such a clause. The second that-clause is a relative clause. Relative clauses can qualify almost any noun, and are not considered to be part of their complementation patterns.

Also considered not to be part of a complementation pattern are prepositional phrases or adverb groups that give information about manner, place or time. Thus in the sentence *He said he'd phone at four o'clock*, the prepositional phrase *at four o'clock* is not part of the complementation pattern of *phone*.

There are a few other cases in which a word is frequently followed by a structural element which is nevertheless not considered to be part of its complementation pattern. These will be discussed in Chapter 4.

Let us turn to the question of the elements which are considered to be part of a word's pattern. As pointed out above, these are usually things that follow the word: its complementation. These patterns are listed in the next section. In some patterns, however, elements are included which precede the word in question. For example, some verbs have to have a plural noun group as their Subject. A plural noun group may consist of one noun group which indicates two or more people or things, as in *the children were always arguing*. Alternatively it may consist of two or more co-ordinated noun groups, linked by *and*, for example *Molly and Simon were always arguing*.

The main class of verbs which have a plural Subject are reciprocal verbs. Reciprocal verbs have two basic patterns:

1. They are used with a plural Subject and it is understood that the people, groups, or things realised by the Subject are interacting with each other. For example, two people can *quarrel, have a chat,* or *meet.*
2. They are also used with a Subject which refers to one of the participants and an Object or Adjunct which refers to the second participant, as in *She quarrelled with her sister, I chatted with him,* and *I met him at university.*

Because reciprocal verbs have these two related patterns, their patterns are usually supplied in pairs: the most frequent combination is **pl-n V** and **V *with* n**.

There is another major group of patterns where elements preceding the verb are included in the pattern. These involve the word *it. It* is considered to be part of a pattern in two different cases. The main one is when it is 'introductory' or 'anticipatory', in sentences like *It is a shame that the press ignored these events,* which has the pattern *it* **V n that**. In this sentence *it* is the Subject, but it may also be the Object, as in *I find it hard to understand your motives.* In this type of sentence, *it* points forward to a clause somewhere else in the sentence. This process is normally referred to as extraposition, but we prefer to avoid this term, on the grounds that it is transformational; it assumes that the non-extraposed version (*That the press ignored these events is a shame*) is somehow more fundamental than the version with *it.* In fact the latter is far more frequent; initial that-clauses seldom occur.

Secondly, *it* may be what we call 'general' *it,* which refers vaguely to a general situation, and does not point anywhere else in the sentence. The *it* used in reporting the weather is of this type: *It was drizzling steadily,* and for reporting time: *It was four o'clock.* Again it may be the Subject, as in these sentences, or the Object, in sentences like *I make it four o'clock.* A list of the major *it* patterns is given in the next section.

Finally there are two other symbols used in the labelling of verb patterns. One is **amount** in sentences such as *I owe her a lot,* or *We beat them 3–2.* The other is **pron** (pronoun), which is used in the patterns of phrasal verbs to indicate that a noun group is not realised by a pronoun. Thus *ring up* has the patterns **V n P** (*ring someone up*) and **V P n (not pron)**, indicating that *ring up him* does not usually occur. (**P**, here, stands for the particle — adverb or preposition — which combines with a verb to make a phrasal verb.)

As for the patterns of nouns, they resemble those for verbs in that they are normally complementation patterns, encoding the elements that follow the noun. Their patterns are sometimes very similar to those of verbs; for example, both verbs and nouns have patterns in which they are followed by a that-clause or a to-infinitive clause.

Like verbs too, there are some patterns which include elements that precede the noun: these include articles, prepositions, and possessive markers, for example *the cosmos, on duty, his junior*. They will be discussed further in the next section.

In the case of adjectives, the patterns are of two main types. First one needs to specify whether an adjective is attributive only (occurs before a noun), predicative only (occurs after a link verb), or both. In CCED the first two of these are coded as **ADJ n** and **v-link ADJ**, respectively. This code may be precede by **usu**, which indicates that this is usually but not always the pattern. Second, complementation patterns must be identified; again, some of them are the similar to those for verbs and nouns, notably those with a that-clause or a to-infinitive clause.

2.5   What kinds of pattern are there?

In general then, the pattern of a word consists of the elements that follow it, but it may also include elements which precede it. Let us look now at the major patterns which we consider to 'belong' to a word. A full list is available in Francis et al. (1996; 1998). In the pattern codes, the part-of-speech that is being focused on is in upper-case.

2.5.1   *The patterns of verbs*

In this section we will list and explain the main verb patterns as used in CCED and in Francis et al. (1996).

1. The verb is followed by a single noun group, adjective group, or clause, yielding the following patterns:

V n

(3)   *I broke my left leg.*

V pl-n

(4)   *The research compares two drugs.*

V pron-refl (reflexive pronoun)

(5)   *I enjoyed myself.*

V amount

(6)   *Two and two make four.*

V adj

    (7)   *He <u>escaped</u> unhurt.*

V -ing

    (8)   *She <u>started</u> walking.*

V to-inf

    (9)   *John <u>began</u> to laugh.*

V inf (bare infinitive)

    (10)   *I <u>helped</u> save these animals.*

V that

    (11)   *We <u>agreed</u> that she was not to be told.*

V wh

    (12)   *A passer-by <u>inquired</u> why the television cameras were there.*

V wh-to-inf (to-infinitive clause introduced by a wh-word)

    (13)   *I <u>have forgotten</u> what to say.*

V with quote

    (14)   *'Hello', he <u>said</u>.*

V so/not

    (15)   *I <u>think</u> so.*

V as if/as though

    (16)   *You <u>look</u> as if you've seen a ghost.*

V *and* v

    (17)   *I'll <u>go</u> and see him.*

2. The verb is followed by a prepositional phrase or adverb group. In some cases, there is a wide range of adverbs and prepositions following the verb, and these cannot be specified. This pattern is

V prep/adv

    (18)   *He <u>ran</u> across the road.*

Sometimes only an adverb can be used. This pattern is

V adv

    (19)   *Sarah has fair skin that <u>burns</u> easily.*

Sometimes only a prepositional phrase can be used. This pattern is

V prep

    (20)   *She <u>chewed</u> on her pencil.*

In other cases, the verb is followed by a noun group, adjective group, '-ing' clause or wh-clause introduced by a specific preposition. This pattern is **V *about* n, V *at* n, V *as* adj, V *by* -ing** etc., depending on the preposition. Examples include

    (21)   *He <u>was grumbling</u> about the weather.*

    (22)   *The rivals <u>shouted</u> at each other.*

The prepositions which are used in patterns like this are as follows:
about, across, after, against, around/round, as, as to, at, between, by, for, from, in, in favour of, into, like, of, off, on, onto, out of, over, through, to, towards, under, with.

    Sometimes the adverb *together* is used in the pattern **pl-n V *together***

    (23)   *The whole team <u>must pull</u> together.*

3. The verb is followed by a noun group and another element such as another noun group, an adjective group, a that-clause, a wh-clause or an '-ing' clause, yielding the following patterns:

V n n

    (24)   *I <u>wrote</u> him a letter.*

V n adj

    (25)   *The darkness <u>could drive</u> a man mad.*

V n -ing

    (26)   *I <u>kept</u> her waiting.*

V n to-inf

    (27)   *My advisers <u>counselled</u> me to do nothing.*

V n inf

    (28)   *She <u>heard</u> the man laugh.*

V n wh

(29)   He _showed_ me where I should go.

V n wh-to-inf

(30)   _I'll show_ you how to do it.

V n with quote

(31)   'We'll do it', she _promised_ him.

V n -ed (the past participle form of another verb)

(32)   I _had_ three wisdom teeth extracted.

4. The verb is followed by a noun group and a prepositional phrase or adverb group. In some cases there is a wide range of adverbs and prepositions following the verb, and again these cannot be specified. This pattern is

V n prep/adv

(33)   Andrew _chained_ the boat to the bridge

(34)   _Stir_ the sugar in.

Sometimes only an adverb can be used. This pattern is

V n with adv, where the adverb comes either before or after the noun group. Examples include:

(35)   He _switched_ the television on.

(36)   He _switched_ on the television.

Sometimes the pattern is formed with the word _way_ and an adverb group or prepositional phrase. This pattern is

V _way_ prep/adv

(37)   She _ate_ her way through a pound of chocolate.

In other cases, the verb is followed by a noun group and another noun group, adjective group or wh-clause introduced by a specific preposition. This pattern is

V n _about_ n, V n _at_ n, V n _as_ adj etc. depending on the preposition. Examples include:

(38)   I _warned_ him about the danger.

(39)   I _saw_ the question as crucial.

The prepositions which are used in patterns like this are almost but not quite the same as those in 2 above:

about, against, as, as to, at, between/among, by, for, from, in, into, of, off, on, onto, out of, over, to, towards, with.

Sometimes the adverb *together* is used in the pattern **pl-n V with** *together*

    (40)   *We <u>stuck</u> the pieces together.*

5. The verb pattern contains the word *it*. The main patterns are as follows.
Introductory *it:*
it **V clause**

    (41)   *It <u>doesn't matter</u> what you think.*

it **V** *to* **n clause**

    (42)   *It <u>sounds</u> to me as if you don't want to help her.*

it **V prep clause**

    (43)   *It <u>came</u> to light that the plane had not been insured.*

it be **V-ed clause**

    (44)   *It <u>is thought</u> that the temple was used in the third century.*

it **V n clause**

    (45)   *It <u>struck</u> me that the story would make a good film.*

it **V adj clause**

    (46)   *It <u>feels</u> good to have finished a piece of work.*

V *it* **clause**

    (47)   *I <u>hate</u> it when she's away.*

V *it to* **n clause**

    (48)   *I <u>owe</u> it to my parents to work hard.*

V *it as* **n/adj clause**

    (49)   *He <u>would take</u> it as an insult if I left.*

    (50)   *He <u>regards</u> it as significant that the Government is suggesting cuts.*

V *it* **n clause**

    (51)   *They <u>felt</u> it their duty to visit her in hospital.*

V *it* adj clause

(52)   *I think it best if you tell him the truth.*

'General' *it*:
it **V**

(53)   *It snowed all afternoon.*

it **V adj**

(54)   *It was very windy.*

it **V adj prep/adv**

(55)   *It's nice here.*

it **V n**

(56)   *It's blowing a gale.*

it **V *to* n**

(57)   *It got to the point where we couldn't bear to be in the same room as each other.*

it **V prep/adv that**

(58)   *It says here that they have live music.*

V *it*

(59)   *They didn't make it.*

V *it* prep/adv

(60)   *My family hated it in Southampton.*

2.5.2   *The patterns of nouns*

The following are the main noun patterns as used in CCED and in Francis et al. (1998).

1. Patterns with elements preceding the noun
a **N;** *the* **N** The noun is preceded by an indefinite or definite article:

(61)   *a cinch, a standstill; the blues, the bourgeoisie.*

poss N The noun is typically preceded by a possessive determiner like *my* or *your*, or a possessive formed from a noun group:

(62)   *She had tidied away her possessions.*

(63)   *I give you my word*

(64)   *My husband's sister came to stay.*

adj N The noun is preceded by an adjective:

(65)   *He was a tough customer.*

(66)   *She's a smart dresser.*

n N The noun is preceded by another noun:

(67)   *A window cleaner was arrested.*

from **N,** *on* **N,** *to* **N** etc. The noun is preceded by a specific preposition:

(68)   *I've been blind in my right eye from birth.*

(69)   *The film was shot on location in Washington.*

(70)   *They went to school together every day.*

The prepositions most frequently used in patterns like this are as follows:
at, by, from, in, into, on, out of, under, with.
supp N The noun is preceded by a range of the elements given above: determiner, possessive determiner or possessive noun group, adjective or noun.

2. Patterns with elements following the noun
N to-inf

(71)   *All four teams have shown a desire to win.*

N that

(72)   *There was a suggestion that the whole thing was a joke.*

N n The noun frequently modifies another noun.

(73)   *They have been exercising mob rule.*

(74)   *The federation is the umbrella body for seventy state organizations.*

N prep The noun is followed by a prepositional phrase introduced by a wide range of prepositions.
N *of* **n, N** *for* **n, N** *from* **n** etc. The noun is followed by a prepositional phrase introduced by a specific preposition.

(75)   *It was the latest in a series of acts of violence.*

(76)   *Their hatred for one another is legendary.*

(77)   *The threat from terrorists is at its highest for two years.*

The prepositions most frequently used in patterns like this are as follows:

about, against, among, as, at, behind, between, for, from, in favour of, in, into, of, on, over, to, towards, with.

In addition there is the pattern **N with supp**, which means that the noun is both preceded by a range of the elements mentioned above, and followed by them.

2.5.3   *The patterns of adjectives*

The following are the main adjective patterns as used in CCED and in Francis et al. (1998).

ADJ -ing

> (78)   *I felt <u>uncomfortable</u> watching him.*

ADJ to-inf

> (79)   *The print was <u>easy</u> to read.*

ADJ that

> (80)   *I am absolutely <u>horrified</u> that this has happened.*

ADJ prep The adjective is followed by a prepositional phrase introduced by a wide range of prepositions.
ADJ *as* n, ADJ *of* n, ADJ *on* n etc. The adjective is followed by a prepositional phrase introduced by a specific preposition.

> (81)   *We felt <u>inadequate</u> as parents.*
> (82)   *I think he's fully <u>aware</u> of those dangers.*
> (83)   *He's always been very <u>dependent</u> on me.*

The prepositions most frequently used in patterns like this are as follows:

about, against, as, as to, at, between, by, for, from, in, into, of, off, on, with.

It must be stressed that the patterns listed above are only the major ones. There are many more; full lists can be found in Francis et al. (1996; 1998).

2.6 Looking at patterns from all sides

So far we have treated patterns as though they are the discrete properties of words; patterns 'belong' to specific words. But this is to oversimplify: it is possible to look at patterns from different angles. Any sentence or utterance can be seen in terms of the pattern of any one of its lexical items. Consider the following sentence:

> (84) *A fire safety officer said it was important that residents in high-rises were aware of fire safety procedures and equipment in their particular buildings.*

1. The whole of the sentence after the Subject is a **V that** pattern belonging to the verb *say: A fire safety officer <u>said</u>...*
2. There is the pattern **it V adj that**, *it <u>was</u> important that...* where the pattern belongs to the verb *be*.
3. The same pattern can be seen as belonging to the adjective *important*, in which case it would be coded as **it v ADJ that**.
4. There is a pattern **V adj** belonging to the verb *be: ...residents in high-rises <u>were</u> aware of...*
5. The same pattern can be seen as belonging to the adjective *aware,* in which case it would be coded as **v-link ADJ *of* n.**

The ways in which all these patterns flow into each other will be explored in Chapter 8.

2.7 Different forms of a pattern

Patterns, especially those of verbs, are not always straightforward: their elements do not always occur in the order given in the explanations above. What follows is a list of the different forms a basic verb pattern can have. (This information and some of the examples below are taken from Francis et al. 1996: 611–615.)

1. Subject not before verb
In straightforward utterances the Subject comes before the verb, but this is not always the case. Sometimes the Subject comes earlier in the clause, or is not mentioned explicitly in the clause. For example, the verb exemplified may itself be part of the pattern of another verb and be in the to-infinitive form or '-ing' form.

> (85) *We want to **<u>ensure</u> that there is care and comfort available for them.***
> (pattern is **V that**)

> (86) *I enjoy **telling** people I was born in Brixton.*
> (pattern is **V n that**)

In other cases there is no Subject as such: the agent can be inferred from the context.

(87)   *The idea is to **use** conflicts as opportunities to show youngsters how*
        to observe siblings' feelings.
        (pattern is **V n** *as* **n**)

There is usually no Subject when the verb is in the imperative.

2. Passive voice

When a verb is in the passive, the order of the elements is different, with the
Object of the active sentence functioning as the Subject of the passive sentence.
As mentioned above, a strict adherence to the surface description would perhaps
involve the treatment of the passive as a separate pattern. However, for the sake of
convenience and simplicity, it is considered here as a variant of the active pattern.

(88)   *King Conrad **was elected** German king in 911.*
        (active pattern is **V n n**)

3. Questions and reported questions

In a 'yes/no' question, the order of the elements are the same as in an ordinary
clause, except that the Subject comes after the auxiliary.

(89)   ***Have** you **found** it yet?*
        (pattern is **V n**)

In a wh-question, the order of the elements is normal when the question relates
to the Subject, but if it relates to the Object or Complement then the order
changes, with the Subject coming between the auxiliary and the main part of the
verb. When there is a preposition following the verb, this remains in its position
after the verb.

(90)   *Who **said that**?*

(91)   ***What did** you **say**?*
        (pattern is **V n**)

(92)   ***What are** you **looking for**?*
        (pattern is **V** *for* **n**)

(93)   ***What did** he **train** as?*
        (pattern is **V** *as* **n**)

With reported questions, the wh-word comes first but the order is normal after
that: the Subject comes before the whole verb group.

(94)   *They asked me who I **could trust**.*
        (pattern is **V n**)

(95)   *Perhaps in the back of my mind I knew* **what I <u>was looking for</u>.**
      (pattern is **V *for* n**)

4. Relative clauses

When the relative pronoun is the Subject of the verb in the relative clause, there is no change in the order of the elements.

(96)   *The man who <u>shot</u> him was immediately overpowered.*
      (pattern is **V n**)

However, when the relative pronoun is the Object or Complement of the verb in the relative clause, the normal order is changed. The relative pronoun comes before the Subject.

(97)   *Most of the people* **that I <u>met</u>** *were academics.*
      (pattern is **V n**)

(98)   *Inside the ticket hall he dialled the number* **that Mr Furniss <u>had given</u>**
      <u>him</u>.
      (pattern is **V n n**)

(99)   *He tapped the file on Baum* **which Fox <u>had brought</u> in.**
      (pattern is **V n adv**)

When a verb is followed by a prepositional phrase, one of two things can happen. In formal English, the whole prepositional phrase is often used to begin the relative clause (except when the relative pronoun is *that*).

(100)   *The feeling of timelessness was just as strong at the farmhouse* **in**
      which we <u>stayed</u>.
      (pattern is **V prep/adv**)

In other contexts, the preposition remains at the end while the relative pronoun comes first.

(101)   *We have put together several lists of plants* **that you <u>may be looking</u>**
      <u>for</u>.
      (pattern is **V *for* n**)

Often no relative pronoun is used as the Object or Complement of the verb in the relative clause.

(102)   *The people I <u>met</u> at Fairbanks appeared very capable.*
      (pattern is **V n**)

(103) *It sounded exactly like the small town I **was looking for.***
(pattern is **V** *for* **n**)

In the case of the pattern **V that**, the Subject may be preceded by a relative pronoun which is part of the that-clause. The *that* of the that-clause is not realized.

(104) *I shall invite both written and oral observations from any person **who** I **think** **can help me.***
(pattern is **V that**)

5. '-ing' form or to-infinitive as part of a Complement
If a non-finite verb form is used after an adjective or noun as part of a Complement, that verb 'loses' a noun group from its pattern. In the following example, *ready for printing* is the Complement of the verb *be*. The verb *print* has the pattern **V n** (as in *They printed the book*) but in this example the noun group which the verb relates to occurs as the Subject of the clause.

(105) ***The book** is ready for **printing.***

Here are some more examples:

(106) ***Strawberries** are easy to **propagate.***

(107) ***Gina** seemed very likeable and looked easy to **talk to.***

(108) ***The battle** will be fun to **watch.***

6. To-infinitive as qualifier of a noun group
If the to-infinitive form of a verb is used after a noun group, that verb 'loses' a noun group from its pattern. In the following example, *to play* is qualifying the noun group *a rotten trick*. The verb *play* has the pattern **V n** (as in *He played a trick*) but in this example the noun group which the verb relates to occurs before the verb.

(109) *It was a **rotten trick to play.***

Here are some more examples:

(110) *I had a **rather special problem to solve.***

(111) *That was a **silly thing to say.***

7. Fronted elements
Normally the first element in the clause is the Subject: there is a strong tendency for the Subject to be thematised. However, other elements can be fronted for emphasis.
These examples show a fronted Object or prepositional Object:

(112)   *This I __could__ never __have anticipated__.*
(pattern is **V n**)

(113)   *I became known among my friends as the boy who took drugs. **This I**
really __bragged__ of.*
(pattern is **V *of* n**)

(114)   *He put the hat into his holdall. **The gun** he __put__ **in the pocket of his**
raincoat.*
(pattern is **V n prep**)

These examples show a fronted Complement or Object Complement:

(115)   ***Terrible** he __was__. Horrible man.*
(pattern is **V adj**)

(116)   ***The Butcher**, they __called__ **him**.*

(117)   ***Lucky Alexander**, he __was__ **called**.*
(pattern is **V n n**)

These examples show a fronted Adjunct:

(118)   *In the middle of all this, **in __walked__** Maggie.*
(pattern is **V prep/adv**)

(119)   *Taking a deep breath, **in** he __went__.*
(pattern is **V prep/adv**)

Note that there is verb-Subject inversion except where the Subject is a pronoun.
These examples show a fronted wh-clause:

(120)   ***Why I did this** I __cannot say__.*
(pattern is **V wh**)

(121)   ***How he got in** I __do not know__.*
(pattern is **V wh**)

8. Cleft structures

If you want to focus on a noun group, you can use a cleft structure instead of
using that group as the Subject or Object of a sentence. In a cleft structure the
Subject is *it*, the verb is *be*, and the noun group you are focusing on is the
Complement. The noun group is followed by a relative clause giving the rest of
the information.

(122)   *He found a telephone and dialled the Kent number. It was Bird who*
__answered__.

In this example, the cleft structure represents an alternative to *Bird answered*. As with ordinary relative clauses, when the noun group you are focusing on is the Object of the verb, the normal word order is changed. The Subject comes after the relative pronoun if there is one, or after the Object.

> (123)   *If it's **gossip** you **want**, you've come to the right place.*

> (124)   *It was **you** I came to **see**.*
>   (pattern is **V n**)

9. Pseudo-cleft structures

In a pseudo-cleft structure, a clause beginning with *what* is the Subject of the verb *be*, focusing on new information following the verb. The word *what* can be the Subject or Object of the clause, but always comes first. If *what* is the Subject, the word order is normal. If *what* is the Object, it comes before the Subject.

> (125)   *What **worries me** is that there has been a huge influx of drivers with very little experience.*

> (126)   ***What** we **need** is democracy.*
>   (pattern is **V n**)

A clause beginning with *all* can be used in a similar way.

> (127)   ***All** they **want** is a quiet life.*
>   (pattern is **V n**)

10. Comparisons

When a comparative noun group is followed by a clause beginning with *than*, there is no noun group after the auxiliary, verb, or preposition in the clause.

> (128)   *They knew much more than we **did** about the problems ahead.*

> (129)   *I have much more money than I **need**.*

> (130)   *It may be a better job than it **looks**.*
>   (pattern is **V n**)

> (131)   *We got far more than we **had bargained for**.*
>   (pattern is **V for n**)

When a noun group beginning with *as* is followed by a clause beginning with *as*, there is no noun group after the auxiliary, verb, or preposition in the clause.

> (132)   *Please give as much notice as you **can** before you vacate the premises.*

(133) *Fit a Venetian blind which can be angled to let in as little or as much*
       *light as you **like**.*
       (pattern is **V n**)

(134) *We have as much support as we **ask for**.*
       (pattern is **V *for* n**)

A similar thing happens when an adjective group or adverb group is followed by
a clause beginning with *than* or *as*. There is no adjective or adverb after the verb
or auxiliary in the clause.

(135) *He's smarter than I **am**.*

(136) *This is not as simple as it **sounds**.*
       (pattern is **V adj**)

(137) *They did better than we **did**.*
       (pattern is **V adv**)

Similarly there is no that-clause following the verb.

(138) *Obtaining access to Wu took a little longer than she **had promised**.*

(139) *I'm not as disheartened as people **think**.*
       (pattern is **V that**)

The patterns of nouns and adjectives, too, may be superficially different in
similar ways as those described above. (See Francis et al. 1998: 547–550.)
Firstly, the pattern of a noun may be affected by a verb pattern. In the following
example a noun with the pattern **N to-inf,** *duty,* is used with a verb, *impose,*
which has the pattern **V n *on* n**. The prepositional phrase beginning with *on*
comes before the to-infinitive clause:

(140) *Section 221 of the Companies Act 1985 imposed a **duty** on a company*
       ***to keep accounting records**.*

Secondly, the noun pattern may be interrupted by a verb group, as shown by the
following example, where the pattern is **N that**:

(141) ***Rumours** quickly spread **that Mr Yeltsin had been the victim of an***
       ***assassination attempt**.*

Thirdly, the noun may be separated from the other elements in the pattern by a
verb group and an adjective group. The following example has the pattern **N that:**

(142) ***Rumours** are rife **that the Prime Minister may be about to resign**.*

In the same way, adjective patterns may occur in a different form when interrupted by another pattern. The following example shows the pattern **ADJ** *at* **n/-ing**:

(143) *Sam Rosen was a **good** man **at explaining things**, and Kelly a good questioner.*

These, then, are the basic ways in which patterns operate. The next chapter will explore some issues which complicate the notion of pattern.

CHAPTER 3

Problems in identifying patterns

One of the appealing aspects of corpus linguistics is that it appears to open many doors in terms of the automatic processing of texts. One possible application of automatic text processing would be to identify the patterns that a given word has. This might appear to be a relatively easy task: the computer would simply have to recognise that a word is often followed by a particular preposition, by a to-infinitive or an '-ing' form, for example, and a pattern would have been identified. Manual work with patterns, however, suggests that the situation might not be so simple. There are several obvious complications. One is that the computer would have to recognise the different forms that a pattern can take (see Chapter 2). Secondly, it would need to distinguish between sequences which in formal terms are the same but which in pattern terms are not. Here are some examples:

a. The computer would need to distinguish between *that* introducing a relative clause, as in *Daniel didn't miss the look of annoyance that flickered on Brenda Goldstein's face* and *that* introducing an appositive that-clause, as in *If anything, my mood is more one of annoyance that we haven't been winning when we have played so well in so many matches*.

b. It would need to distinguish between a to-infinitive that is part of a pattern, as in *But then things started to go wrong* and a to-infinitive that simply means 'in order to', as in *A group of young children passing by stopped to watch us*.

c. It would need to distinguish between the preposition *as*, as in *I went along dressed as a Japanese lady* and the conjunction *as*, as in *Rock queen Tina Turner didn't feel quite dressed as she stepped aboard Concorde yesterday*.

In this chapter we identify three further phenomena that can confuse the human being and would almost certainly mislead the computer. In doing so we raise further issues around the question 'what is a pattern?' This question has been answered by exemplification in Chapter 2. In this chapter we turn to problem cases and ask 'what is not a pattern?' Our main argument in this chapter is that frequency and pattern are not necessarily the same thing.

3.1 Which word does the pattern belong to?

The first point to make is that a pattern does not always directly accompany the word that it 'belongs to'. Consider as an example the nouns *annoyance* and *satisfaction*, both sometimes followed by *that*. In the following sample concordance lines, the clause following *that* is an appositive that-clause belonging to *annoyance* and *satisfaction* (the pattern **N that**).

```
uld be 'not guilty'. He expressed annoyance that the judge was obviously
ho was the pilot, did express his annoyance that he could not start it,' M
  lightly, clearly concealing his annoyance that Voloshin knew this, as his
 in the Tonga. It started with my annoyance that the newsmen who were makin
I can now see it stemmed from my annoyance that she should have implied, n
his over-riding emotion is one of annoyance that he wasn't warned about the
British Embassy in Rome expressed satisfaction that the Italian authorities
        the Lithuanians expressed satisfaction that the meeting had occurre
and for the voters.' He expressed satisfaction that people are increasingly
   I felt an incredible amount of satisfaction that the perpetrators of thi
the full variety of wares, a smug satisfaction that yet another client has
   I didn't want them to have the satisfaction that they were getting to me
```

In other cases, however, the that-clause belongs to a verb that precedes the noun. This happens particularly when the noun is part of a phrase such as *to one's annoyance/satisfaction* or *with annoyance/satisfaction*. In the following examples, the verb with the pattern **V that** is underlined.

```
times, but Yul decided to his own satisfaction that the sickness was the fa
  It is easy to prove to your own satisfaction that you are worth many time
broad-rimmed hats and notes with satisfaction that in Australia sunscree
the airport itself. She saw with satisfaction that the less maneuverable
the same time he remembered with satisfaction that he was, in a sense,
viewing head, Brunner noted with satisfaction that in a few places rough
       out. Ruth found, to her annoyance, that far from quieting her
ossroads, he found to his intense annoyance that brave Horatius had taken
cab home and find, to my intense annoyance, that I can't put any weight on
   for they had found to their annoyance that, thanks to Peierls's shred
   didn't reply. Hart noted with annoyance that his brother hadn't respond
```

Too cursory a glance at the concordance lines would overestimate the number of occurrences of *annoyance* and *satisfaction* with an appositive that-clause.

Another example where the careless observer might be tempted into making an error is the adjective *rife*. This occurs 1114 times in the 300 million word Bank of English. It is followed by *that* introducing a that-clause no fewer than 113 times, and the t-score for *rife* followed by *that* is 9.5, which clearly indicates a significant collocation (see p. 231). A sample of the concordance lines, however, shows that these figures may be misleading.

```
    Rumours were rife that Knin had been taken
   Suspicion was rife that there were Mid-east connections
Speculation has been rife that the glamour forward could leave
   Rumour had been rife that Mr Andrew's return to the
      rumours were rife that he'd suffered a recurrence of
     With rumours rife that ringleaders of both sets of
```

```
      Speculation is rife that Grant's handlers have scripted
   Rumours had been rife that if war came the ground would
         Suspicion is rife that the bond-arbitrage profits were
        concern is now rife that citizens with burnt fingers
      Speculation is rife that the shake-out could trigger the
          fears were rife that bankruptcy moves on Britain's
      Speculation is rife that he will become life president
      Speculation is rife that there could be a flood of new
    speculation was rife that Offiah would be on his way
          rumour is rife that Dorothy's job is still in
      Speculation is rife that it will tumble back through the
```

The that-clause in each of these lines belongs to the noun, mainly *rumour/s, suspicion* and *speculation*. Clearly it is significant that *rife* comes between the noun and its that-clause in a large number of cases, but the adjective *rife* does not have the pattern **ADJ that**.

A similar issue arises if we consider the word *enough* following an adjective and followed by a to-infinitive clause. If the adjective is *big*, for example, the to-infinitive clause 'belongs to' *enough*:

```
    troughs of flowers scarcely big enough to decorate a gnome's summerhou
          The back seat is even big enough to hold the occasional adult if
   another room. The laundry is big enough to take a standing ironing boar
    Do it when the seedlings are big enough to handle.
 also eminently practical — it's big enough to take four adults and thei
in addition to designing a stage big enough to take large-scale opera
     to the more apprehensive eye, big enough to drown a suburban church
    grow up to 15 cm tall and are big enough to catch small fishes.
       Just a little girl, not even big enough to drive a car or go out
no one else has an indoor space big enough to throw this kind of party
```

This pattern is unique to *enough*. It might be expressed as **adj *enough* to-inf**.

If the adjective is *easy*, however, the same pattern does not occur. If *enough* is followed by a to-infinitive clause, that clause belongs to *easy*, not to *enough*. The following examples all begin with *it*.

```
                It is easy enough to find two who wish that his
                It is easy enough to make if you buy the pastry
        and it was easy enough to follow
                It was easy enough to understand why their
       but it is easy enough to speculate on their
     But it was easy enough to tell then that there was
                It is easy enough to explain the preponderance
          it was easy enough to persuade him that the
                It was easy enough to hear the clatterings of
                It was easy enough to seed a mine, bringing in
                It was easy enough to tell Alice was fresh
                It is easy enough to look at your course
With hindsight it is easy enough to see the two main errors
```

In most cases, the pattern is *it* **v-link ADJ to-inf**. In lines 2 and 3, however, the *it* is anaphoric reference, not introductory *it* and the pattern is **ADJ to-inf**. In either case, the presence of *enough* does not affect the pattern. *Enough* here is a post-positional grading adverb, similar to *fairly*, but following the adjective.

The adjective *bad* is, for the most part, similar to *big* above. If it is followed by *enough* and a to-infinitive, the to-infinitive belongs to *enough*:

```
so bad that I couldn't get up but bad enough to prevent my doing anything
                 I don't think it's bad enough to give it up
tuation in Indian Kashmir appears bad enough to persuade thousands to make
              Disaster — this is bad enough to put us out of business
thought 'bout whether I wanted it bad enough to smoke it anyways
ond-degree burns on his tail were bad enough to force him to stop
               The result was not bad enough to force him to call an early
               The fog was just bad enough to make overtaking dangerous
even with back and sinus problems bad enough to bring the trainer on
```

This pattern is, again, **adj *enough* to-inf**. However, if the adjective is preceded by an introductory *it*, we find a pattern that needs a different kind of explanation. Here are a few concordance lines:

```
        It is bad enough to lose a length casting, let alone
        It is bad enough to suffer the control of our
        It was bad enough to realise it — she could not
        it was bad enough to know that their father had
        It was bad enough to lose, Admiral, worse to be
He said it was bad enough to break a precedent by
```

and some expanded examples:

(1)   *It is bad enough to suffer the control of our minds by the modern media; we don't want to be completely programmed by the scientists.*

(2)   *It was bad enough to lose, Admiral, worse to be unable to accept it.*

(3)   *It is bad enough to lose your prisoners, but injuring your customers through ignorance of procedures will be a criminal responsibility.*

Here the to-infinitive belongs to *bad*, in the pattern *it* **v-link ADJ to-inf**, but there is also an association between *bad enough* and the clause that follows. The clause *bad enough* indicates a bad situation, and this is followed by the second clause which indicates a still worse scenario. This is an example of 'clause collocation', which will be discussed in more detail in Chapter 8.

The sequence 'adjective *enough* to-infinitive', then, is ambiguous in terms of pattern, and the adjective must be specified for the pattern to be correctly identified. A computer programme would have difficulty, then, in recognising the correct pattern for an adjective it had not been taught to deal with.

Pattern ambiguity may also occur with a single word. The following two sets of concordance lines have the same sequence of words but exemplify, first, the pattern **v *it* ADJ to-inf** and, second, the pattern **ADJ to-inf**. In other words, the first set of lines comprise a pattern with introductory *it* as Object, whilst in the second set the *it* is anaphoric reference.

```
oft conditions though, and make it awkward to mow to the lawn's edge
he protruding perches will make it awkward to position the cages within
```

```
on your social life (making it awkward to eat out) and the lack of
        adding bulk and making it awkward to write comments in the margins
    intervention. That makes it awkward to look too hard at the pre-
nders that the usual stubs make it awkward to write.
    Alongside the halyards makes it awkward to operate if another control li
oll after printing, which makes it awkward to read and file. Also, the
small but heavy enough to make it awkward to carry. I rested it on the
        radioactive. That makes it awkward to store and handle, but it make
on the bottom of the tube made it awkward to use. It's expensive too.
```

We do not know exactly how the human reader decides which pattern interpretation is the correct one. Possibly he or she asks, on encountering *it* 'is there
something that this might refer to?' and asks, on encountering the to-infinitive 'is
this clause complete or does it refer back to *it*?' Both retrospective operations are
beyond the capacity of current computer programmes. If a computer were given
the task of assessing how many lines of the pattern *it* **v-link ADJ to-inf**, with the
adjective *awkward*, occurred in a particular corpus, it would be highly likely to
give an inaccurate answer.

Our point in this section is that the raw data of concordance lines needs to
be interpreted for patterns to be identified correctly. We have focused here on
points of difficulty, where interpretation is particularly important and where
automatic processing is likely to fail. For the human researcher, however, all the
problems raised in this section are highly solvable. In the next section we turn to
problems that are open to debate even by the human corpus-user, and which
challenge us to define more precisely what we mean by pattern.

3.2 When is a pattern not a pattern?

Our argument in this chapter is that frequent co-occurrences of words do not
necessarily indicate the presence of a pattern, and that interpretation of concordance lines is necessary to the identification of patterns. In the previous section
we suggested cases where a computer (or an inattentive human researcher) might
mistake frequent occurrence for pattern. In this section we look at cases where
the identification of pattern is open to interpretation.

The first example is the verb *train* (in the sense of 'study' or 'teach'),
which is commonly followed by a variety of prepositions, notably *as, at, for, in*
and *with*. The verb *train* can be interpreted as having two sets of patterns: **V** *as*
n and **V n** *as* **n** (or the passive *be* **V-ed** *as* **n**); **V** *in* **n** and **V n** *in* **n** (or the passive
be **V-ed** *in* **n**). These are illustrated briefly by the following concordance lines:

```
    dog trainer, Gary Jackson, has trained Yandi as a narcotics-detect
ventually the Chinese Government trained her as a librarian and she f
t in Africa, Asia and Europe. He trained as a teacher, and at present works
        Feb 15), interesting. I trained as a nurse in Brisbane where both
```

```
by the Americans and were being trained as an opposition commando force.
said that she had a son who was trained as an engineer but that he was an
the Celtic races, women warriors trained boys in the arts of combat.
mprehensive religious education, trained the boarders in the use of
for the last eight years. I have trained in counselling, hypnotherapy and
    cheek and passion. Ningali has trained in dance but never as an actor
        Armani was never formally trained in design, though he says he must
raggerman and they are specially trained in underground rescue. Each of
```

Saying that these lines illustrate patterns belonging to the verb *train* essentially means that the use of the preposition *as* or *in* is constrained by the choice of verb, and, conversely, that the choice of verb is constrained by the preposition. In other words, and in accordance with the idiom principle, *train(ed) as* and *train(ed) in* are selected by the speaker as single units.

The same is not true when the verb is used with other prepositions. *At* is usually used to indicate a place, *for* to indicate a time, and *with* to indicate equipment or companions. The verb often means 'prepare for a sport' as well as 'learn or be taught a skill'. The preposition *in* is sometimes also used to indicate place: in this case, it is not an instance of the pattern **V *in* n**. The concordance lines below illustrate the use of *train* with a preposition where this does not constitute a pattern.

```
om practice in that England will train at Wembley on the Saturday before
go. Stone said it was a bonus to train at the Finland Institute for two
me offering her a scholarship to train at a college in Idaho. America
sandbagged roads outside, troops trained at great expense to defend Western
    of whole problems than those trained at first-rate schools (and) worked
    friend William Hewlett, who had trained at MIT before returning to

was. After all the best way. She trained for a year, perfected what speech
powerfully controlled as if he'd trained for years. Altering his gait
e fact that his goal ace has not trained for three weeks because of shin
rtley said yesterday he had been training for a couple of weeks and thought
easant army that Marcos has been training for 10 years move out from the

    Damien Marsh left Brisbane to train with Torrence in Atlanta in April
t of ordering the players not to train with the Super League clubs but
ing up the sport. Weight lifters train with weights, but in a very
    passport and I'm not allowed to train with the other players, but nothing
    after the Brazilian midfielder trained with the team yesterday, despite a

le drive into Belfast where they train in the gymnasium run by their
n the USA and Britain, the group trained in New York and have performed in
from his father Francis, who was trained in Paris at the famous Larue
```

The case of *train* is relatively straightforward, in that there is a clear difference between *train as a teacher* and *train at a college*. In some cases, however, the interpretation of a frequent sequence as a pattern or not is much more difficult and open to debate. As a first example, consider the concordance lines below, which show the adjective *available* followed by a variety of prepositions. Although here only a few lines are shown, they are representative of large number of occurrences (in the Bank of English) of each preposition following *available*.

```
       slips into a pocket or handbag.  Available  at chemists, supermarkets and
         first quality tile prices are  available  at The Tile Bin, next door to
      of a ribbon and these were made  available  at all venues. A 10p donation in
        is artistic, and most of it is  available  at reasonable prices. But even
          There are very few rooms  available  at any Forte hotel. But even

        except for Jakovich should be  available  for our first practice match, he
         with McCaw Cellular, was not  available  for comment. A public statement
    ange of commodities and services  available  for cash, the commercialization
   isfied that the child is legally  available  for adoption and that the natura
   not have to be filed but must be  available  for inspection.

       of the trails. Full details are  available  from the Park Authority. Both
      onies. Explanatory leaflets are  available  from most GP's surgeries
         and Norwich. Full details  available  from World Development Movement
      Chesterfield, the sofa is  available  from Robert's shop, Carless
   one of the lowest everyday rates  available  from any major credit card

        blaming a lack of hotel beds  available  in Glasgow for the 8 May
     ly 17 of 125 toothpaste formulas  available  in Australia. The toothpaste
     made. Further places may become  available  in the coming weeks. If parent
    not be new as long as it's still  available  in the shops. Write to: Lena
   French and Czech lagers (widely  available  in supermarkets and off-licences

   d design projects. The product is  available  in ten strong colours in rolls
            The new Nubrollis are  available  in 45 and 50 inch diameters at
          Kit costs £2.19 and is  available  in 15 different colours. The
   creamer, sugar bowl and vases. Available  in Gold, Purple, Blue, Ruby Red
   is scratch resistant. Frames are  available  in traditional tortoise or ebon

   Allotments. But none of these is  available  on the open market. Goods can
   or allegedly misusing information  available  on a shared computer network, b

   alls for the allowance to be made  available  to more women, paid at a higher
   said there were four alternatives  available  to Homestake shareholders: acce
   Users and street cops agree it is  available  to virtually all who want it,
   med local telephone calls will be  available  to all consumers from 1997 as
   basic married couple's allowance  available  to those aged under 65.
```

In the case of most of these prepositions, we would not consider the prepositional phrase to be part of a pattern with *available*. This is certainly true of the prepositions *at, from* and *on*. The information given in the prepositional phrase is relatively trivial (the phrase indicates place or time in most cases), the prepositional phrase can (arguably) be moved to a different part of the clause, and in each case the association of the prepositional phrase with *available* is not important. Admittedly, none of these criteria is at all watertight. Triviality is a subjective quality, and it is one of the principles of corpus work that a potential transformation (or movement) is not particularly valid evidence (for an alternative view see Rudanko 1996). The final criterion — that it matters what the adjective is — is perhaps the most telling but also somewhat subjective. Let us take an example from the above lines:

(4)   *There are very few rooms available at any Forte hotel…*

We would argue that this information can be phrased in many ways, not using *available* or another adjective that might belong to the same meaning group: *You can't stay at any Forte hotel; At any Forte hotel rooms are in short supply; There are very few rooms at any Forte hotel* and so on. Thus the adjective *available* is not significant to the prepositional phrase *at any Forte hotel*.

There are three types of example in the concordance lines above where it is possible to argue for a closer association between adjective and preposition. These are: the second group of *for* examples, such as *the child is legally available for adoption...*, the second group of *in* examples, as in *The product is available in ten strong colours*, and the *to* examples, such as *it is available to virtually all who want it*. Attempts at rephrasing would give us:

(5)   *The child has been brought to us for adoption; The child is to be considered for adoption; ?You can take the child for adoption.*

(6)   *The product can be bought in ten strong colours; The shop stocks the product in ten strong colours; The product is manufactured in ten strong colours.*

(7)   *The product can be sold to virtually all who want it.*

The first two sets of rephrasings suggest that *for adoption* and *in ten strong colours* are phrases in their own right that are used with a range of other lexical items. The presence of *available* is not significant to the use of those prepositional phrases. Thus, *available* does not have the patterns **ADJ *for* n** or **ADJ *in* n**. The phrase *to virtually all who want it*, on the other hand, is not so flexible. It can be used with the verb *sell*, but only because that verb has the pattern **V n *to* n**. It is therefore important for the prepositional phrase that the adjective is *available*, or we might say that the pattern 'selects' this adjective and not other words. Therefore the adjective has the pattern **ADJ *to* n**.

On the whole, the question of whether something is or is not a pattern is especially difficult to answer in the case of nouns and adjectives. The preposition *in* is particularly problematic. Here are some concordance lines for the sequence 'possessive + *aim/purpose* + *in* + -ing form'. The question they raise is: Do the nouns *aim* and *purpose* have a pattern **poss N *in* -ing**?

```
1  Renewed – and this should be your  aim in  applying similar methods at home
2  pposition claims the government's   aim in  expanding the Supreme Court is t
3  mself has repeatedly insisted his   aim in  going was purely humanitarian, t
4  it has stayed the same brain. Her   aim in  pursuing these courses was to
5   before he achieved his principal   aim in  retaking Jerusalem. That the
6  peror's wedding, her more serious   aim in  travelling to China was to meet
7          disease. Vogel's express   aim in  writing Vital Circuits is to
8  atever the therapy discipline. My   aim in  writing this book was to give
9  yone can be bought. Franco's real purpose in  arranging the meeting finall
10     has told me himself – that his purpose in  coming here was to hold
11    and among lesbians. This was my purpose in  creating the book. A Lesbian
12 s got to be in charge. Part of my  purpose in  going is to see how we appro
13 roaches (Box 21.1). Part of their  purpose in  protesting, in fact, is not
14  act as parliamentary adviser.. My purpose in  putting the amendments down
15    at home, the taxpayer's primary purpose in  sending her to a public high
16    edition, Seafield explained his purpose in  writing the book: The great
```

The answer to this question is not easy. On the one hand, there is clearly a frequently-occurring, variable sequence of words that comprises 'someone's aim or purpose in doing something'. This is the kind of sequence that a teacher may well find it useful to teach a learner of English. Furthermore, there is clearly a group of nouns with similar meanings (*aim, purpose, intention, motivation, target*) that occur in this sequence. On the other hand, the prepositional phrase beginning with *in* is very mobile. Rephrases of some example lines, such as *In pursuing these courses her aim was to...* (line 4); *In writing this book my aim was to give...* (line 8); *In coming here his purpose was to hold...* (line 10); *In creating the book, this was my purpose...* (line 11) are very acceptable, although of course they alter the weight of information given. In addition, the preposition *in* seems to have a meaning that is expressible in other ways. For example, line 1 is rephrasable as *This should be your aim when you are applying similar methods at home*, and line 5 might be rephrased as *He achieved his principle aim which was to take Jerusalem*. Furthermore, the examples might be rephrased with the prepositional phrase but without the key words *aim* or *purpose*. Line 6, for example, might be rephrased *What she wanted to do in travelling to China was to meet...* or *She expressed the wish that in travelling to China she might meet...* On balance, it seems that we do not here have a pattern **poss N *in* -ing**, but the question does remain open to debate.

In our study of adjectives with the pattern **ADJ *in* n** (Francis et al. 1998), we have distinguished between adjectives where the occurrence of *in* is dependent on the adjective, making a genuine adjective pattern, and those adjectives where the occurrence of *in* is less dependent on the adjective, so that the sequence is not a genuine adjective pattern, although the adjective and preposition occur together so frequently that it is unreasonable simply to omit them from consideration. In those cases where the preposition is not dependent on the adjective, the prepositional phrase indicates an aspect of the situation to which the adjective is relevant.

The genuine pattern groups include the following:

1. *absorbed, bogged down, concerned, disinterested, embroiled, engaged, engrossed, enmeshed, entangled, immersed, implicated, interested, involved, locked, mixed up, tied up, uninterested, wrapped up*

(8)   *Universities need to be more <u>involved</u> in student life.*

2. *deficient, lacking, wanting*

(9)   *There's a need for people to teach literacy and numeracy to kids who are <u>deficient</u> in those skills.*

3. *implicit, inherent, present*

    (10)   *All the mistakes point up the limitations <u>inherent</u> in the technology.*

4. *awash, high, low, poor, rich*

    (11)   *Keep your meals <u>low</u> in fat and sugar.*

5. *long, quick, slow, tardy*

    (12)   *Success was not <u>long</u> in coming.*

The groups for which the pattern is not genuine (that is, where the preposition is not dependent on the adjective) include the following:

6. *adamant, forthright, firm, frank, loud, resolute, steadfast, unequivocal, vehement, vocal, vociferous*

    (13)   *She is <u>adamant</u> in her refusal to make any statement.*

7. *assiduous, relentless, rigorous, ruthless, vigorous*

    (14)   *His ancestors were much more <u>ruthless</u> in their exploitation of the workers than he was.*

8. *attired, clad, clothed, dressed, garbed, shod*

    (15)   *She was <u>clothed</u> in a red top, grey slacks and shoes.*

9. *banded, bathed, bedecked, coated, cocooned, dappled, edged, plastered, shrouded, smothered, upholstered*

    (16)   *As I recovered my senses I realised I was <u>bathed</u> in a cold sweat.*

10. *beneficial, helpful, invaluable, unparalleled, useful, useless, valuable*

    (17)   *I understand celery seed extracts are <u>helpful</u> in the treatment of arthritis.*

Thus the question of what is and is not a pattern is one that is not always easy to answer. The existence of a particular pattern with a particular verb, noun or adjective is a factor not only of the frequency of a given sequence of items but of the dependency of the potential pattern on the key word. To a certain extent, that dependency can be tested by attempts at rephrasing, but, at the present time at least, intuition seems also to play a part.

    In the next section we look at cases where patterns as we have described them up to now seem insufficiently specific for the description of the behaviour of some words.

3.3 Do patterns over-generalise?

3.3.1 *Introduction*

In the previous section we referred to a possible pattern **poss N *in* -ing**, and discussed whether the nouns *aim* and *purpose* might be said to have this pattern. This pattern would be different from most mentioned in this book in that it specifies, not only what comes after the key word but also what comes before it.

In general, our topic in this book is complementation patterns, that is, the specification of items that follow the key word. Some patterns do involve other elements (see Chapter 2). For example, patterns involving the 'dummy Subjects' *there* and *it* specify what comes at the beginning of a clause. Similarly, some of the patterns associated with reciprocal verbs specify that the Subject must be plural. An example of a pattern of this kind is **pl-n V**, exemplified by *They argued*, where the plural Subject indicates reciprocity ('A argued with B and B argued with A') as well as simple plurality. Mostly, however, information is restricted to what follows the verb, noun or adjective.

In addition, our patterns involve a fairly high degree of generalisation. For example, our coding **n**, as in the pattern **V n**, usually means either a noun or a pronoun. When an adjective pattern involves a verb, we distinguish between link verbs and others, but we do not make any finer distinctions. In this respect, our work is not entirely in step with that of Sinclair, who stresses the idiosyncratic behaviour of individual word forms and the phraseological patterning of particular lexical items. Where Sinclair seeks to differentiate, we seek to draw parallels and make generalisations. Our generalisations are not as broad as those of traditional grammar, but the principle of generalisation is there.

In this section we look at a number of cases where it might be argued that our patterns need to be specified in greater detail. We also point out the problems inherent in trying to adopt this greater specificity.

3.3.2 *'It's been a privilege to know you'*

The first example involves the nouns *privilege* and *honour*. For both these nouns, a frequent pattern is **N *of* -ing**, as in 'the privilege/honour of knowing you'. In the Bank of English corpus, there are 557 examples of this pattern with *privilege* and 338 examples with *honour*. A less frequent pattern is **N to-inf**, as in 'the privilege/honour to know you' (177 and 149 examples respectively). However, this second pattern typically occurs only as part of three longer patterns. These are:

*it be a/***poss N to-inf**, as in *It was my privilege to watch the game* or *It was an honour to meet him and talk to him*;
have the N to-inf, as in *..all those who had the privilege to know him* or *I have the honour to remain your obedient servant*;
what a/an N to-inf, as in *What a privilege to drive a car of this calibre* or *What an honour to share Christ's name!* This pattern might be said to be a variant of the first: an ellipted version of 'what a privilege/honour it is to do something'.

Strictly speaking, then, it is incorrect to say that these nouns have the pattern **N to-inf**. On the other hand, it would be incorrect to say that *privilege* and *honour* cannot be followed by a to-infinitive. Rather, the to-infinitive forms part of a set of longer, more specific patterns.

3.3.3   *'Adamant in her refusal'*

Our next example comes from the adjective pattern **ADJ *in* n**. One group of adjectives with this pattern comprises words such as *adamant, forthright, firm, frank, loud, resolute, steadfast, unequivocal, vehement, vigorous, vocal* and *vociferous*, which indicate that someone believes something strongly or talks about something as if they believe it strongly. Examples of these adjectives with this pattern, taken from Francis et al. (1998), include:

(18)   *She is <u>adamant</u> in her refusal to make any statement.*

(19)   *Both men are military officers and <u>firm</u> in their belief that the nation's interests and their own are one and the same.*

(20)   *Last week the fans were <u>loud</u> in their support for their manager, his players and his tactics.*

(21)   *Even Greenpeace UK, so <u>vocal</u> in its opposition to Sellafield, said that their independent scientific advice was that low-level radiation posed no threat.*

The noun groups in this pattern share two features: Firstly, the noun itself realises a way of thinking, such as *belief*, a way of talking, such as *support* or *opposition*, or an absence of the same, such as *refusal*. Secondly, the noun group begins with a possessive determiner (*her, their, its*) that refers to the Subject of the clause (*She...her; Both men...their; the fans...their; Greenpeace UK...its*). If we adopt Halliday's distinction between congruent and metaphoric representations, then *She is adamant in her refusal to make any statement* might be said to be a metaphoric realisation of the congruent *She adamantly refused to make any statement*, and the other examples can be interpreted in the same way.

None of this information is captured by the pattern representation **ADJ** *in* **n**. We might change this to **ADJ** *in* **poss n** (which would in turn change the meaning of **n** from 'noun group' to 'noun'), but this would still not capture the fact that particular kinds of noun are used here.

3.3.4 *'Her success as a designer'*

The next example concerns a noun pattern: **N** *as* **n**. Two nouns that are used with this pattern are *success* and *failure*. These nouns are used with this pattern, however, only under certain circumstances, that is, when the pattern **N** *as* **n** occurs as part of a more specific pattern. There are three such specific patterns, exemplified by the following (taken from Francis et al. 1998):

(22) *I knew I **could be a success** as a fighter and a human being*. (**v-link N** *as* **n**)

(23) *Bella is modest about **her success** as Young Designer of the Year*. (**poss N** *as* **n**)

(24) *We need more research and reports on the **failure of men as fathers and housekeepers** and on the growing burdens imposed on working mothers*. (**N** *of* **n** *as* **n**)

Note that the second of these patterns is unsatisfactory from the point of view of consistency, as the first **N** means 'noun' but the second **n** means 'noun group'.

Apart from that problem, these examples highlight a dilemma of doing grammar as pattern: how much phraseological information on individual words can be included. The nouns *success* and *failure* behave idiosyncratically, and differently from the other nouns (*performance, potential* and *record*) in their meaning group. The details of their phraseology perhaps belongs in a dictionary rather than a grammar book (though it would be a rare dictionary that could spare the space for so much detail), but the generalised pattern **N** *as* **n** is clearly missing some vital information.

3.3.5 *'It's illogical to believe'*

This example is from the pattern *it* **v-link ADJ to-inf**. One meaning group associated with this pattern (in Francis et al. 1998) consists of the following adjectives:

accurate	*illusory*	*obvious*
fair	*inaccurate*	*plain*
fallacious	*inconceivable*	*plausible*
false	*incorrect*	*true*
fanciful	*incredible*	*untrue*
illogical	*logical*	*valid*

All these adjectives indicate a judgement about an idea, that it is accurate, obvious, true, untrue and so on. We can give three further pieces of information about this meaning group and this pattern.

Firstly, the verb in the to-infinitive clause is typically one which indicates a mental process, as in these examples:

(25)   *It is illogical to believe that old age or a love of privacy should entitle her to expect special treatment.*

(26)   *It is at least plausible to conclude that rainfall patterns shift and a drought will occur.*

A second type of verb which frequently occurs in the to-infinitive clause is the verbal process type, such as *say, state* and so on. However, when these verbs are used, the link verb typically includes a modal. The adjectives *accurate, fair, obvious, true* and *untrue* are most often used in this way, as in these examples:

(27)   *Anita did not take much notice of the types of people present. It would be more accurate to say that she did not see them.*

(28)   *It may seem obvious to state this, but I am constantly amazed at the small percentage of patients who, given that they feel better avoiding a food, still can't wait to go back to eating it.*

The third observation concerns only one of the adjectives, *plain*, which is typically used with the verb *see* in the to-infinitive clause:

(29)   *Why did she make those awful chewing movements with her mouth when it was plain to see she hadn't anything to chew?*

Again, an accurate portrait of how these adjectives are used requires more than can be captured by the simple pattern representation.

3.3.6   *'She qualified as a doctor'*

Our final example concerns the pattern **V** *as* **n**. In our coding, **n** stands for 'noun group', which in principle includes both nouns, and their associated modification, and pronouns. With some verbs that have the pattern **V *as* n**, however, the pronoun option does not apply. (This was pointed out to us by Mike Scott.) For example, for the verbs *volunteer* and *moonlight* there are no occurrences in the Bank of English where they are used with *as* followed by a pronoun. The verb *work* has just one example (out of a total of 6714 occurrences of *work|works| working|worked as*) where *as* is followed by a pronoun:

(30)   *Enrico would rather act as a tough guy than <u>work</u> as one.*

Notice here that the pronoun is *one*, and could not be replaced by a personal pronoun such as *it* or *him*. Similarly *qualify*, with 1016 lines of the verb followed by *as*, has only four lines where *as* is followed by a pronoun, the pronouns being *both, either, one* and *that* (e.g. *'They were really creating this extraordinary new information medium.' 'When you call it a medium, how does it <u>qualify</u> as that?'*). In all four lines, the meaning of *qualify* is 'be interpreted in that way' rather than 'be fitted for a career'.

One possible solution to this would be to adopt the coding used in CCED for phrasal verbs. For example, the verb *hand in* (as in 'hand in your notice') has one pattern **V n P** where the **n** indicates either a noun group or a pronoun (e.g. *He handed his notice in* or *He handed it in*), and another pattern **V P n (not pron)** where the **n (not pron)** indicates a noun group but not a pronoun (e.g. *He handed in his notice* but not *He handed in it). We could, then, adopt a coding **V *as* n (not pron)** for examples such as *She qualified as a doctor*. That would be only partially accurate, however, because *qualify* can be used with a pronoun, but only a pronoun of a particular kind, and such uses occur only rarely, as we have described above. A coding such as **V *as* n (not pers pron)** seems perversely clumsy. Of the many possible almost-truths, we have so far settled for **V *as* n**, but it might be argued that the alternatives are preferable.

In all these examples, then, we have suggested that patterns may be made far more specific than they currently are. Such specificity would not allow simple grammar codes of the type we have used here, however. An increase in information, therefore, would be paid for by a loss of transparency. Groupings would become much more complex. As work at the interface of lexis and grammar progresses, it is possible that other compromises will be reached between specificity and generalisation, between what is accurate and what is simple to represent.

CHAPTER 4

Patterns and Meaning

4.1 Meaning groups: some examples

One of the most important observations in a corpus-driven description of English is that patterns and meaning are connected. Following his description of the senses and uses of the word *yield*, in which he finds that each sense of the word is strongly associated with a single pattern of use, Sinclair (1991: 65) concludes: "It seems that there is a strong tendency for sense and syntax to be associated." Francis (1993) adds more evidence from a different perspective, by noting that in a pattern such as **v** *it* **adj**, the range of lexical items that appear frequently in either the verb or the adjective position is limited, suggesting that the meanings that the pattern can make are also limited. Taking these two pieces of evidence together we can hypothesise, firstly, that the different senses of words will tend to be distinguished by different patterns, and secondly, that particular patterns will tend to be associated with lexical items that have particular meanings. It is the second of these hypotheses that we explore here.

The question of how far we may take this observation that meaning and pattern, or sense and syntax, are associated, and what the theoretical implications are, will be taken up later in this chapter. Meanwhile it is enough to say that more extensive work with a larger corpus has tended to confirm the initial observations. One outcome of this is the Collins COBUILD Grammar Patterns series (Francis et al. 1996; 1998), in which the words that occur with each pattern are listed in meaning groups. We will now look at some of these patterns to explain this in more detail.

Example 1: V *of* **n**
Here is a list, in alphabetical order, of the 32 verbs from the Collins COBUILD English Dictionary (CCED) that have the pattern **V** *of* **n**:

approve	*come*	*daydream*
beware (infinitive and	*complain*	*despair*
imperative)	*conceive*	*die*
boast	*consist*	*disapprove*

dispose	*reek*	*tell*
drain	*repent*	*think*
dream	*smack*	*tire*
hear	*smell*	*warn*
know	*speak*	*weary*
learn	*stink*	
partake	*taste*	
permit	*talk*	

With some of the items in this list, the sense or senses of the verb that has/have this pattern is/are not the most obvious. For example, two, fairly infrequent, senses of the verb *come* have this pattern: 'result from something', as in *Some good may come of all this*, and 'belong to a family', as in *She comes of a family of painters*. The verb *speak* occurs with this pattern in the obvious sense of 'talking' but also in the sense of 'being evidence of', as in *His behaviour spoke of an early maturity*. The verb *conceive* with this pattern means both 'plan something', as in *They conceived of a plan to rob the Kremlin*, and, in the negative, 'disbelieve', as in *She couldn't conceive of a worse plan*. The sense of *drain* in this pattern is as in *Her face drained of colour*.

Another, perhaps obvious, point is that putting a word in this list does not account for all the behaviours of that word, nor does it imply that any word in the list behaves the same as the other word in the list, except that they all occur reasonably frequently with the pattern **V** *of* **n**. For example, *talk* and *warn* share some patterns (e.g.,'talk/warn of something') but not others (e.g.'warn/*talk someone about something'). The list tells us about an area of shared behaviour, but by itself it does not give us anything like complete information about any of the verbs in it.

To return to our main point concerning meaning: the list is a varied one, and includes many words that share nothing with each other in terms of meaning. It would be difficult to find a connection, for example, between *partake* and *complain*, or between *reek* and *repent*. On the other hand, there are sets of words in this list that do share something in the way of meaning. Here are some examples:

approve and *disapprove* both mean 'like' or its opposite;
despair and *repent* both indicate a (mental) reaction to a situation;
boast and *complain* both indicate a (spoken) reaction to a situation;
speak (in its usual meaning), *talk* and *tell* all mean 'talk about';
reek, smell, and *stink* all mean 'smell';
smack and *taste* both mean 'taste';
dream and *daydream* have similar meanings that are related to *think*;

tire and *weary* both mean 'become tired or bored';

know and *learn* are clearly connected in meaning, and *hear* is similar in meaning to *learn*;

dispose and *drain* both mean that something goes from a place, although with *dispose* the Subject causes the removal (*We disposed of the garbage*) and with *drain* the cause is not mentioned in this pattern (*Her face drained of colour*).

It is not difficult to find larger groupings that will account for all of the original thirty-two verbs:

a. verbs that mean 'talking' include *boast, complain, speak, talk,* and *tell.* To these we can add *warn*, making a total of six verbs;

b. verbs connected with mental activity include *approve, disapprove, despair, repent, dream, daydream,* and *think.* To these we can add the two senses of *conceive.* Some people might want to include *tire* and *weary* in this group, others would keep them separate. This gives us a total of eight or ten verbs;

c. verbs connected with the senses include *reek, smell, stink, smack,* and *taste.* If we take a broader view of this meaning, and take it to mean 'give evidence of' we might include the less frequent sense of *speak* as well, giving a total of six verbs.

We are left with two small groups:

d. verbs meaning to know or come to know: *know, learn, hear,* a total of three verbs;

e. a possible very small group of two verbs: *dispose, drain*;

and five further verbs that do not fit into any of these groups: *beware, come* (both senses), *die, partake* and *permit.*

From the evidence of this pattern, some conclusions may be drawn about the association of pattern and meaning. First, we must point out what it does not mean. There is no one-to-one correspondence — it is not the case that a single pattern occurs with verbs of a single meaning. It does not even mean that *all* the instances of a particular pattern can be covered by a set of meaning groups — we are left with a 'ragbag' of five verbs that do not fit in any group.

We must also say that the association of pattern and meaning is not entirely predictive, in the sense that not every verb with a meaning similar to those given above will share the pattern **V** *of* **n**. For example, although *warn* has this pattern, *threaten* does not. *Complain* has this pattern, but *gripe* does not. *Boast* has this pattern, but *gloat* and *swank* do not. (But see the discussion of language change in Section 4.2.2 below. For approaches that argue for a more deterministic relationship between semantics and syntax see Levin 1995 and Rudanko 1996.)

Second, it must be conceded that the division into meaning groups, such as that given above for **V** *of* **n**, is not achieved through anything other than the intuition of the person looking at the list. Different researchers or teachers may well come up with a different set of meaning groups, and even the same observer may on different occasions and for different purposes wish to propose different groups. In Francis et al. (1996), for example, the meaning groups given in the section '**V** *of* **n**' (p211–214) are similar to but not the same as the groups suggested above. This is largely because the verbs in the groups are not synonyms of each other, but simply share an aspect of meaning, and different observers would prioritise different aspects. On the other hand, any observer could identify some meaning groups, and it is probable that most observers would arrive at meaning groups that were very similar to each other.

Thus a weak statement of the association between pattern and meaning would be that a list of verbs frequently having a particular pattern is not totally random with respect to meaning. A strong statement would be that a word has a particular pattern because it has a particular meaning. A medium view would be that, given a list of words occurring with a particular pattern, the majority will be divisible by most observers into reasonably coherent meaning groups. We have found no counter-examples to this latter view. It is important to recognise, however, that the weak and the medium statement alike make no theoretical claims and do not ascribe causality. They merely give a shape to a set of observations. The strong statement is a theoretical claim, but is as yet insufficiently substantiated, in our view.

So far we have talked about 'pattern' and 'meaning' as though these were separate, as though the pattern were a framework into which words with particular meanings could be slotted. This is essentially a matter of convenience: it allows us to talk about a word 'having' a pattern and to compile a dictionary entry for a word which lists the patterns it 'has' (this is done in CCED). Moreover, it allows us to generalise about patterns, and to list them as if they existed as an entity apart from the words that occur at their core. This approach, however, runs counter to the work of Sinclair, for example, whose investigations into the behaviour of particular lexical items (e.g.1991, 1994 and see the discussion in Section 1.4) stress the uniqueness of each 'meaning unit'. We would come closer to the spirit of Sinclair's work if we defined a pattern as a sequence of elements including the core. For example, *approve of something* would be one pattern, *disapprove of something* would be another, *complain of something* another, *boast of something* another, and so on. Instead of grouping words that had a common pattern, we would group patterns that shared a common feature (the preposition *of* in this case). In both cases, the words or patterns would be subdivided in terms of meaning. In the second case, however, the 'meaning' would belong to the whole pattern rather than to a single lexical item.

In the example given above (**V** *of* **n**), it makes little practical difference whether we say that *reek, smack, smell, stink* and *taste* share a meaning, or whether we say that *something reeks of something, something smacks of something, something smells of something*, and so on, share a meaning. Sometimes, however, the word and its pattern means a lot more than the word on its own. For example, one group of adjectives that occur with the pattern **v-link ADJ** *about* **n** comprises the following words (Francis et al. 1998):

adult	*funny*	*nice*
beastly	*good*	*odd*
brave	*gracious*	*ok/ okay*
brilliant	*great*	*reasonable*
cool (= reasonable)	*heavy (= unreasonable)*	*sweet (= kind)*
excellent	*lovely*	
fine	*marvellous*	
foolish	*mature*	

At first glance, this is a strange list, containing many words that appear to be unrelated to each other. In this case, however, it is not the words themselves that belong together but the way they are used with the pattern '**v-link ADJ** *about* **n**'. With this pattern, they all indicate that someone reacts to a situation in a particular way. It is not the words in the list that have this precise meaning, but the whole phrase of which they are a part.

Having discussed some of the issues involved in the construction of meaning groups in some detail, we will now give briefer examples of a verb pattern, a noun pattern, and an adjective pattern.

Example 2: V n n

The pattern **V n n** is familiar to language teachers and linguists in two guises. Firstly, the traditional ditransitive verbs have this pattern, as in *I gave him some bread* and *He made me a sandwich*. Secondly, verbs followed by an Object and an Object Complement have the same pattern, as in *She called them all idiots*. There is a third possible structure: verbs occuring in clauses such as *They beat us three-nil* also have the pattern **V n n**, with the restriction that the second noun group is an amount. More properly speaking, then, the pattern is **V n amount**, the first noun group being an Object and the second noun group (the amount) being an Adjunct. Following these traditional distinctions we can identify the following meaning groups (taken from Francis et al. 1996: 272–280):

Verbs with two Objects

Meaning group 1: verbs and phrasal verbs concerned with giving someone something, or refusing to do so

accord	deny	offer	set
advance	feed	pass	show
afford	give	pay	slip
allocate	give back	pay back	sneak
allot	grant	permit	spoon-feed
allow	hand	proffer	stand (someone a
assign	hand back	promise	drink)
aware	lease	refund	throw
bequeath	leave	refuse	tip
chuck	lend	render	toss
concede	loan	sell	vouchsafe
deal (someone	make	serve	
some cards)			

Many smaller groups could be made from this large group, such as giving, selling, lending, offering, not giving, allocating money, resources, or tasks.

Meaning group 2: verbs concerned with doing something for someone

assure	cut	knit	pour
bear (someone a	do	land	prescribe
child)	fetch	leave	secure
book (someone a	find	make	sing
room)	fix	mix	wangle
bring	get	order	
buy	guarantee	play	
carve			
cook			

Meaning group 3: verbs concerned with talking, writing, or otherwise communicating something to someone

ask	cast (someone a	flash (someone a
bid (someone-	look)	smile)
farewell)	concede	kiss (someone good-
cable	fax	bye)

mail	*shoot* (someone a	*throw* (someone a
pen	glance)	look)
post	*spin* (someone a	*wire*
quote	tale)	*write*
read	*teach*	
send	*tell*	

Meaning group 4: verbs and phrasal verbs concerned with giving someone a benefit or a disadvantage

cause (someone	*dock* (someone	*lose*	*spare*
harm)	money)	*save*	*take* (someone
charge	*earn*	*set back*	time)
cost	*intend* (someone		*win*
do (someone a	harm)		
favour)			

Meaning group 5: verbs concerned with feeling and attitudes

| *(not) begrudge* | *envy* | *excuse* | *forgive* |

Other verbs and phrasal verbs

bear	*let off*	*set*
bet	*owe*	*turn off*
give	*put off*	*wish*

Verbs with Object and Object Complement

There is only one meaning group here: verbs and phrasal verbs concerned with putting something into a category, either by naming or labelling (e.g.*acclaim*), or by putting someone or something into a particular position (e.g.*anoint*), or by thinking (e.g.*adjudge*), or by causing (e.g.*make*).

acclaim	*bring up*	*declare*	*find*
account	*call*	*deem*	*hail*
adjudge	*christen*	*designate*	*label*
anoint	*code-name*	*dub*	*make*
appoint	*consider*	*elect*	*be misnamed*
be born	*count*	*fancy*	*name*
brand	*crown*	*fell*	*nickname*

nominate	prove	rule	vote
ordain	rate	tag	
proclaim	re-elect	term	
pronounce	rename	title	

There is one other verb with this pattern and structure:

hold (someone prisoner)

Verbs with Object and Adjunct

Again there is only one meaning group here: these verbs are all concerned with winning or losing in a game or sport.

beat (a team 2–1) *lose* (a game 2–1) *win* (a game 2–1)
defeat (a team 2–1)*thrash* (a team 2–1)

One additional point needs to be made before we leave this pattern. In most cases, the lists are exhaustive in that in the Collins COBUILD English Dictionary there are no other verbs with this pattern. For example, the list given under the heading **Verbs with Object and Object Complement** (including *hold*) gives all the verbs common enough to be in the dictionary which have this pattern and this structure. We can be reasonably confident that none are omitted. There is one exception, however. The list given under the heading *Meaning group 2: verbs concerned with doing something for someone* is not complete, and it is probably not possible to give a complete list of the verbs that are used in this way. As Francis et al. (1996: 274) point out, any verb that indicates an activity that you can do on behalf of someone else, or to benefit someone else, may be used in this pattern. The verbs given in the list are only the most frequent. We will return to this point in Section 4.2.3 below.

Example 3: N *in* n
In this pattern, the noun is followed by a prepositional phrase beginning with *in*. The meaning groups below are based on Francis et al. (1998: 166–172).

Meaning group 1: increase, decrease, or change

acceleration	change	dent	explosion
adjustment	collapse	deterioration	fall
advance	cut	diminution	falling-off
alternation	cutback	dip	flare-up
boom	decline	downturn	fluctuation
bulge	decrease	drop	gain

growth	moderation (mak-	shake-up	turn
improvement	ing less)	shift	turnabout
increase	pick-up	slip	turnaround
increment	relaxation	slowdown	upsurge
innovation	resurgence	slump	upswing
jump	reversal	surge	upturn
leap	reduction	transformation	
lessening	rise	trend	

Meaning group 2a: involvement in something

absorption	immersion	lead	toehold
acquiescence	interest	part	vested interest
assistance	interference	participation	voice
complicity	intervention	role	
foothold	investment	share	
help	involvement	stake	

Meaning group 2b: someone who is involved in something

contender	partner	prime mover
force	pawn	shareholder
participant	player	stakeholder

Meaning group 3: something that is involved in or is part of something else

component	factor	ingredient
element	fixture	keystone

Meaning group 4: an event in history or in someone's life

breakthrough	development	landmark	watershed
chapter	high point	turning point	

Meaning group 5: part of a period of time or of an event

age	era	period	stage
epoch	moment	point	time

Meaning group 6: problem affecting the course of something

hiccup	setback	stumbling block

Meaning group 7: (temporary) stop

breach	hiatus	lapse	pause
break	interlude	let-up	
breakdown	interruption	lull	

Meaning group 8: hole, groove, or dent

chink	gap	hollow	rut
crack	groove	incision	slit
dent	hole	leak	

Meaning group 9: fault in something

defect	flaw	irregularity	weakness
error	gap (metaphorical)	loophole	
fault	hole (metaphorical)	mistake	

Meaning group 10: pain

ache	numbness	tingling
cramp	pain	

Meaning group 11: difference or similarity

contrast	discrepancy	imbalance	similarity
difference	disparity	inconsistency	variation

Meaning group 12: belief

belief	confidence	faith	trust

Meaning group 13: feelings

delight	interest	pride
disinterest	pleasure	

Meaning group 14a: skill, experience, or advantage

ability	expertise	prowess	superiority
edge	proficiency	skill	track record

Meaning group 14b: person who is skilled or knowledgeable

expert	past master	specialist
master	pioneer	

Meaning group 15a: education

chair (= profes- sorship) class course crash course	degree diploma first grounding	lectureship lesson pass professorship	qualification training tuition

Meaning group 15b: people connected with education

graduate	lecturer

Meaning group 15c: metaphors of education and research

essay exercise	experiment lesson	object lesson

Meaning group 16: employment

career	employment	job

Meaning group 17: commercial transactions

market	traffic	trade

Meaning group 18: success, delay, and failure

blockage delay	difficulty progress	success tardiness

Meaning group 19: other nouns

entry immersion irony	kink presence rarity	split taste use

Example 4: ADJ that

In this pattern, the adjective is followed by a that-clause. The meaning groups below are based on Francis et al. (1998: 400–403).

Meaning group 1: having a reaction to a situation

This group can be subdivided according to the nature of the reaction.

amazed astonished astounded	bemused curious incredulous	puzzled shocked surprised

angry	furious	irate
annoyed	incensed	livid
cross	indignant	mad

appreciative	encouraged	gratified	pleased
chuffed	flattered	happy	proud
content	glad	heartened	thankful
ecstatic	grateful	jubilant	thrilled

envious	jealous	resentful

disappointed	regretful	sad	sorry

concerned	disturbed	perturbed	worried

aghast	disgusted	frustrated	outraged
ashamed	dismayed	heartbroken	unhappy
bitter	distraught	horrified	

(feel) bad	(feel) good

awestruck	critical	impatient	impressed

Meaning group 2: being certain or uncertain

certain	content	persuaded	sure
comfortable	convinced	positive	uncertain
complacent	doubtful	satisfied	unconvinced
confident	dubious	sceptical	

Meaning group 3: knowing or being ignorant of something

aware	conscious	mindful
cognizant	ignorant	unaware

Meaning group 4: having a reaction to something that may happen

This group can be subdivided according to the nature of the reaction.

afraid	desperate	petrified	terrified
anxious	fearful	scared	wary
apprehensive	nervous	suspicious	worried

confident	eager	keen
determined	hopeful	

optimistic	pessimistic

Meaning group 5: two or more people agreeing with each other

agreed   *unanimous*

Meaning group 6: saying something in a forceful way

adamant	*definite*	*firm*
categoric	*emphatic*	*insistent*
categorical	*explicit*	*resolute*

Meaning group 7: being careful

careful   *sure*   *vigilant*

Meaning group 8: being lucky or unlucky

fortunate   *lucky*   *unlucky*

Meaning group 9: having the correct information

correct   *right*

In this section we have given some fairly straightforward examples of patterns and meaning groups, and we have begun a discussion about the relationship between pattern and meaning. This discussion will continue in the next section, in which we look at creativity in pattern use.

4.2 Creativity in pattern use

4.2.1   *Introduction*

In this section we take up some further issues which relate to the question of what it means precisely to say that there is an association between pattern and meaning. So far we have taken the medium view of this association, stating simply that of a list of words which have a given pattern, the majority will be assignable into meaning groups. In addition we have said that the meaning belongs to either the words in the list, or to the phrases consisting of each word and the given pattern. The topics discussed in this section suggest, by contrast, that in some cases at least it may be the pattern itself which might be said to have meaning.

Owen (1993) has questioned the validity of lists of words with particular patterns, on the grounds that they do not successfully distinguish between words which can be used in a certain way, however rarely they are actually used, and those which cannot be used in that way. If one subscribes to the view that to know a language means to be able, potentially, to generate all and only the sentences in that language, then such an omission is serious indeed. The previous section (4.1) was based on the premise that complete lists of words with a given pattern are indeed possible. In this section we look at some examples which suggest that complete lists are not always possible.

4.2.2   *Pattern and analogy*

The crucial observation that lies behind the notion of a lexical grammar is that patterns occur with restricted lexis. What this means is that in the case of most patterns:

most of the words that occur with that pattern do so very frequently;
there may be a small number of words that occur with the pattern very infrequently;
the native or expert user of the language can in most cases make a judgement about whether a particular word is 'likely' or 'unlikely' to occur with a particular pattern, that is, he or she can made a judgement of acceptability;
the distinction between the list of words that have the pattern and other words that do not have it is very clear.

We argued above (Section 4.1) that the association between pattern and lexis cannot be used to predict that a word has a particular pattern just because it shares a meaning with other words that do. Now we take the other side of the coin: it does seem to be the case that speakers of a language sometimes use a word with a pattern it does not typically have. We might speculate that, when a pattern is used with words with a particular meaning, speakers begin to use other words with a similar meaning with the same pattern, by a process of analogy, so that at any point in time, what words belong to a list is in a state of flux.

Numerous examples of this apparent use of analogy can be found with relation to individual words. Here are some brief examples:

a. In Section 4.1 we discussed the pattern **V** *of* **n**. The verbs listed as having that pattern do so relatively frequently. There are other verbs, however, that have the pattern very occasionally, apparently by analogy with some of the verbs in the list. For example, *expire*, which has a meaning similar to *die*, occurs with the pattern **V** *of* **n** six times in the Bank of English, out of a total of 3519 occurrences of all forms of *expire*. Similarly, *foretell*, which has a meaning similar to *warn*, occurs five times with the pattern **V** *of* **n**, out a total of 330 occurrences.

Such limited occurrences are not sufficient to warrant saying that the verb concerned 'has' the pattern; on the other hand, it would not be correct to say that the verb does not have the pattern at all.

b. As Owen (1996) has noted, the verb *require* is less often found followed by a passive to-infinitive clause, than the similar verb *need* is, but there are nonetheless numerous instances of *require to be* followed by a past participle in the Bank of English corpus. (With *require*, however, the past participle is nearly always of a specific verb, such as *prune* or *examine*, rather than a verb with a general meaning such as *do*. Owen's hypothetical teacher, who objects to a learner's use of *requires to be done,* is correct to do so, but not on the grounds that '*require* is not followed by a passive to-infinitive'.)

c. Although *provide* is typically used with the pattern **V n *with* n** ('provide someone with something'), there are a handful of occurrences in the Bank of English of 'provide something to someone' (the pattern **V n *to* n**), presumably by analogy with *give*.

It is possible that the use of analogy the mechanisms of language change. For example, examination of the instances of the verb *impact* in the Bank of English shows a large number with the pattern **V *on* n** (...*this has impacted on its profits*), and a much smaller number with the pattern **V n** (...*factors which directly impacted the dealer's income*) and its passive equivalent ***be* V-ed** (*margins were impacted*). The sources of the pattern **V n** are for the most part American English, but this is not absolute: there are a number of British examples too. It seems that the word *impact* has changed from a noun (*have an impact on*) to a verb followed by the preposition *on* (*to impact on*) and finally to an ordinary transitive verb (*to impact something*). The analogy might be with the verb *affect*, which has a similar meaning and which also has a cognate noun with the pattern **N *on* n** (*have an effect on*). It also seems likely that the change in this word has been led by American speakers of English, with their British counterparts following suit.

Unfortunately, it is not possible to verify this hypothesis regarding language change in general, as we do not have corpora of the size of today's corpora for the language fifty, thirty, or even ten years ago. (The equivalent of the Bank of English that was used to compile the Collins COBUILD English Language Dictionary in the 1980s, for example, was much smaller than the current corpus.) For this reason, it is not possible to say for certain that a particular, infrequent usage is new just because it occurs in a later (and larger) corpus but not in an earlier (and smaller) one.

For another example, consider verbs which occur in the patterns **V -ing** and

V to-inf. As is commonly known, there are a number of verbs which are used in both these patterns, and some which are used in only one. For example, *omit* occurs both as in 'omit doing something' and as in 'omit to do something'; *postpone* occurs as in 'postpone doing something' but not as in 'postpone to do something'; and *fail* occurs as in 'fail to do something' but not as in 'fail doing something'.

There is, however, a certain amount of 'leakage' across the two patterns, and some verbs which are normally thought to have the pattern **V to-inf** only do actually sometimes occur with the other pattern, **V -ing**. Table 4.1 gives some examples. We speculate that the process of analogy is at work here, and that a word commonly used with the pattern **V -ing** is acting like a magnet for the less frequently-used word.

Table 4.1

Verb	Number of occurrences in 'V -ing'	Total occurrences of verb in 300 million words	Possible analogy with	Example
attempt	18	24061	try	*Paul did not attempt qualifying for Wimbledon.*
confess	8	6871	admit	*...any officer who confesses being corrupt.*
deprecate	4	399	dislike	*The French deprecated mining the Rhine.*
neglect	8	4536	omit	*Many of us neglect drinking enough water.*
repent	3	432	regret	*He might repent sitting up so late.*

We might speculate that a process of language change is in progress here, though, as discussed above, there is insufficient evidence to be certain of this.

4.2.3   *Patterns with less restricted lexis: N that and it v-link ADJ of n to-inf*

In the pattern **N that**, a noun is followed by an appositive that-clause (see Francis 1993 for a detailed discussion of nouns of this kind; also Francis et al. 1998). Some of the nouns that are found in this pattern indicate an reaction to a situation. These include: *amazement, anger, annoyance, anxiety, astonishment,* *concern, delight, disappointment, expectation, fear, guilt, outrage, satisfaction, sorrow* and *surprise*. As well as some nouns that frequently occur with the pattern there are some that only occasionally do so. Here are some examples of nouns sometimes or often found with the pattern, with the number of occurrences in the 300 million word Bank of English corpus given for comparison.

concern	about 2000	*annoyance*	33
fear	about 2000	*sorrow*	24
expectation	669	*bitterness*	11
disappointment	223	*fury*	11
surprise	200	*despair*	11
anxiety	129	*jealousy*	9
satisfaction	111	*happiness*	8
anger	107	*horror*	7
guilt	88	*embarrassment*	6
delight	67	*joy*	6
outrage	65	*envy*	5
amazement	50	*anguish*	3
astonishment	35	*admiration*	2

It is possible, of course, to give a list of the nouns with this general meaning that are reasonably frequently used with this pattern, as is done in Francis et al. (1998: 111). The list cannot, however, be complete, in that it cannot include all the nouns with this general meaning that are sometimes used with this pattern or which might be used with this pattern. Instead, it gives what we might call the 'core' words. Beyond that, however, there is an area of flux, comprising nouns that are occasionally used with the pattern and of which no complete list can be given. From the list given above, the following nouns might be said to be 'core' for the pattern **N that** : *amazement, anger, annoyance, anxiety, astonishment, concern, delight, disappointment, expectation, fear, guilt, outrage, satisfaction, sorrow* and *surprise*, while the following are 'non-core': *admiration, anguish, bitterness, despair, embarrassment, envy, fury, happiness, horror, jealousy* and *joy*.

In the pattern *it* **v-link ADJ** *of* **n to-inf**, the adjective is followed by a prepositional phrase beginning with *of* and by a to-infinitive clause (see Francis et al. 1998: 501–502). The Subject of the clause is an introductory *it*. The function of utterances with this pattern is to evaluate the action indicated by the to-infinitive clause. For example, in *it was courageous of him to speak out*, 'that he spoke out' is evaluated as *courageous*, and in *it was nice of you to come*, 'that you came' is evaluated as *nice*. The adjectives used with this patterns belong to three very general meaning groups: those meaning 'good in some way' (e.g.*big,* *brave, clever, courageous, decent, fair, generous...*); those meaning 'bad in some way' (e.g.*absurd, arrogant, cheeky, childish, churlish, clumsy, cruel...*); and those meaning 'typical or not typical' (*characteristic, typical,* and *uncharacteristic*).

As well as adjectives which occur reasonably frequently in the Bank of English with this pattern, there are many, with similar meanings, which occur only once or twice. Table 4.2 gives some examples:

Table 4.2

Adjectives which occur fairly frequently	Adjectives which occur only once or twice
good; great; lovely; nice	*brilliant; magnificent; terrific*
clever; prudent; sensible; smart	*diplomatic; rational; subtle*
disgraceful; immoral; shameful; unkind; unworthy	*beastly; disgusting; horrible; horrid; lousy*
absurd; foolish; silly	*ludicrous*
hypocritical; rude; selfish; thoughtless	*inhuman; insensitive; tacky*

However big a corpus was consulted, it would not be possible to give a definitive and exclusive list of adjectives which occur with this pattern. For example, here are a selection of adjectives which do not occur in the Bank of English with this pattern, but which intuition suggest are perfectly possible: *appalling* ('it was appalling of him to...'); *sensitive* ('it was very sensitive of you to...'); *devious* ('it was devious of them to...'); *obtuse* ('it was obtuse of me to...'); *careful* ('it was very careful of you to...').

The solution to the problem posed by these patterns might be to say that in these cases the pattern is not restricted as to lexis, but is restricted as to meaning. That is, any noun may occur with the pattern **N that** if it indicates a feeling towards a situation, and any adjective may occur with the pattern *it* **v-link ADJ** *of* **n to-inf** if it indicates judgement of an action in term of 'good', 'bad', or 'typical'.

4.2.4   *Patterns with a meaning: V way prep/adv*

In some cases, it is possible to go further and say that it is the pattern itself, not the words with which it occurs, that has the meaning. For example, one of the meaning groups associated with the pattern **V** *way* **prep/adv** comprises verbs which are concerned with talking. When the verb is used in this pattern, the meaning of the whole phrase is that someone uses clever, devious, or forceful language to achieve a goal, usually extricating themselves from a difficult situation, or getting into a desirable situation. Examples include:

(1)   *Armed with a sheaf of sketches and photographs, he <u>talked</u> his way into the post of chief costume designer.*

(2)   *Make sure your child is not afraid to own up, so she does not try to <u>lie</u> her way out of trouble.*

(3)   *He was more able than anyone else to <u>argue</u> his way out of tough situations.*

The verbs from this meaning group used most frequently in this pattern are as follows (numbers indicate the frequency in the 300 million word Bank of English corpus):

talk	162
negotiate	81
bluff	72
charm	40
lie	26
argue	12
wheedle	10

But there are, in addition, many verbs which occur fewer than ten times in this pattern:

reason	08
bluster	06
blag	05
bullshit	04
cajole	04
joke	04
sweet talk	04

In addition there are verbs that occur only once or twice each. It is almost impossible to obtain a complete list of these verbs, but here are some examples of these rare uses:

apologise	02
blather	01
communicate	01
discuss	01
flatter	02
haggle	02
persuade	01

plead	02
rationalise	01
verbalise	01
whinge	02
wrangle	01

This set of verbs does not meet any of the criteria set out in Section 4.2.2 above. The apparent lack of restriction on lexis here suggests that the pattern itself carries meaning.

4.2.5   *Are there restrictions in a pattern?: V n into -ing*

The pattern **V n *into* -ing** is exemplified by utterances such as *He talked her into going out with him.* Some of the verbs associated with this pattern are concerned with making someone feel something, usually fear. These verbs are: *frighten, intimidate, panic, scare, terrify*, and, extending the range of emotions, *embarrass, shock* and *shame.* These verbs are all concerned with negative emotions and it is perhaps not surprising that other verbs indicating negative emotions are also used with this pattern occasionally. Here are some examples, with number indicating the frequency in the Bank of English:

annoy	03
awe	01
baffle	01
bore	02
frustrate	02
irritate	04

Perhaps more surprising is the extension of this list to include verbs associated with positive emotions:

embolden	01
excite	06
relax	02

Again, it must be stressed that this list is far from exhaustive. If we can say that someone *annoys* or *irritates* someone into doing something, then presumably we could also say that someone *angers* or *infuriates* someone into doing something. The lack of corpus evidence does not indicate that the missing occurrences are 'incorrect English'. If we can say that someone *relaxes* someone into doing something, can we also say that someone *calms* or *soothes* someone into doing something? This seems, intuitively, less likely, but only, perhaps, because the process of analogy has not yet progressed so far.

This raises the question of whether there are any limits to the creativity of speakers: can we state categorically that something 'cannot' be said? This issue, raised for example by Owen (1993; 1996) is important if we regard the purpose of a grammatical description to be to delimit the boundaries of a language: to draw the line between what 'is English' and what 'is not English'. It may be discussed with respect to another group of verbs from the pattern **V** n *into* -**ing**. These verbs are all concerned with speaking, and with this particular pattern they indicate that someone uses language cleverly, deviously, or forcefully, in order to make someone else do something, as in *She talked them into agreeing to her plan*. Verbs used frequently with this meaning and this pattern are:

talk	317
coax	67
cajole	56
charm	28
browbeat	26
persuade	22
badger	19
sweet-talk	14
nag	10

These verbs occur fewer than ten times:

bluff	07
flatter	07
tease	06
wheedle	04

There are also some verbs that occur a handful of times. Here are some examples:

argue	03
boss	03
chivvy	03
needle	03
counsel	02
pester	02
debate	01
scold	01

Some verbs that are not found with this pattern in the current Bank of English include: *advise, recommend, suggest* and *warn* (predicted by analogy with *persuade*) and *discuss* and *dispute* (predicted by analogy with *argue* and *debate*). Intuition suggests that these verbs could not be used with this pattern, but intuition is a poor guide here. (Our intuitions reject 'persuade someone into doing something', yet there are no fewer than 22 examples in the Bank of English.) Instead we might propose two hypotheses:

a verb that is to be used with the pattern **V n *into* -ing** does not mean 'talk reasonably, gently and without force';
a verb that is to be used with the pattern **V n *into* -ing** is also used with the pattern **V n**.

Most of the verbs in the lists above fit the first hypothesis. The exception is *debate*, which will be discussed further in Section 4.2.6 below. Most fit the second hypothesis, but there are a few that do not, namely *talk, argue* and *debate*. Rather than converting our hypotheses into rules, then, we might need to convert them into probabilities:

a verb is most likely to be used in the pattern if it meets the two conditions named above;
a verb is less likely to be used in the pattern if it meets only the first of the two conditions named above;
a verb is still less likely to be used in the pattern if it meets only the second of the two conditions;
a verb is unlikely to be used in the pattern if it meets neither of the two conditions.

It would seem the formulations of this 'more or less' type must be made if we are to specify conditions for the use of a pattern.

4.2.6   *Exploiting the prosody of patterns: V n into -ing and V n as n*

The term 'semantic prosody' was coined by Sinclair (1991) and further developed by Louw (1993) and more recently by Stubbs (1995; 1996). Hunston (1995: 137) summarises the notion of semantic prosody thus: "Briefly, a word may be said to have a particular semantic prosody if it can be shown to co-occur typically with other words that belong to a particular semantic set."

Examples include *set in* ('something bad sets in'); *utterly* ('something is utterly bad'); *cause* ('something causes something bad'); *brook* ('someone brooks no disagreement') (see Sinclair 1991; Louw 1993; Stubbs 1995; Sinclair 1994). One of the important observations concerning semantic prosody is that it can be exploited. If a collocation is chosen which is at odds with the usual semantic set, an 'extra' meaning will be implied which may convey irony or even insincerity (see Louw 1993; 1997). For example, if someone is described by the phrase [*He]* *brooked little discussion* (*discussion* does not belong to the semantic set exemplified by *disagreement*), this may be interpreted as implying that the person concerned sees all discussion as opposition, and that this in turn indicates arrogance or unreasonableness (Hunston 1995: 138). One way of interpreting this is to say that there is a pattern ('**V** *no/little* **n**') which occurs with the verb *brook* and which assigns to any noun occurring in that pattern the meaning 'opposition or disagreement'. This in turn leads to the ironic interpretation of *he brooked little discussion* as 'He was arrogant and unreasonable'.

We have spoken above of patterns themselves having meanings, and we can now consider some cases where that meaning can be thought of as a kind of semantic prosody which can be exploited for ironic effect. First, however, we may note a less dramatic, but related, phenomenon, where the sense of a word appears to be determined by the pattern in which that word appears. Above we discussed the pattern *it* **v-link ADJ** *of* **n to-inf**, noting that the function of the pattern is to evaluate the action indicated in the to-infinitive clause. Now consider the example

(4)   *It was big of you to take the risk.*

In this example, *big* does not have its usual meaning of 'large in size' but instead takes on the evaluative meaning of 'courageous' or 'generous', in keeping with the meaning of the pattern. Another example is the pattern ***there*** **v-link** ***something*** **ADJ** ***about*** **n**, which has the function of evaluating the person or thing indicated in the noun group following *about*. Even when potentially neutral words such as nationality words, or words such as *masculine* and *feminine*, are used in this pattern, they take on an evaluative meaning, as in these examples:

(5)   *Kouchner has that rare thing among prominent Frenchmen: the common touch. There is something almost American about the minister's informality.*

(6)   *Whether you're swanning about at Glyndebourne or sitting in a poppy field, there's something very British about picnics, especially if you use a traditional wicker basket.*

(7)   *Richard was starting to enjoy the atmosphere. There was something masculine about the dark wood dining room. In a difficult situation, it gave him a certain comfort.*

In all these examples, the meaning of an adjective is affected by the pattern it occurs with, but there is no actual conflict between the meaning of the pattern and the usual meaning of the adjective. Returning to the notion of semantic prosody, however, let us consider two examples where there is such a conflict, with a resulting 'extra' meaning.

The first example is one that has been met above, but which is shown here with a larger co-text. The writer is describing her childhood with a father who had wanted a son rather than a daughter:

> (8)   *I studied night and day, in an effort to please him... I learned eight*
> *languages, but none spoke to his granite heart. I rode like a centaur,*
> *I fenced, I learned marksmanship. I honed my intellect as if by doing*
> *so I could debate him into loving me, force him to logic or ethic or*
> *morality.*

As was noted in the discussion of the pattern **V n *into* -ing,** the verbs that occur with this pattern usually indicate some kind of forcefulness or even coercion. Verbs which mean 'talk reasonably' are not normally found with this pattern. What, then, of *debate him into loving me*? A look at the co-text shows that the writer is describing something which is, firstly, unsuccessful — a futile attempt to use reason to achieve something not amenable to reason, and which is, secondly, a misuse of a mode of discourse — debate — for an ulterior motive. The essence of that evaluation is carried by the mismatch of verb and pattern.

The second example makes use of the pattern **V n *as* n,** which is typically used with verbs such as *consider, describe, interpret, label, perceive, portray, regard, represent, see* and *view*. These verbs all indicate that the description, interpretation etc is a matter of opinion, not of fact. An example is:

> (9)   *His father had regarded him as a wastrel and playboy.*

We might say, then, that the pattern in itself indicates an opinion being held. In the following example, there is a tension between the meaning of the pattern and the meaning of the verb used with it. The writer has asserted that politicians and the media tend to create 'moral panics' about crime, which make ordinary citizens unreasonably afraid that there is more crime in the society than there actually is. He goes on to assert that this 'moral panic' cannot come from politicians and the media alone: society has to be ready to believe it. He says:

> (10)   *Society must be predisposed to panic about crimes. There has already*
> *to be a tendency to discover crime as the cause behind worrisome*
> *social ills.*

In the second sentence, the writer uses the verb *discover* in the pattern **V n** *as* **n**. Not only is this verb itself uncommon with this pattern (there are 6 examples in the Bank of English corpus), but the meaning of 'finding out something that is a fact' is at odds with the 'opinion' meaning of the pattern. The implication of the sentence might be paraphrased as 'People think it is a fact that crime is the cause of social ills, but actually it is only an opinion'.

4.3 Summary of Chapter 4

In this chapter we first explored the connection between pattern and groups of words based on meaning. We then considered in some detail exceptions to the generalisation that patterns occur with restricted lexis. These exceptions throw doubt on the observation that it is possible to give complete lists of all the words that occur with a particular pattern.

Some of the explanation for these exceptions can be found in the notion of analogy and language change. It is argued that speakers sometimes use an unusual word with a pattern by analogy with a word that more typically occurs with that pattern, and that because of this the full complement of words that occur with a given pattern is constantly open to change. Whereas it is possible, therefore, to give a list of 'core' words, there will always be a more fuzzy set of words around the periphery of a pattern, as it were, that is, words that are occasionally used with that pattern and which cannot be said *not* to occur with the pattern. It is extremely difficult to give a complete list of these words.

In the case of nouns and adjectives in particular, it was argued that some patterns are relatively unrestricted in terms of actual lexis, though they are restricted in terms of the kind of word that can occur with them. Looking at the concordance lines for words of this kind, the observer sees, not a few words with many lines each, but many words with a few lines each. Speaker creativity is particularly common here.

We also considered two cases of verb patterns which had an extremely wide range of lexis, and where the meaning might be said to belong to the pattern itself rather than to the lexis that typically occurs with it.

Finally, we considered cases of semantic prosody, where a tension between the meaning of the pattern and the meaning of the word used with the pattern was exploited by a skillful writer or speaker to imply meaning not explicitly stated.

CHAPTER 5

More on pattern and meaning

5.1 From meaning to pattern: lexis and function

5.1.1 *Using a 'meaning finder'*

One of the outcomes of the process of assigning words that share a common pattern to meaning groups is that it is possible to collect together meaning groups from different patterns which have something in common. In Francis et al. (1996: 616–622) this is done in an index with the title 'Meaning Finder'. Entries in the Meaning Finder have titles such as 'Attacking and doing harm', 'Beginning, continuing and ending', 'Bodily functions and movements', 'Changing', 'Talking, writing and gesturing', 'Fighting and competing', 'Giving, getting and paying for things' and 'Learning and finding out'. Each of the groups under these titles will be termed a 'notional group' in the discussion below.

For example, one meaning that appears more than once in Francis et al. (1996) is that of 'eating, drinking or smoking', that is, the notion of consuming something. Meaning groups in this general notional group appear under the patterns shown in Table 5.1 (verbs and most examples from Francis et al. 1996).

Two very obvious points need to be made about this table. First, the verbs and patterns by no means 'mean the same thing'. Examples using different verbs, or the same verb with a different pattern, are not paraphrases of each other. Rather, the table suggests the range of meanings that can be made in the general semantic area of 'eating, drinking and smoking'.

Second, not all the verbs in the table in fact belong to this specific notional group. The additional verbs given in small print in the table are those which in Francis et al. (1996) are in the same meaning groups as those meaning 'eating, drinking and smoking'. A thesaurus of verbs in the notional group in question would have to exclude those verbs. This is particularly the case with the pattern **V** *into* **n**, where verbs concerned with biting something (*bite, crunch, eat* and *sink*) have been placed into the same meaning group as verbs that indicate other ways of making a hole or indentation (*bore, dig* and *drill*).

To appreciate the significance of this is it important to realise that the

Table 5.1

Pattern	Verbs	Example
V	e.g.(most frequent verbs only): *drink, eat, feed, smoke*	*Most of the people I know don't smoke.*
V n	e.g.(most frequent verbs only): *drink, eat, have, leave, take, (not) touch, use;* *drink up, eat up, finish off, finish up, get down, get through, keep down, shoot up, take in, use up* Other verbs in the same meaning group: *burn, burn off, burn up*	*The children went in, and ate the biscuits.*
V *at* n	*chew, gnaw, nibble, nip, peck, pick, puff, sip, snap, suck;* *munch away, nibble away*	*He chewed at the end of his pencil, thinking out the next problem.*
V *from* n	*drink, eat, sip*	*The mechanic drank from the bottle with enthusiasm.*
V *into* n	*bite, crunch, eat, sink* Other verbs in the same meaning group: *bore, dig, drill*	*Weatherby bit into a digestive biscuit.*
V *on* n	*binge, browse, chew, choke, crunch, dine, draw, feast, feed, gnaw, gorge, live, munch, nibble, overdose, puff, pull, snack, suck;* *fill up, munch away, nibble away*	*He chewed on his toast, taking his time.* 'So what are the options?' Mr Clarke *asks, puffing on his small cigar.*
V *way* prep/adv	*booze, chain-smoke, chew, chomp, drink, eat, feast, gasp, gnaw, graze, guzzle, lick, munch, nibble, nosh, peck, puff, slice, slurp, smoke, taste, work*	*Mrs Lorimer chewed her way through a large helping of apple tart.* *Fiona amazed onlookers by puffing her way through three cigarettes and swigging red wine and schnapps.*
V n/pron-refl *on* n	*feed, gorge*	*Sometimes she fed the baby on milk and water.* *The whole point about chocolate cake is that you gorge yourself on it.*

meaning groups in Francis et al. (1996) were compiled for each pattern independently, and reflect what appeared to be a sensible grouping for each pattern. The grouping together of meaning groups in the Meaning Finder was a subsequent stage. The lack of straightforward 'fit' or uniformity between meaning groups under different patterns may be seen as a drawback and as the result of a fault in methodology. On the other hand, it does confirm the suspicion that notional groups, and the semantic areas they reflect, are extremely fuzzy entities. In this case, for example, the notional group 'consuming something' shades into the notional group 'making a hole or indentation'. The two areas are not entirely separate, but neither are they part of a superordinate grouping. To begin with the idea of certain notional groups, and to require meaning groups under individual patterns to conform to these, would be misleadingly artificial. We shall return to this discussion in Section 5.3.1 below.

5.1.2   *Further examples of notional groups*

Before returning to our discussion of notional groups, let us give two more examples of these groups, both based on the Meaning Finder in Francis et al. (1996). The examples that have been selected are: 'Logical relations' and 'Making someone do something'. These examples have been chosen because the semantic areas they represent are likely to be found in a functional/notional teaching syllabus. In these examples, only those verbs which belong to the notional group concerned are listed; other verbs which may be found in the same meaning group under the relevant pattern are omitted.

Logical relations. This notional group comprises verbs which, in Halliday's terms, realise relational processes. Halliday (1994: 119) comments that these processes do more than indicate existence; rather, 'a relation is being set up between two separate entities'. These entities may be simple ones realised by ordinary concrete nouns; often, however, they are themselves processes and are realised by nominalisations or by other nouns that realise complex ideas and processes. Halliday (1994: 343ff) refers to this type of complexity as 'ideational metaphor' and notes that it is more typical of academic, written language than of casual, spoken language. Familiarity with the verbs indicating logical relations and the patterns they occur with is, therefore, an essential component of training in academic writing.

The term 'logical relations' of course covers a variety of meanings. Three are particularly common, and these may be glossed as: (i) be evidence for; (ii) make (im)possible or (un)necessary; (iii) be a result of.

Logical relations (i) 'be evidence for'
V n (most frequent verbs only): *confirm, indicate, mark, mean, prove, reflect, reveal, show, suggest, support, tell; bear out*

 (1) *The latest experiments <u>have</u> also <u>confirmed</u> earlier results.*

 (2) *The test scores <u>tell</u> a different story.*

V that: *confirm, demonstrate, denote, illustrate, imply, indicate, mean, prove, reveal, show, signal, signify, underline, underscore*

 (3) *The large size <u>implies</u> that the gaps were created by a star rather than a planet.*

V wh: *confirm, demonstrate, illustrate, indicate, prove, reveal, show, signal, underline, underscore*

 (4) *The incident <u>underlines</u> how easily things can go wrong on holiday.*

V *to* n: *attest, point, testify*

 (5) *…all the evidence <u>points</u> to her guilt.*

V amount *about* n/-ing: *reveal, say*

 (6) *The way you present information <u>says</u> a lot about the way you do business.*

Logical relations (ii): 'make (im)possible or (un)necessary'
V n (most frequent verbs only): *afford, allow, carry, decide, demand, determine, encourage, ensure, invite, involve, mean, need, require, take; rule out, set off, set up, touch off; call for, count towards, cry out for, enter into, go with, lead on to, lead up to, lie behind, make for*

 (7) *The interaction of the teaching and research interests of staff <u>ensures</u> a stimulating intellectual atmosphere.*

 (8) *The maximum number of wolves … is too small to <u>rule out</u> a high degree of inbreeding.*

V -ing: *allow, entail, involve, justify, mean, necessitate, permit, preclude, prevent, save*

 (9) *Taking the engine out <u>necessitates</u> removing the front panel.*

V that: *dictate, ensure, guarantee, mean*

 (10) *Survival needs <u>dictate</u> that infants have to be self-orientated.*

V wh: *decide, define, determine, dictate, influence*

(11)   *The final exam determines whether you can sit for university entrance or not.*

V *in* n/-ing: *result*

(12)   *The operation resulted in the arrest of one alleged kidnapper.*

V *of* n/-ing: *permit*

(13)   *His nerves had been steady enough to permit of his returning to the office.*

V n -ing: *entail, involve, justify, mean, necessitate*

(14)   *A move there would involve him taking a cut in salary.*

V n -ed: *get*

(15)   *Anything at all that can get you noticed is good news in this business.*

it **V that**: *follow; come about*

(16)   *Since sound is actually the motion of molecules, it follows that the fastest speed with which the air molecules can get out of the way is the speed of sound.*

Logical meaning (iii): 'be a result of'
V *from* n/-ing: *arise, come, develop, flow, follow, result, spring, stem*

(17)   *Alzheimer's ... is unlikely to result from a defect in a single human gene.*

V *on* n/-ing: *depend, hang, hinge, pivot, rely, rest, ride, turn*

(18)   *A great deal hangs on the answer to these questions.*

V *out of* n/-ing: *arise, develop, grow*

(19)   *The trouble appears to have arisen out of demands that several senior police officers should be forced to stand down.*

V n *on* n/-ing: *base, build, ground* (usu passive), *predicate* (usu passive), *be premised*

(20)   *The whole thing is predicated on whipping up demand for the tournament hotline.*

(Talking about) making someone do something. This notional group comprises ways of reporting utterances which perform the speech act of 'directive' (Searle 1979; Leech 1983), and of describing non-verbal ways of influencing what someone does. Just as there are several ways in English of performing a directive, so there are many patterns and verbs that can be used to report a directive. In those patterns that include a clause, the action that is influenced is indicated by that clause. For example, in

> (21)   *I <u>recommend</u> all readers to follow the manufacturer's instructions,*

where the pattern is **V n to-inf**, the advised action is indicated by the non-finite clause: *to follow the manufacturer's instructions*. In those patterns which do not include a clause, the action is indicated by a noun, or may not be explicitly indicated at all. In the first pattern given below (**V n**), for example, the action itself remains implicit, and some considerable 'unpacking' is necessary to retrieve it. In

> (22)   *I attempted to <u>talk</u> them <u>down</u>,*

the desired action may be made more explicit as follows: 'I attempted to persuade them <u>to reduce their asking price</u>'. Similarly, the passive example

> (23)   *The spokesman refused to <u>be drawn</u>*

may be rephrased as 'People tried to persuade the spokesman <u>to talk about the issue</u> but he refused'. An example such as

> (24)   *He <u>motioned</u> Arnold to a chair*

with the pattern **V n prep/adv** may be unpacked as 'He invited Arnold <u>to sit down</u>'.

The patterns and verbs belonging to this notional group are as follows:

V n (most frequent verbs only): *attract (people or animals), bind (Laws...people), call (a doctor or witness), draw (a crowd), draw (a speaker), force, push, use, work; beat down (a seller), buy off, call out (a doctor), draw out, head off (a person or vehicle), hold back, move along, move on, order around/about, pick up, pull back (troops), pull in (crowds), pull out (troops), pull over (a driver), pull up, push around, set off, start off, talk down (a pilot or a seller), talk up (a buyer), throw out, turn back, turn out*

> (25)   *Family doctors are fed up with <u>being called out</u> on home visits late at night.*

(26)   *The spokesman refused to be drawn. 'We do not comment on the reasons for people either joining or leaving the company,' he said.*

V n (Ergative Verbs) (see Section 7.2.2): *assemble, demobilize, disband, disperse, mass, mobilize, muster, organize* (*workers*), *reassemble, redeploy, regroup, relocate, reorganize, resettle, reunite, rotate, scatter, settle, unite, withdraw; bunch up, hold together, line up, pull back, pull out, split up, turn back*

(27)   *Washington had to disband part of his army for lack of clothing.*

assimilate, feed, graze, hush, integrate, nurse, overwork, quiet, quieten, rearm, reform, retrain, run (*a horse*), *stampede, train; dry out, hold back, liven up, move along, pull up, quiet down, quieten down, shut up, slow down, sober up, trip up*

(28)   *He blamed his heart attack on his employer for overworking him.*

V to-inf: *apply, ask, beg, bid, campaign, clamour, demand, petition, plead, pray*

(29)   *The police asked to use Keith's video as evidence.*

V at n to-inf: *bark, bawl, bellow, hiss, holler, scream, screech, shout, snap, yell; go on, keep on*

(20)   *I shouted at her to run.*

V for n to-inf: *agitate, appeal, ask, call, campaign, gesture, holler, motion, petition, plead, pray, press, push, shout*

(21)   *She got up from her desk and motioned for Wade to follow her.*

V on/upon n to-inf: *call, prevail*

(22)   *So we call on everyone to seize this opportunity and to look at it positively.*

V with n to-inf: *collaborate, connive, conspire, contract, plead, vie*

(23)   *I pleaded with her to stop but she wouldn't. ...she conspired with others to perform illegal campaign services.*

(Note: *collaborate, connive, conspire* and *vie* are reciprocal verbs (see Section 2.5))

V n -ing: *have, keep, leave, send, set*

(24)   *The show generated an electric atmosphere that lit up the audience and had them cheering till they were hoarse.*

(Note: The Subject often indicates something inanimate.)

V n to-inf: *admonish, advise, approach, ask, beckon, beg, beseech, bid, call, caution, challenge, command, counsel, dare, defy, direct, enjoin, entreat, exhort, forbid, be given, implore, importune, instruct, invite, mandate, motion, order, petition, recommend, remind, request, summons, tell, warn, wire; bind over*

(25)   *She looked at him, waiting for him to <u>ask</u> her to come with him.*

badger, cajole, chivvy, coax, encourage, incite, nag, nudge, pester, press, pressure, pressurize, prod, urge; egg on

(26)   *My education was the most important thing to my mother, and she <u>pestered</u> my father to pay for me to go to the best schools.*

bind, blackmail, brainwash, bribe, (cannot) bring, cause, coerce, compel, condemn, condition, constrain, convince, discipline, doom, drive, entice, force, get, impel, induce, lead, be made, manipulate, nerve, obligate, oblige, pay, persuade, push, rouse, sentence, steel, stir, tempt; rope in

(27)   *Even now she <u>couldn't bring</u> herself to tell John the whole truth.*

V n inf: *bid, have, make*

(28)   *I wanted to find some way to <u>make</u> her commit herself to the group.*

V n prep/adv: *allow, ask (out), assign, beckon, boo, book (in), call, check, chivvy, coax, direct, dispatch, divert, drag, drive, entice, exile, flush (out), force, gallop, get, help, herd, hurry, hustle, invite, jostle, kick (off), let (in/out), lure, march, motion, move, nudge, order, persuade, post, put, route, second, settle, shoo, show, shunt, shuttle, set, steer, summon, take, tempt, throw, transfer, urge, usher, warn, wave, whisk; sit down*

(29)   *He <u>motioned</u> Arnold to a chair.*

(30)   *I never saw Daddy again. Three months later I <u>was summoned</u> home to his funeral.*

V n *against* n/-ing: *caution, warn*

(31)   *Many of his advisers <u>had warned</u> him against involving himself in a complicated foreign conflict.*

V n *in* n/-ing: *embroil, employ, engage, implicate, include, involve; be caught up*

(32)   *Riding in the car offers a wonderful opportunity to <u>engage</u> your child in observing the surroundings.*

V n *into* n:
badger, blackmail, bludgeon, bounce, browbeat, bulldoze, bully, chivvy, coerce, cow, drag, dragoon, force, frighten, goad, intimidate, nag, panic, press, press-gang, pressure, prod, provoke, push, railroad, scare, stampede, steamroller, suck, talk, terrify, whip; whip up

> (33)   *...police <u>terrified</u> him into a false confession.*

bamboozle, con, deceive, dupe, entrap, fool, inveigle, lure, trap, trick

> (34)   *Luisa <u>inveigles</u> Paco into a plot to swindle Trini out of her savings.*

cajole, charm, seduce, sweet talk, tempt

> (35)   *The ingredient he brought to the job was a talent for <u>charming</u> his opponents into submission.*

galvanize, jolt, nudge, persuade, propel, seduce, spur, steer, stir, tempt

> (36)   *The friendship could be extremely good for her, for she will catch the enthusiasm and energy and <u>be spurred</u> into action.*

chasten, condition, lull, manoeuvre, rush, shame, sidetrack

> (37)   *The intention was to <u>shame</u> young drivers into better behaviour on the roads.*

V n *into* -ing:
badger, blackmail, bludgeon, bounce, brainwash, browbeat, bulldoze, bully, chivvy, coerce, co-opt, cow, dragoon, force, frighten, goad, intimidate, manipulate, nag, panic, press, press-gang, pressure, pressurize, prod, provoke, push, railroad, scare, shock, stampede, steamroller, talk, terrify

> (38)   *He tried to <u>frighten</u> people into doing what he wanted.*

con, deceive, delude, dupe, entrap, fool, hoodwink, inveigle, lure, mislead, sucker, trap, trick

> (39)   *Can a machine be built that <u>could fool</u> a human judge into thinking it was a person?*

beguile, bribe, cajole, charm, coax, entice, flatter, sweet talk, tempt

> (40)   *Henry <u>charmed</u> and <u>cajoled</u> people into parting with thousands of pounds.*

galvanize, jolt, lead, nudge, persuade, propel, seduce, spur, steer, stimulate, stir, tempt

(41)   *Some new acquaintances persuaded us into spending the summer near Kiev.*

chasten, condition, embarrass, lull, manoeuvre, rush, shame, sidetrack

(42)   *Somehow the authorities have to manoeuvre the markets into demanding a cut in interest rates.*

V n *out of* n: *bomb, boot, chase, chuck, drive, drum, flush, force, hound, jolt, kick, knock, order, put, shake, throw, turf, turn, vote, winkle*

(43)   *She fears the authorities might kick her out of Barbados.*

coax, persuade, talk

(44)   *David Gower has been coaxed out of retirement.*

V n *to* n: *admit, assign, banish, commit, confine, consign, deport, direct, extradite, refer, relegate, restrict, send, transfer, transplant; bundle off, pack off, take out*

(45)   *I ended up directing him to a cut-rate travel agent in San Bruno.*

drive, incite, incline, lull, move, predispose, reduce, rouse; bring round, put up, spur on, work up

(46)   *The party agreed not to incite its supporters to violence.*

V n *towards/toward* n: *draw, incline, push*

(47)   *This pushed him towards resignation in 1983.*

5.1.3   *Notional groups in teaching languages*

The notional groups exemplified above have a clear relevance to the functional/notional approach to language course design that came to prominence in the 1970s and is still widely used in English language teaching coursebooks. An early, and still influential, proponent was Wilkins (1976), who champions a notional syllabus above a structural or situational syllabuses on these grounds:

> The notional syllabus is in contrast with the other two because it takes the desired communicative capacity as the starting-point. In drawing up a notional syllabus, instead of asking how speakers of the language express themselves or when and where they use the language, we ask what it is they communicate through language. We are then able to organize language teaching in terms of the content rather than the form of the language. (Wilkins 1976: 18).

He further argues (Wilkins 1976: 2) that whereas traditional syllabuses are *synthetic*, building up knowledge of a language from the individual 'building blocks' of grammar, notional syllabuses are *analytic*, presenting the learner with meanings and utterances which can be analysed for grammatical information. There are obvious influences here from functional grammar, whose model of grammar is based on the investigation of the meanings that language makes (e.g. Halliday 1994: xvii).

Academic opinion has now moved away from notional or functional syllabuses as the ideal in language teaching (see, for example, Willis 1990), but notions and functions still comprise an important organising principle in many English Language Teaching textbooks and are a key part of the EFL/ESL teacher's repertoire.

The original work on language functions and notions carried out by Wilkins (1976), van Ek (1975) and others was carried out intuitively, without the benefit of extensive corpus analysis. They could only give examples of the ways that particular meanings could be expressed, and they worked 'top-down', that is, starting with a notion or function and suggesting the language forms by which that notion or function might be expressed. By contrast, the notional groups described in Section 5.1.2 are derived in a 'bottom-up' way, working from the individual lexical item, to the pattern and meaning group, to the notion or function expressed. The result is a list (in the Meaning Finder in Francis et al. 1996) of those notions that in English are expressed in a variety of ways, together with a reasonably comprehensive account of the patterns and lexis by which each notion may be expressed. In a sense, then, notional groups from the Meaning Finder are a way of substantiating a notional syllabus and of integrating with it the more recent focus on lexis (e.g. Willis 1990).

There are, however, important differences between the notions identified by Wilkins in 1976, and the functions commonly found in the ELT textbooks, and the notional groups identified in Francis et al. (1996). We would argue that these differences go a long way towards explaining the dissatisfaction many language teachers feel when faced with a list of functions/notions that they are required to teach. To illustrate the differences, let us consider the notion 'Duration', which Wilkins discusses under the heading of 'semantico-grammatical categories'. These are the categories which "express our perceptions of events, processes, states and abstractions" and which are concerned with a meaning that "has been variously called 'ideational', 'cognitive', or 'propositional' meaning" (Wilkins 1976: 21). In short, the ability to express these notions would enable a learner to describe and to narrate.

Wilkins' (1976: 26) suggestions for the language needed to express Duration in English comprise:

prepositional phrases: *for five years, until six o'clock, since Monday, from Monday*
noun groups: *all the day, the whole day, this week, last year*
clauses introduced by *while, when, since* and *until*

Francis et al.'s (1996:618) account of the verbs used to express Duration in English comprises:

verbs followed by a noun group indicating a length of time: *allow, last, occupy, take; fill in, fill up;*
verbs followed by an adverb indicating a length of time: *keep, last, live, run;*
verbs followed by a prepositional phrase, often beginning with *for, from,* or *until: endure, keep, last, live, run;*
verbs followed by a prepositional phrase beginning with *to: live, date back, go back;*
a verb followed by a noun group indicating a person and a noun group indicating a length of time: *take;*
a verb followed by a noun group indicating a person, a noun group indicating a length of time, and a to-infinitive clause indicating an action: *take;*
it followed by a verb, a noun group indicating a person, a noun group indicating a length of time, and a to-infinitive clause indicating an action: *take;*
it followed by a verb, a noun group indicating a length of time, and an '-ing' clause: *take;*
it followed by a verb, a noun group or adverb indicating a length of time, and a clause beginning with *before* or *since: be, seem, take.*

Wilkins' list would produce utterances such as these (all examples invented):

(48) *We travelled for six weeks.*

(49) *We ate well the whole day.*

(50) *We worked until we had finished.*

Francis et al.'s list would produce utterances such as these (all examples invented):

(51) *Our journey lasted six weeks.*

(52) *The journey did not last long.*

(53) *Our rations kept for three days.*

(54) *The vase dates back to the sixteenth century.*

(55) *Our work took us a long time.*

(56) *The work took us several days to finish.*

(57) *It took us several days to finish the work.*

(58)   *It took two hours washing the dog.*

(59)   *It seems ages since we met.*

In the first set of examples, duration is expressed by an optional adverbial, something that is not central to the clause structure. In the second set, duration is expressed by the verb and another necessary part of the clause. In the first set, the Subject indicates a person and the verb indicates what the person did. In the second set, the Subject indicates (for the most part) an abstraction, or is the 'dummy Subject' *it*. The first set represents an event or action in a concrete way ('congruent' in Halliday's (1994: 343) terms), and might be glossed as 'talking about what people do'. The second set represents an event or action in a more abstract way ('metaphoric' in Halliday's terms), and might be glossed as 'talking about what happens'.

It must be stressed at this point that Wilkins and Francis et al. are undertaking different tasks and do not position themselves in opposition to each other. Ultimately, a learner would need to be able to understand and produce the examples in both of the lists above. The absence from Wilkins' list of verbs that indicate duration, and the consequent omission of the more abstract ways of talking about duration, would lead to an impoverished language repertoire unless supplemented in the ways indicated by the Francis et al. list. We believe that this impoverishment is an unfortunate feature of many functional textbooks.

We can take this argument further if we look at Wilkins' discussion of language forms in the categories 'suasion' and 'requesting', which roughly correspond to the notional group '(Talking about) making someone do something'. Wilkins (1976: 41) makes a distinction between "what we *do* through language and what we report by means of language". He cites

(60)   *If you don't get out, I'll call the police*

and

(61)   *The manager threatened to call the police*

as examples of 'doing' and 'reporting' respectively. This is similar to Hasan's (in Halliday and Hasan 1985) distinction between 'active' and 'reflective' modes of language: language is used both to do and to talk about or reflect on doing. From the account of the notional group 'Making someone do something' above it is clear that the utterances associated with the group belong to Wilkins' 'reporting' function and to Hasan's 'reflective' mode. In fact, the title of the notional group should properly be 'Talking about making someone do something'. (The same of true of other notional groups. For example, the concept described above as

'Eating and drinking' should really be described as 'Talking about eating and drinking', and so on.)

Wilkins (1976: 42) comments that:

> Language learning has concentrated much more on the use of language to report and describe than on doing things through language. ... While *reporting* and *describing* are acts that we would like to carry out through language and which we can perform largely with a knowledge of the semantico-grammatical categories, they are by no means the only ones that are important for the learner of a foreign language.

He proceeds to redress the balance by giving ways of doing suasion and requests. These are by now familiar to any language teacher, and include many variations of the type *Shall we go to the zoo.. How about us going to the zoo... The best course seems to be for you to take the job... Would you be good enough to shut the window...* and so on (Wilkins 1976: 47–51). In addition, he indicates ways of reporting these functions, giving lists of verbs such as *persuade, suggest, advise, recommend, advocate, exhort, beg, incite, propose* (Wilkins 1976: 46) and shows which of seven verbs (*authorize, allow, consent to, agree to, permit, approve, tolerate*) occur in various combinations of four patterns, which in our terms would be **V n, V n to-inf, V that, V n -ing**.

Wilkins was undoubtedly right to insist that 'doing' was as important a function for the language learner as 'reporting'. His advice has certainly been taken to heart by the English Language Teaching world, to the extent that many textbooks tend to concentrate on 'doing' functions at the expense of 'reporting' functions. Perhaps it would be truer to say that whereas textbook writers go to considerable trouble, as Wilkins did, to list various ways of performing a function, such as 'requesting', they handle the complexity of a function such as 'reporting requests' with a less sure hand. As our notional group 'Making someone do something' indicates (see above), a considerable variety of lexis and pattern is involved. (Wilkins' (1976: 43) comment that "...there will be no single, unambiguous, grammatical structure by which a function is realized" applies just as much to reporting as to doing.) If 'reporting' is made secondary to 'doing', the result is, as we said before, a sense of impoverishment in the language being taught, and it is this sense of impoverishment that lexical approaches to language seek to compensate for.

A further point might be made here about Wilkins' distinction between 'doing' and 'reporting'. Wilkins appears to regard the reporting function as separate from the cut-and-thrust of everyday interaction (Wilkins 1976: 41–43) and seems to imply that reporting may be carried out in the classroom, using a decontextualised lexico-grammatical system. If learners wish to interact in genuine situations with native speakers of a language, Wilkins implies, they must learn the 'doing' functions. Certainly, a learner who can say *If you don't get out, I'll call the police* sounds admirably assertive and involved, whilst one who can only aver *The manager threatened to call the police* sounds, by contrast, insipid and detached. The study of verbs reported in Francis et al. (1996), however, implies that a great deal of English lexis is used, typically, to report and describe, and that the ability to handle the complexity of these functions is central to the language learner's task. At the post-elementary level, interaction in genuine situations with native speakers is as likely to involve reflective as active uses of language.

Rather than considering 'reporting' and 'describing' as just two functions among many, textbook writers should perhaps introduce an 'active–reflective' distinction into each functionally-based unit. For example, a unit on 'requests' would include 'making requests' and 'talking about influencing someone'. A unit on 'agreeing and disagreeing' would include 'talking about agreeing and disagreeing'. At the very least, textbooks should include a fair balance of active and reflective language and should take account of the fact that what matters is not the monolithic functions 'reporting' and 'describing', but the particular notions 'reporting persuasion', 'describing (dis)agreement' and so on.

5.2 Mapping meaning on to pattern

5.2.1 *Patterns and roles*

One of the things that a consideration of notional groups and patterns makes obvious is that a single aspect of meaning might be realised in different ways, depending on the pattern, so that various configurations of meaning and pattern are possible. For example, with respect to two of the ways of talking about duration (see Section 5.1.3), the meaning expressed by *the journey* in *The journey from London to Southampton took three hours* is practically the same as that expressed in the to-infinitive clause in *It took three hours to travel from London to Southampton*.

Continuing this theme, let us consider each of the patterns that occur with the verb *take* to indicate duration.

V n:

(62)   *The journey took seven hours.*

V n n:

(63)   *The journey* <u>took</u> *us four days.*

V n n to-inf:

(64)   *The model* <u>took</u> *him six months to complete.*

it **V n to-inf**:

(65)   *It* <u>takes</u> *time to learn about finance.*

it **V n n to-inf**:

(66)   *It* <u>took</u> *them twelve days to finish the face.*

it **V n -ing**:

(67)   *It* <u>took</u> *ages getting through London.*

it **V n/amount before/since**:

(68)   *It* <u>took</u> *nine months before the case came to court.*

If we use Halliday's (1994: 107ff) terminology of 'process', 'participant' and
'circumstance', we might note that in each of these examples, in addition to the
process realised by the verb *take*, there is one additional process (travelling,
learning about finance and so on) and a circumstance (the time period: *seven
hours, four days* and so on), and in many of them there is a participant (*us, him,
them*). Referring to each of these (process, participant and circumstance) by the
neutral term 'role', we can see that these roles can be mapped on to the patterns
in three distinct ways, as in Table 5.2.

Table 5.2a

Activity		Time period
	V	**n**
The journey	*took*	*seven hours.*

Table 5.2b

Activity...		Person	Time period	...Activity
	V	**n**	**n**	
The journey	*took*	*us*	*four days.*	
	V	**n**	**n**	**to-inf**
The model	*took*	*him*	*six months*	*to complete.*

Table 5.2c

		Time period	Activity
It	**V**	**n**	**clause**
It	*takes*	*time*	*to learn about finance.*
It	*took*	*ages*	*getting through London.*
It	*took*	*nine months*	*before the case came to court.*

Table 5.2d

		Person	Time period	Activity
it	**V**	**n**	**n**	**to-inf**
It	*took*	*them*	*twelve days*	*to finish the race.*

In these examples, the mapping of role on to pattern depends on the pattern that occurs with *take*. However, the mapping of role on to pattern depends on the verb as well as on the pattern. For example, continuing the theme of duration, we find that *last, occupy* and *take*, with the pattern **V n**, have a consistent mapping of role on to pattern, but *allow*, with the same pattern, has a different mapping, as tables 5.3a and 5.3b illustrate.

Table 5.3a

Activity		Time period
	V	**n**
The concert	*lasted*	*two hours.*
Sewing the quilt	*occupied*	*three months.*
Analysis of the data	*took*	*another ten days.*

Table 5.3b

Person		Time period
	V	**n**
You	*should allow*	*at least two days.*

We have illustrated two observations here: firstly, that two utterances with different patterns may exemplify the same roles, though in a different order; secondly, that two utterances with the same pattern may demand different role-mappings if the lexical items in them are different. Another illustration of the first observation is a group of verbs that occur in two patterns: **V n prep/adv** and **V n *with* n.** In each case, the noun group following the verb in the first pattern realises the same role as does the noun group following *with* in the second pattern. Table 5.4 shows some examples, with the roles mapped on to them (for details of the verbs involved, see Francis et al. 1996: 442–443).

Table 5.4a

Actor		Small things or material	Area or Container
	V	**n**	**prep/adv**
We	*draped*	*banners*	*across the walls.*
He	*loaded*	*cartons*	*into the van.*
I	*splashed*	*water*	*on my face.*
They	*plastered*	*dung*	*over the wall.*

Table 5.4b

Actor		Area or Container			Small things or material
	V	**n**	***with***		**n**
We	*draped*	*the walls*	*with*		*banners.*
He	*loaded*	*the van*	*with*		*cartons.*
I	*splashed*	*my face*	*with*		*water.*
They	*plastered*	*the wall*	*with*		*dung.*

As another example of a single pattern requiring different role mapping depending on the lexical item involved, consider some verbs with the pattern **V n *to* n** (Francis et al. 1996: 427). Five verbs with this pattern belong to a meaning group which is concerned with a person or group starting to like or approve of someone or something. In the case of the verbs *commend, endear* and *recommend*, the noun group following the verb indicates the object of liking, while the second noun group indicates the person who likes. In the case of *attract* and *draw*, however, the roles are reversed: the noun group following the verb indicates the person who likes, and the second noun group indicates the object of liking. This is shown in Table 5.5.

Table 5.5a

		Object of liking/approval		Person who likes/approves
	V	**n**	***to***	**n**
These qualities	*recommend*	*him*	*to*	*the electorate.*

Table 5.5b

	Person who likes/approves		Object of liking/approval
V	**n**	*to*	**n**
The company wants to attract	*investors*	*to*	*something new.*

It is not only verb patterns that exemplify this kind of variation. For example, *She is plastered in make-up* exemplifies the pattern **ADJ *in* n**, while *His face was plastered on giant billboards* exemplifies the pattern **ADJ *on* n**. In the first example, *she* represents a place and *make-up* is something that is put in the place. In the second example, the roles are reversed: *his face* represents the thing that is put and *billboards* represents the place. Occasionally, a single lexical item in a single pattern may represent two alternative role-mappings. For example, in *[The play] is ... rather lacking in laughs*, *the play* represents a (metaphoric) container and *laughs* are the thing it does not contain; whereas in *...an intellectual challenge was lacking in her life*, the first noun group — *an intellectual challenge* — represents the thing and the second noun group — *her life* — represents the container.

Traditional SVOCA analyses go some way towards accounting for examples of this type by assigning different functional labels. For example, there is a traditional distinction made within the pattern **V n n** (where the verb is followed by two noun groups) between the configuration Verb-Object-Object Complement and the configuration Verb-Indirect Object-Direct Object. An example of the first is

(69)   *We elected her President*

and an example of the second is

(70)   *She gave him a book.*

The term 'Indirect Object' itself is an attempt to represent the role similarity between *him* in *She gave him a book* and in *She gave a book to him.*

Case grammar (e.g. Fillmore 1968), and in particular the participant roles proposed by Halliday (1994), represent the most effective way of dealing with this kind of variation in mapping. Halliday, for example, notes that, following verbs with the pattern **V n**, the noun group may realise a 'goal':

(71)   *Toxins attack the connective tissue,*

a 'phenomenon':

(72)   *You could hear the cheering for miles around,*

an 'experiencer':

    (73)   *These stories surprised me,*

or 'range':

    (74)   *He gave out a scream of pain.*

The role realised by the noun group depends entirely upon the choice of verb; thus the grammatical configuration is determined by lexis.

    Halliday uses a small, finite number of such participant roles, and links each type of process to a particular set of roles. So, for example, the verb *see*, which realises a mental (perception) process, is associated with the participant roles 'phenomenon' and 'senser'. Such generalisations lead to a grammatical description of great explanatory power. However, they also make necessary on occasion dual analyses. For example, Halliday (1994: 346) quotes the example

    (75)   *The fifth day saw them at the summit*

and comments that two analyses are possible. The first treats the process involved as a mental process, and yields Table 5.6a (based on Halliday 1994: 346).

Table 5.6a

Senser	Mental Process: Perception	Phenomenon	Place
The fifth day	*saw*	*them*	*at the summit.*

This is clearly only partially satisfactory, as it involves treating a period of time as something animate and able to see. The alternative analysis is more in keeping with our experience of the world, but involves a re-wording of the clause (see Table 5.6b).

Table 5.6b

Actor	Material Process	Place	Time
They	*arrived*	*at the summit*	*on the fifth day.*

Halliday (1994: 346) terms the second analysis 'congruent' and the first 'metaphoric'. Note that Halliday is precluded from proposing an analysis such as

The fifth day	=	Time
saw	=	Mental process (Perception)
them	=	Actor
at the summit	=	Place

by his linking of particular participants and circumstances to particular process types. Mental processes are associated with the participants Senser and Phenomenon, not with Actor, Time and Place, so the above analysis is impossible.

We, however, are concerned with individual lexical items rather than with process types. We would thus associate roles, not with process types but with notional groups, or meanings. We are then able to propose that *see* with a Subject that realises a point of time requires a very different set of roles than does *see* with a human Subject. Francis et al. (1996: 318) point out that *see* and *find* are both used in the way illustrated by Halliday above, in the pattern **V n prep/adv** (verb followed by a noun group and either a prepositional phrase or an adverb), and give the following examples, shown in Table 5.7a with possible roles mapped on to them.

Table 5.7a

Point of time			Actor	Place or Situation
	V	**n**		**prep/adv**
Dawn	*found*	*us*		*on a cold, clammy ship...*
The last night of the course	*saw*	*a group of us*		*nearly in tears...*

If the clauses were re-written in a more 'congruent' way, the role analysis would be the same, but the pattern analysis would be different:

Table 5.7b

Actor		Place or Situation	Time
	V	**prep**	**prep**
We	*were*	*on a cold clammy ship*	*by dawn.*
A group of us	*were*	*nearly in tears*	*on the last night of the course.*

A further step in the account of pattern and meaning in English, then, would involve the creation of 'mapping tables' such as those above, not only for each pattern, but for each word-pattern combination. A possible objection to such an approach might be that it leads to a proliferation of roles, which is of course undesirable in any analytical system (cf. Sinclair and Coulthard 1975: 15–16). The answer may lie in the notion of 'local grammar', wherein any utterance is deemed to have a particular function, and a restricted set of roles that are uniquely associated with that function (see Barnbrook and Sinclair 1995; Hunston and Sinclair 2000; Allen 1999). Taking the notional groups discussed in Section 5.1, then, each notional group would have its own set of roles, which would be mapped on to each verb-pattern combination.

One function which has been investigated in these terms is that of 'evaluation' (Hunston and Sinclair 2000). The roles involved in the process of evaluation may be mapped on to the patterns of words which are associated with that function. There are various ways of illustrating this, one obvious one being to take several patterns that belong to a notional group with the title 'evaluation', list the lexical items in them, and map role on to pattern. To do so, however, masks some of the problems that would occur if this principle were ever to be applied to the computer analysis (without human intervention) of naturally-occurring text. The computer would then run into several difficulties caused by pattern sequences and different forms of patterns (see Chapter 2). To illustrate these as well as the principle behind the exercise, we instead choose to analyse two specific lexical items: the adjective *difficult* and the noun *difficulty*. In the next two sections we consider each word in turn. In each case we present 100 randomly-selected concordance lines from the Bank of English corpus, identify the patterns represented therein, and map the roles on to each pattern.

5.2.2   The patterns of <u>difficult</u>

The 100 randomly-selected concordance lines for the adjective *difficult* are given in the Appendix to this chapter. We exclude from discussion two lines of the hundred, which use the meaning of *difficult* as 'having awkward behaviour' (*I'm not trying to be difficult* and *I hope I haven't been too difficult*).

For the purposes of role-mapping, it is necessary to separate out all different forms of a pattern and all instances of pattern sequence, treating them as separate patterns. If this is done, no fewer than 21 different patterns occurring with the adjective *difficult* may be identified. A complete list, with examples from the concordance lines, is given here:

1. **v-link ADJ**

   (75)   *Some of it is, well, really quite difficult. ... will perhaps prove rather difficult.*

2. *make* **n ADJ**

   (76)   *to make things more difficult*

3. **ADJ n**

   (77)   *...to place a difficult adult, ...in this difficult area of the environment ...often under the most difficult conditions ... you do ask some difficult questions ... Difficult questions are invaluable...*

4. v-link ADJ n

(78)   *...city governments in Poland can be difficult business partners ... the question of peace was a very difficult one*

5. v-link ADJ n to-inf

(79)   *it was a very difficult decision to make ... it would be a difficult trick to pull off twice ...*

6. *make* n ADJ to-inf

(80)   *modifiers make a sentence difficult to understand*

7. v-link ADJ *for* n to-inf

(81)   *it's quite difficult for us to do ... this last need is quite difficult for most of us to understand*

8. v-link ADJ *for* n

(82)   *Life is therefore difficult for males with a family in tow.*

9. v-link ADJ to-inf

(83)   *The materials are difficult to find ... account deficit that may prove difficult to finance*

10. *it* v-link ADJ to-inf

(84)   *It is getting difficult these days to sit down to the... it is difficult to see the future .. it is difficult to generalise ...*

11. *find it* ADJ to-inf

(85)   *he found it difficult to succeed ... they will find it difficult to pull back*

12. *it* v-link ADJ *for* n to-inf

(86)   *it's going to be very difficult for business to match declines*

13. *make it* ADJ *for* n to-inf

(87)   *make it really difficult to large cars to use the roads*

14. *it* v-link ADJ -ing

(88)   *it was pretty difficult over the last 18 months reading...*

15. ADJ-SUPERL *of* n

(89)   *...this most difficult of concessions*

16. **v-link *as* ADJ *as* n/-ing**

    (90)   *...wasn't nearly as difficult as coping with the feeling...*

17. **v-link ADJ-COMPAR *than* n/-ing**

    (91)   *...might be more difficult than its efforts...*

18. **v-link ADJ-COMPAR *of* n**

    (92)   *The 800m is the more difficult of the two...*

19. ***what* v-link ADJ to-inf v-link n/that/to-inf**

    (93)   *What is difficult to gauge, is the... What is difficult to believe is that*

20. ***the* ADJ n v-link to-inf**

    (94)   *The most difficult thing is to score a goal...*

21. ***how* ADJ *it* v-link to-inf**

    (95)   *How much more difficult it is to imagine a world...*

Omitting, for simplicity's sake, those patterns that occur only with comparative or superlative forms of the adjective (patterns 15, 17 and 18), we can map roles on to these patterns as follows.

The two basic roles associated with evaluation are the Evaluated Entity (using Thetela's 1997 terminology) and the Evaluative Category. In the present study, the Evaluative Category in each case is, of course, *difficult*. The patterns which make use of only these two roles, along with the role mapping, are illustrated in Table 5.8.

Table 5.8a

Evaluated Entity		Evaluative Category
	v-link	**ADJ**
Some of it	*is*	*really quite difficult.*
Economic conditions	*became*	*increasingly difficult.*

Table 5.8b

	Evaluative Category	Evaluated Entity
	ADJ	**n**
Often under the	*most difficult*	*conditions.*
in this	*difficult*	*area of the environment.*
	difficult	*questions…*
You do ask some	*difficult*	*questions.*

Table 5.8c

		Evaluative Category	Evaluated Entity
it	**v-link**	**ADJ**	**to-inf/-ing**
It	*is*	*difficult*	*to see the future.*
It	*is*	*difficult*	*to generalise.*
It	*was*	*pretty difficult*	*reading into a man's mind.*

Table 5.8d

	Evaluative Category			Evaluated Entity
how	**ADJ**	*it*	**v-link**	**to-inf/-ing**
How	*much more difficult*	*it*	*is*	*to imagine a world…*

In the next pattern (Table 5.9), the Evaluated Entity is realised by a verb group in one part of the pattern and a group or clause in another part of the pattern.

Table 5.9

		Evaluative Category	Evaluated Entity…		…Evaluated Entity
what	**v-link**	**ADJ**	**to-inf**	**v-link**	**n/that/to-inf/-ing**
What	*is*	*difficult*	*to gauge*	*is*	*the sentiment of the Cambodians…*
What	*is*	*difficult*	*to believe*	*is*	*that this small yellow flower seed could yield such a nutritious oil.*

In the next set of patterns, there are two more roles involved in addition to the Evaluated Entity and the Evaluative Category. First, in Table 5.10, we consider examples where *difficult* modifies either a general noun that simply fills a grammatical slot in the pattern, or a more specific noun that limits the scope of the evaluation. An example of the first is *the question of peace was a very difficult one*, where *one* simply completes the noun group without adding meaning. An example of the second is *city governments in Poland can be difficult business partners*, where the Evaluated Entity is *city governments in Poland*, but where *business partners* gives information about the scope of the evaluation: the city governments are difficult in one respect only. The terms Evaluation Carrier and Evaluation Limiter will be used for these roles.

Table 5.10a

Evaluated Entity		Evaluative Category	Evaluation Carrier
	v-link	**ADJ**	**general noun/pronoun**
The question of peace was		*a difficult*	*one.*

Table 5.10b

	Evaluative Category	Evaluation Carrier		Evaluated Entity
the	**ADJ**	**general noun**	**v-link**	**to-inf**
The	*most difficult*	*thing*	*is*	*to score a goal...*

Table 5.10c

Evaluated Entity		Evaluative Category	Evaluation Limiter
	v-link	**ADJ**	**n**
City governments in Poland	*can be*	*difficult*	*business partners.*

The Evaluation Limiter may be realised by a clause, as in Table 5.11.

Table 5.11a

	Evaluative Category		Evaluated Entity	Evaluation Limiter
	v-link	**ADJ**	**n**	**to-inf**
It	*was*	*a very difficult*	*decision*	*to make.*
It	*would be*	*a difficult*	*trick*	*to pull off twice.*

Table 5.11b

Evaluated Entity		Evaluative Category	Evaluation Limiter
	v-link	**ADJ**	**to-inf**
The materials	*are*	*difficult*	*to find.*
An account deficit that	*may prove*	*difficult*	*to finance.*

The next set of patterns again involve a different role: a person, group or thing that is judged to experience the difficulty. This will be called the Affected Entity. Table 5.12 shows these patterns.

Table 5.12a

Evaluated Entity		Evaluative Category		Affected Entity	Evaluation Limiter
	v-link	**ADJ**	*for*	**n**	**to-inf**
It	*'s*	*quite difficult*	*for*	*us*	*to do.*
This last need	*is*	*quite difficult*	*for*	*most of us*	*to understand.*

Table 5.12b

Evaluated Entity		Evaluative Category		Affected Entity
	v-link	**ADJ**	*for*	**n**
Life	*is*	*difficult*	*for*	*males with a family in tow.*

Table 5.12c

		Evaluative Category		Affected Entity	Evaluated Entity
it	**v-link**	**ADJ**	*for*	**n**	**to-inf**
It	*'s going to be*	*very difficult*	*for*	*business*	*to match declines...*

Table 5.12d

Affected Entity				Evaluative Category	Evaluated Entity
	find	***it***	**ADJ**		**to-inf**
He	*found*	*it*	*difficult*		*to succeed.*
They	*will find*	*it*	*difficult*		*to pull back.*

The final set of patterns involve the verb *make*, and another role, which we will call the Causer. These are shown in Table 5.13.

Table 5.13a

Causer		Evaluated Entity	Evaluative Category
	make	**n**	**ADJ**
Joni's possessiveness	*made*	*the change*	*difficult.*

Table 5.13b

Causer		Evaluated Entity	Evaluative Category	Evaluation Limiter
	make	**n**	**ADJ**	**to-inf**
Modifiers	*make*	*a sentence*	*difficult*	*to understand.*

Table 5.13c

Causer			Evaluative Category	Affected Entity		Evaluated Entity
make	*it*	**ADJ**		*for*	**n**	**to-inf**
I	*'d make*	*it*	*really difficult*	*for*	*large cars*	*to use the road.*

The tasks for an automatic parser that might perform this analytical task without human intervention would include:

identifying *difficult* as an evaluative adjective;
identifying the patterns associated with *difficult* and correctly parsing each concordance line or occurrence of *difficult* in context;
differentiating between different lexical items, for example, between *make* and *find*, and between general nouns and specific nouns (in the pattern **v-link ADJ n**); assigning the correct role label to each part of each pattern.

Having established a set of role labels, let us apply these to a similar word from a different word-class: *difficulty*. Because the word-class is different, the patterns are expected to be different, but the role labels might be expected to be the same.

5.2.3   The patterns of **difficulty**

The 100 randomly-selected concordance lines in the Appendix to this chapter yield 25 different patterns. These are shown below. Some of the lexical items are shown in square brackets to indicate that other lexical items with a similar meaning might occur in the same pattern.

1. **N *in* -ing**

   (96)   *Difficulty in relating to a partner ... The evident difficulty in making the policy trade-offs...*

2. ***have* N**

   (97)   *if you do have difficulty... Mr Shamir has no such last-minute difficulty*

3. **v-link N**

   (98)   *...is another difficulty*

4. **[*have/find*] N *in* -ing**

   (99)   *anyone has a difficulty in accepting... We had great difficulty in driving people out of... Rock complained of difficulty in breathing*

5. **[*have*] N -ing**

> (100) *Mr Howard recently had difficulty remembering what discussions...*
> *you encounter difficulty reading a passage*

6. **[*have*] N *with* n**

> (101) *students who are having difficulty with the exercises ... most women*
> *have some sort of difficulty with food*

7. **N *of* -ing**

> (102) *the engineering difficulty of passing very hot gases..*

8. **poss N v-link that**

> (103) *His difficulty is that...*

9. **v-link poss N**

> (104) *That is Mr Gummer's difficulty*

10. **poss N *in* -ing**

> (105) *...my difficulty in defining...*

11. **_in_ N**

> (106) *those in difficulty ... franchising is already in difficulty*

12. **_with_ N**

> (107) *with difficulty*

13. **_without_ N**

> (108) *without much difficulty*

14. **_there_ v-link N _in_ -ing**

> (109) *There is a great deal of difficulty in working things through...*

15. **_the_ N _of_ -ing/ _the_ N _of_ n -ing**

> (110) *The difficulty of peeling chestnuts ... the difficulty of a non-Jewish*
> *Israeli getting...*

16. **_the_ N _of_ n**

> (111) *the difficulty of the subject*

17. **N v-link wh/that/n/to-inf/-ing**

> (112) *the difficulty is that I'm not going... The difficulty is how does he get*
> *through*

18. **N *for* n v-link that/wh/n/to-inf/-ing**

   (113)   *The difficulty for the government is that...*

19. **v n *as* N**

   (114)   *what some people see as a difficulty*

20. **n [*cause*] N**

   (115)   *part of the verse has caused difficulty*

21. **n [*cause*] n N**

   (116)   *causing the Irish line-out endless difficulty*

22. **N [*arises from*] n**

   (117)   *Another difficulty arises from the limited viewpoint...*

23. **reason for N v-link that**

   (118)   *The reason for this difficulty is that...*

24. **N v-link adj**

   (119)   *Chile's more recent difficulty is similar... ...the underlying difficulty is not organic*

25. **N v**

   (120)   *...the difficulty is likely to increase ...This difficulty extends to the very origins of...*

The first point to be made here is that not all these patterns include both Evaluative Category and Evaluated Entity. That is, in some cases 'the thing that is difficult' is not specified. This is true of the following patterns:

have N e.g.*if you do have difficulty... Mr Shamir has no such last-minute difficulty*
in N e.g.*those in difficulty ... franchising is already in difficulty*
N v e.g.*...the difficulty is likely to increase ...This difficulty extends to the very origins of...*

and the patterns which specify a Causer:

n [*cause*] N e.g.*part of the verse has caused difficulty*
n [*cause*] n N e.g.*causing the Irish line-out endless difficulty*
N [*arises from*] n e.g.*Another difficulty arises from the limited viewpoint...*
reason for N v-link that e.g.*The reason for this difficulty is that...*

The pattern **N v-link adj** is an interesting one, in that the adjective may realise the role of Causer, as in *the underlying difficulty is not <u>organic</u>*, but it may not realise any evaluative role category at all, as in *Chile's more recent difficulty is similar*. In this last example, as in the others where the Evaluated Entity is not realised in the pattern, that entity must be found elsewhere in the discourse.

Turning now to the patterns which do realise the roles Evaluated Entity and Evaluative Category, we find those illustrated in Table 5.14.

Table 5.14a

Evaluative Category		Evaluated Entity
N	***in***	**-ing**
Difficulty	*in*	*relating to a partner...*
The evident difficulty	*in*	*making the policy trade-offs...*

Table 5.14b

		Evaluative Category		Evaluated Entity
there	**v-link**	**N**	***in***	**-ing**
There	*is*	*great difficulty*	*in*	*working things through.*

Table 5.14c

Evaluated Entity		Evaluative Category
	v-link	**N**
Finding work in the first place	*is*	*another difficulty.*

Table 5.14d

Evaluative Category		Evaluated Entity
N	***of***	**-ing/n**
The difficulty	*of*	*peeling chestnuts...*
The difficulty	*of*	*the subject...*

Table 5.14e

Evaluative Category		Evaluated Entity
N	**v-link**	**wh/that/n/to-inf/-ing**
The difficulty	*is*	*that I'm not going to get through.*
The difficulty	*is*	*how does he get through.*

The patterns *with difficulty* and *without difficulty* also indicate the role of Evaluated Entity, but this is realised by the clause to which the phrase is attached, not in the pattern itself (Table 5.15).

Table 5.15

Evaluated Entity...	Evaluative Category	...Evaluated Entity
clause...	**with/without N**	**...clause**
She carried	*with difficulty*	*a great skin bag...*
One thing we had decided	*without difficulty*	*was that the Arts Fund lodged uncomfortably in the City.*

The next group of patterns, shown in Table 5.16, include the role Affected Entity. They include primarily patterns with *have* or with a possessive determiner.

Table 5.16a

Affected Entity		Evaluative Category		Evaluated Entity
	[*have/find*]	**N**	***in***	**-ing**
Anyone	*has*	*a difficulty*	*in*	*accepting and owning these rights.*
Rock	*complained of*	*difficulty*	*in*	*breathing.*

Table 5.16b

Affected Entity			Evaluative Category	Evaluated Entity
	[*have/find*]	**N**		**-ing**
You	*encounter*	*difficulty*		*reading a passage.*

Table 5.16c

Affected Entity		Evaluative Category		Evaluated Entity
	[*have*]	**N**	**with**	**n**
Most women	*have*	*some sort of difficulty*	*with*	*food.*

Table 5.16d

Affected Entity	Evaluative Category		Evaluated Entity
poss	**N**	**v-link**	**that**
His	*difficulty*	*is*	*that he finds himself the leader of a secular crusade.*

Table 5.16e

Evaluated Entity		Affected Entity	Evaluative Category
	v-link	**poss**	**N**
That	*is*	*Mr Gummer's*	*difficulty.*

Table 5.16f

Affected Entity	Evaluative Category		Evaluated Entity
poss	**N**	*in*	**-ing**
My	*difficulty*	*in*	*defining what is and is not art.*

Table 5.16g

Evaluative Category		Affected Entity		Evaluated Entity
N	*for*	**n**	**v-link**	**that/wh/n/to-inf/-ing**
The difficulty	*for*	*the government*	*is*	*that such tactics may well involve political costs.*

One pattern remains, that introduces a new role. This pattern is illustrated by the example

(121)   *Some people see this as a difficulty,*

in which the evaluation is reported rather than averred. In all the examples met so far, the Evaluator (the person doing the evaluating) has remained implicit. In other words, the Evaluator is the speaker or writer. In reported evaluation, however, the Evaluator is realised in the pattern (see Table 5.17).

Table 5.17

Evaluator		Evaluated Entity		Evaluative Category
	v	**n**	*as*	**N**
Some people	*see*	*this*	*as*	*a difficulty.*

5.2.4   Summary of Section 5.2

In this section, we have considered how participant roles might be mapped on to patterns to give information about the aspects of meaning involved in particular notional groups and to show the various grammatical configurations possible. Those configurations depend both on pattern and on lexical items.

One of the applications of such an exercise is the parsing of naturally-occurring text, either by a human being or, more ambitiously, by a computer. If a computer were to perform this task, the various pattern combinations and forms that the computer was likely to meet would have to be accounted for. As an illustration of the kind of issues involved, a representative 100 lines of *difficult* and *difficulty* were taken and the various patterns found therein were mapped on to roles. This mapping shows that the task, though difficult, can be achieved.

5.3 Semantic word groups and their pattern distribution

The observation that meaning and pattern are associated is not a new one, although we believe that our corpus-driven work has added a new dimension to traditional concerns. Valency grammarians and transformational grammarians in particular have established a tradition of semantic classes, between which fine distinctions can be made, depending on the behaviour of the words, typically verbs, in each class. In a ground-breaking work, Levin (1995) lists dozens of semantic groups, each of which contains verbs which behave alike and which share meaning. The groups are distinguished from each other in both behaviour and meaning. Levin (1995: 11) concludes that

> verbs in English and other languages fall into classes on the basis of shared components of meaning. The class members have in common a range of properties, including the possible expression and interpretation of their arguments, as well as the existence of certain morphologically related forms.

This is an argument that is very similar to our own. Levin goes on to argue that if the semantic properties of a particular verb are defined accurately and finely enough, additional information about the behaviour of the verb is unnecessary, as it will be derivable from the semantic properties. In other words, once the precise semantic group that a verb belongs to has been identified, it can be assumed that it will behave like other verbs in that group, so information about its behaviour is superfluous. We would take issue with this argument, not because we believe that Levin is mistaken in her own terms but because we are using a somewhat different definition of 'syntactic behaviour'. We shall return to this point below.

First, however, it is necessary to examine in more detail the similarities and differences between Levin's work and our own. Francis et al. (1996) contains a chapter on 'Pattern Combinations', which lists verbs that share two or more patterns. For example, the verb *call* is listed among those that occur in the two patterns **V n adj** and **V n n** but not among those that occur in the patterns **V n *as* adj** or **V n *as* n** (Francis et al. 1996: 592). That is, we say 'I called him stupid' and 'I called him an idiot' but not 'I called him as stupid/an idiot'. The same information is to be found in Levin (1995: 182), but it is stated more explicitly, because Levin is concerned to give information on what is *not* said as well as what is said. Similarly, the chapter on 'Ergative Verbs' in Francis et al. (1996: 474–509) gives information that overlaps with that given in Levin's section on 'Causative Alternations' (Levin 1995: 26–32).

The use of a large corpus leads us in some instances to different observations from those made by Levin. It is considerably easier to see what *has* been said than to introspect what *can* be said. In particular, the pitfalls associated with trying to specify what *cannot* be said can be avoided. For example, Levin (1995: 182) lists the following verbs as occurring with the pattern **V n n/adj** but not with the pattern **V n *as* n/adj** (though the pattern terminology is, of course, ours rather than Levin's): *adjudge, adjudicate, anoint, assume, avow, baptize, believe, brand, call, christen, confess, consecrate, crown, declare, decree, dub, fancy, find, label, make, name, nickname, presume, profess, pronounce, prove, rule, stamp, style, suppose, term, think, vote, warrant*. Of these, there is no evidence in the 300 million word Bank of English for the following verbs being used in the pattern **V n n/adj**: *adjudicate, assume, avow, stamp, warrant*. The following verbs are used in that pattern only a handful of times: *decree, suppose*. Conversely, there is corpus evidence for the following verbs being used in the pattern **V n *as* n/adj**: *anoint, brand, dub, fancy, label, name, stamp* and *term*. If something is not found in the corpus, it is always possible to argue that the corpus is too small, or badly skewed in its contents, but if something is found, it is difficult to argue that it does not exist in English.

The most significant differences between our work and that of Levin's, however, arise from the fact that, whereas Levin deals with a limited number of possible patterns that a verb may or may not have, Francis et al. (1996) covers a large number of patterns. Potentially, then, more may be said about each semantic set than Levin does. For example, Levin (1995: 213–217) distinguishes seven groups of verbs which have to do with eating or drinking. Some of the patterns she identifies, translated into our terminology but exemplified with her examples, are:

V

(122)   *Cynthia ate.*

V n

> (123) *Cynthia ate the peach.*

V pron-refl adj

> (124) *Cynthia ate herself sick.*

V *at* n

> (125) *Cynthia nibbled at the carrot.*

V *on* n

> (126) *Cynthia nibbled on the carrot.*

V n n

> (127) *Teresa bottlefed the baby soy milk.*

V n *to* n

> (128) *Teresa bottlefed soy milk to the baby.*

(We should point out that Levin uses other evidence, that does not translate so easily into our terms, to distinguish between the various groups. Our over-simplification of her work here is not intended to detract from it.)

Let us consider in a little more detail four of Levin's sets. These are:

'*Eat*' Verbs: *drink, eat* (only)

These occur in the patterns **V, V n, V *at* n, V pron-refl adj**

'*Chew*' Verbs: *chew, chomp, crunch, gnaw, lick, munch, nibble, peck, pick, sip, slurp, suck*

These occur in the patterns **V, V n, V *at* n**

'*Gorge*' Verbs: *exist, feed, flourish, gorge, live, prosper, survive, thrive*

These occur in the pattern **V *on* n**

'Verbs of feeding': *bottlefeed, breastfeed, feed, forcefeed, handfeed, spoonfeed*

These occur in the patterns **V n n, V n *to* n**

Francis et al. (1996) confirm that *eat* and *drink* share the patterns **V** and **V n** but disagree that these verbs also occur with the pattern **V *at* n**. That is, we find no evidence that *eat* (in the sense of a human being ingesting something) or *drink* are used in a pattern with the preposition *at* (although they do occur with prepositional phrases that are not part of a pattern, as in *They ate at a diner*).

Furthermore, we add a further pattern **V *from* n**, which is found with *eat* and *drink,* but also with *sip.* This spoils the sharp distinction between *eat* and *drink* on the one hand and the 'chew' verbs on the other. The 'chew' group is further upset by the pattern **V *into* n**, which, according to Francis et al. (1996: 205) occurs with *crunch* and also with *bite,* a verb which is not strictly speaking a member of the 'ingesting' set at all. To the verbs of feeding we add the pattern **V n *on* n** with *feed,* although a variant of this pattern, **V pron-refl *on* n**, is also found with *gorge,* but with no other verbs in that group.

This may appear to be little more than over-zealous fault-finding, but there is a more important principle at stake. This is that allowing all patterns of a verb to be considered, instead of just a few, might militate against the consistent formation of semantic groups. As we have pointed out before, the meaning groups in Francis et al. (1996) are not necessarily consistent between patterns. In the section dealing with the pattern **V *into* n**, for example, the verbs *bite* and *crunch* are included with verbs such as *bore, dig* and *drill,* which do not necessarily have anything to do with eating. This suggests that the traditional semantic sets may not be as fixed as might have been thought, that there might be prototypical members of each set, but that other verbs might slide between one set and another. If true, this would throw doubt on Levin's assertion, quoted above, that the syntactic behaviour of a verb can be uncontroversially determined by a description of its semantic properties.

As further illustration, let us consider the verb *die.* Levin (1995: 260) classes this among the 'Verbs of Disappearance' that comprise *die, disappear, expire, lapse, perish* and *vanish.* She points out that these verbs allow little variation. We say 'Somebody died' but not (probably) 'There died three soldiers on the battlefield' or 'On the battlefield died three soldiers' and definitely not 'The executioner died the prisoner'. (These examples are invented in line with Levin's examples, which use the verb *vanish.*)

Francis et al. (1996: 8) also group *die* with verbs of cessation of existence, such as *disappear,* with the pattern **V**. However, other patterns used with *die* suggest different groupings. Examples such as

(129)   *It is better to die a hero*

(with the pattern **V n**) link *die* with *depart, leave* and *retire,* but also with *live. Live* and *die* are also associated together by **V n** examples such as

(130)   *She continued to live the life of an invalid* and

(131)   *He died a painful death.*

Yet another pattern, **V -ing** associates *die* with verbs concerned with finishing, rather than with disappearing:

(132) *I'd die feeling guilty...*

(133) *Their boat finished up pointing the wrong way ...*

(134) *I ended up having dinner.*

The pattern **V *from* n** associates *die* with *reel, smart* and *suffer:*

(135) *He died from a heart attack,*

while in the pattern **V *of* n** *die* is associated with no other verb:

(136) *He died of natural causes.*

In other words, although our evidence supports the general point that Levin makes about the non-random associated of syntax and semantics, we would have to argue that the semantic set that *die* belongs to changes according to the pattern with which the verb is used. *Die*, in fact, belongs to several sets: one with the meaning 'disappear', one where it is connected with *live*, one with the meaning 'finish' and one with the meaning 'suffer'. At the very least, this adds considerably to the task involved in defining semantic sets.

5.4   Conclusion to Chapter 5

In this chapter we have continued our discussion of the nature of the association between meaning and pattern. In Section 5.1 we gave examples of how a particular language notion — a semantic area — may be described in terms of the lexis and patterns that realise it and compared this with the notional approach to language teaching pioneered by Wilkins. In Section 5.2 we took this a step further and considered how meaning roles may be mapped on to patterns, linking this to the concept of a Local Grammar, and comparing it with Halliday's approach to participant roles and grammatical metaphor. Finally, in Section 5.3, we compared our work with that of Levin.

Appendix to Chapter 5

100 concordance lines for 'difficult'

```
s challenge will be that much more difficult. <p> EDWARDS: The BBC's Daniel
   later described her as 'the most difficult" actor he had ever worked with
 s virtually impossible to place a difficult adult # I know I couldn't have
   particularly sexual abuse, can be difficult and take time but if it prevents
```

no choice other # than to make very difficult and very awkward and sometimes
physically and/or psychologically difficult, and all too many take out their
        <p> It is not unusual in this difficult area of the environment, where so
the twins over wasn't nearly as difficult as coping with the feeling of
City, Reid's former club, have a difficult assignment away to Leicester
recent weeks. <p> It's been a very difficult baptism for him and he has
city governments in Poland can be difficult business partners, not because
to particular genes has proved very difficult. But Cookson is confident that
We are aware that it will be very difficult, but not impossible, to put the
<f> broer, <f> I'm not trying to be difficult but this Antigone! No! Please
to create, often under the most difficult conditions. On the tenth
        <p> In the long and increasingly difficult decade since 'mad cow" disease
thing to do. <p> But it was a very difficult decision to make." <p> Three
conditions became increasingly difficult during 1990 as a result of the
to pay you more money during these difficult economic times? Despite the
democracy. 'It will now be very difficult ever to build a bridge between
a peaceful settlement. 'It is not difficult for President Saddam Hussein to
If I had my way I'd make it really difficult for large cars to use the roads.
loss by St George would make it difficult for them to qualify for this year
have made winning these seats more difficult for the Labor Party; <p> asset-
the <ZG0> example I mean it's quite difficult for us to do. <M0X> Well but true
up the sky and makes it more difficult for us to see the stars.
is geographical: 'It makes things difficult for artists and curators later;
for life. <p> Life is therefore difficult for males with a family in tow.
needs. This last need is quite difficult for most of us to understand.
From now on it's going to be very difficult for business to match declines in
loss) faces one of the most difficult futures. But until recently, says
Some of it is, well, really quite difficult. 'I bought Paul Muldoon's The
shoot: 'I hope I haven't been too difficult. I like working off negative
grim and driving conditions were difficult in Surrey. <p> The odds against a
land will perhaps prove rather difficult. Indeed, the very attempt to do
out on top. And to make things more difficult, international human rights
million years ago. How much more difficult it is to imagine a world with
may be unattractive, its ideas difficult, its construction awkward. On the
happen that your elders, after the difficult journey and the trials they have
about new media because this is a difficult magazine with an aesthetically-
the strength to deliver this most difficult of concessions. <h> KASHMIR:
training. <p> The 800m is the more difficult of the two because Mozambique's
the question of peace was a very difficult one which required the
such as tying in stems, which are difficult or impossible with bulky
to prepare them. The materials are difficult (or impossible) to find outside
She said: 'I'll admit it was pretty difficult over the last 18 months reading
Market Day but should be renamed Difficult Parking Day. <p> I drive around
Mhm. <M01> Particularly with rather difficult patients who haven't got much
feelings and to examine some difficult personal issues. I'm going to try
said: 'Retailing is in a difficult position and there are no signs
perhaps the most common — and most difficult — problem faced by divorced and
<ZF0> <M01> Mm. <M02> that's a very difficult process <M01> Mm. <M02>
        <M02> Gosh you do ask some difficult questions. <tc text=coughs>
questions than to deal with them. Difficult questions are invaluable for
All this can add up to an extremely difficult situation in which you both can
helping the Soviet Union with its difficult task of transformation. In the
first 7.3 miles to Ballacraine a difficult test, but Boardman was clearly on
of sexual harassment might be more difficult than its efforts against racial
easier to pass should be made more difficult, the Government's chief
Simon, host: <p> It is getting difficult these days to sit down to the
<F0X> Yeah. <F01> that's the difficult thing. <F0X> Yeah. <F01> And like
right pass and so on. But the most difficult thing I think is to score a goal.
with the human condition during difficult times, do we know what to choose?
If we continue as we are, it is difficult to see the future # We can join
feet every second. It is also very difficult to concentrate on two things at
Griffith University was finding it difficult to maintain an operation up here
Griffith University, argues it is difficult to generalise about Queensland.
mind it could make it much more difficult to follow what Grendon is all
Still, wouldn't it be more difficult to live your life never knowing
in each other's pockets, it's difficult to try to work with a
as well. Er I'm one I'm very difficult to read and secondly <ZF1> the
ve kept they've found it very very difficult to visualize things # <F01> Mm #
heat. The ICRC is finding it difficult to ensure fair distribution of
There's no petrol, and so it's very difficult to transport goods. Because of

```
     Sir Bob also complained that it was difficult to plan ahead because the
          not grab him first. Somehow it is difficult to see where the profit might
       more important than the bands. It's difficult to explain what made it so great.
         any identification, making it more difficult to spot any Iraqi saboteurs among
       how big this spill is, since it's difficult to measure a spill once it is in
            reconciliation. <p> Wang: What is difficult to gauge, however, is the
          paleness of his face. <p> It was difficult to see what was happening. He
       That winter was in the wings was difficult to believe yet. <p> He went to
       and once hooked, they will find it difficult to pull back. <p> Once they
           powers for centuries. What is difficult to believe is that this small
       advance of civilization it is not difficult to quote an instance of modern
       the paucity of reliable data, it is difficult to categorize Belgium as being
       the son of a policeman, he found it difficult to succeed in a white man's
          very windy and it would have been difficult to sit in one place for any
           to keep down the weeds. It is more difficult to fit crops in in the summer
           will probably fall. It will be difficult to keep direct personal taxation
           pain that we change. It can be difficult to see our loved ones hurting but
       health officials often found it difficult to monitor radiation hazards. It
               modifiers make a sentence difficult to understand when they come
           will find it increasingly difficult to resist the pressures for
       account deficit that may prove difficult to finance. <h> THE ECONOMY </h>
           Middle America, finding it difficult to make ends meet in a
       one of these 'so-what" arguments — difficult to become emotionally involved in
       Edberg admitted it would be a difficult trick to pull off twice. <p> In
       s sex life had hitherto been 'difficult, unsatisfactory and a constant
       to get on as things become more difficult you have to start being subtle
```

100 concordance lines for 'difficulty'

```
          from parents or relatives. <p> Difficulty in relating to a partner due to
       is most helpful if anyone has a difficulty in accepting and owning these
       significantly, however, it has a difficulty in explaining why only some
       round what some people see as a difficulty. If people have the same general
       contracted severe headaches and difficulty in breathing whenever exposed to
       work in the first place is another difficulty, unless you set up as freelance
       part of the verse has caused difficulty: literally the Heb. means 'love
       which they seem to have certain difficulty with from time to time when we
           them because you encounter difficulty reading a passage. Circle
       causing the Irish line-out endless difficulty. Blessed with such unlikely
       the problems are the engineering difficulty of passing very hot gases just a
       be a watershed year. The evident difficulty in making the policy trade-offs
       level. The company has experienced difficulty in renewing some of its
       very uncertain due to the extreme difficulty in obtaining suitable classroom
       one other TEC is in financial difficulty and others under increasing
       of sinners, and it seems they find difficulty in recognising the rights of
       NBL is saying it will have great difficulty disciplining the other clubs?"
       a friend of mine is having great difficulty John and it's erm <M01> Yeah.
       told the newspaper: We had great difficulty in driving people out of the
           caused them to have great difficulty in firing. <p> Polley: Johnston
       understood object. She had great difficulty in formulating questions — when
       of Agriculture is having great difficulty getting the Dutch to specify
       feet, Brother Cirillo with greater difficulty on account of his wounds and his
           races and I find the greatest difficulty in expressing my gratitude to our
       Webb had in any case the greatest difficulty in imagining them injecting
       Howard. <p> Mr Howard recently had difficulty remembering what discussions he
       plywood plinth that would have had difficulty supporting the weight of past
       Still he hadn't seen her, he had difficulty facing the so many faces. Then
       otherwise Tansey would have had difficulty in finding the place. It was on
       of 'baby talk." In school he had difficulty concentrating, could not sit
       far-right National Front Party had difficulty in winning more than 1 # of the
           <p> THE French have always had difficulty in coming to terms with the less
       his sudden retreat, which he had difficulty selling to his rank and file, by
           In the wild, the male has difficulty supplying all the food needed by
       age say <M02> Yeah. <M01> has difficulty understanding the form er <ZF1>
       you can find them." If she has difficulty, call out 'hot" or 'cold" to give
       up. <p> She is still in pain, has difficulty swallowing and can no longer take
       so that the patient may have difficulty # speaking distinctly or loudly
       shifts. Often couples have difficulty managing such a transition.
       next section. But if you do have difficulty, and if the passage is important,
       the mystery, Oslear may have difficulty persuading Cowdrey to reopen
```

to help students who are having difficulty with the exercises, all on the
and fewer youngsters having difficulty deciding what they want to do in-
Hughes <p> I have been having difficulty deciding my football personality
a successful disengagement. His difficulty is that he finds himself the
enables the majority of those in difficulty to remain in their homes when the
said: 'Franchising is already in difficulty and is in need of subsidy." He
not only would have had little difficulty finding a place in the game of
is put. Is science having a little difficulty explaining X? No problem. Don't
Mr Shamir has no such last-minute difficulty, he will head a government which
part, Prince Charles has had more difficulty in finding a role for himself. He
Hitler was persuaded without much difficulty would be impracticable after the
<p> March 3, 1993. I told KA of my difficulty in defining, for the benefit of
get out of control? We have no difficulty in rounding up all the usual
should find that he will have no difficulty in settling down to life at
Another, less obvious, difficulty arises from the limited viewpoint
<p> There is a great deal of difficulty in working things through these
<p> In 1981 Rock complained of difficulty in breathing and chest pains.
But most women have some sort of difficulty with food. The way women think
that I in fact come in to a lot of difficulty with money and that so <F01>
for in functional terms. One difficulty in accounting for grammar on the
seemed to have particular difficulty in refraining from critical or
develop serious health problems. difficulty in thinking clearly, making
power. <p> Chile's more recent difficulty is similar. The old dictator,
anachronism. That is Mr Gummer's difficulty. His family may believe him and
alters, but they have similar difficulty developing an integrated
were controversies over the difficulty of a non-Jewish Israeli getting
in that thing. Then there is the difficulty of drawing cartoons: 'It's like
<p> Contrast, as well, the difficulty the Government seems to have had
playing for us next week. <p> The difficulty is how does he get here through
communities. <p> Previously the difficulty is one of familiarity," she told
of neglect? <p> Leaving aside the difficulty of defining or identifying a true
of its construction and the difficulty of setting it up accurately.
<F02> but <ZF1> the <ZF0> the difficulty is I suppose that I'm not going
It's # <M01> Mm # <F0X> I mean the difficulty I've always found in the past #
of strikes and violence. The difficulty for the government is that such
Wearing, for instance, cites the difficulty of finding a style of dialogue -
on a course, depending on the difficulty of the subject. <p> At Macquarie
perhaps rather difficult. And the difficulty is likely to increase." <p> He
probably the best solution of the difficulty. Lloyd George handled Haig's
acknowledges, for example, the difficulty of ensuring that competency
are now from Spain and Italy. The difficulty of peeling chestnuts has
for love and support. And the difficulty in coping with these stresses
to the Galilean tradition. The difficulty the Gospel writers had in trying
problems. First, there is the difficulty of translating pledges into
slowly. <p> If Labour wins, the difficulty may be the opposite. The new
Tim's far-from-tiny coffin. The difficulty is that the escape has more to do
back." <p> Venables knows the difficulty will be to break down a
1973, pp. 40-42). The answer then: difficulty in finding conscientious
either inwards or outwards. This difficulty extends to the very origins of
whatsoever. The reason for this difficulty is that the spiritual nature of
indication that the underlying difficulty is not organic. The same can be
previously made only with difficulty in the laboratory. Five-
could be repopulated only with difficulty. In this sense, time is on the
gate. <p> She carried, with difficulty, a great skin bag full of fresh
because the Jews were able with difficulty to keep a secondary line open
he would heave himself up, with difficulty, as if he were a great burden to
duly blown up — though not without difficulty. The engineers had to be
of which have passed off without difficulty. <p> The UN officials are just as
One thing we had decided without difficulty, however, was that the Art Fund

CHAPTER 6

Pattern and structure

6.1 Relating pattern to structure

6.1.1 *Introduction*

The approach to complementation patterns described in this book is new in that it focuses on the formal components of a pattern rather than on a structural interpretation of those components. For example, the coding **V n** is preferred to 'Verb plus Object' or 'Verb plus Complement'. In addition, the notion of pattern is not restricted to *verb* complementation but is extended to all word classes. The notion of verb complementation patterns, however, has a long history, and many people, including the language teachers who were the imagined audience of our original studies (Francis et al. 1996, 1998), are very much more familiar with the 'Verb plus Object' notation than with our pattern notation.

For this pragmatic reason we decided to offer an interpretation of all our verb patterns in terms of the traditional structural categories. Thus, the pattern **V n** in Francis et al. (1996) is presented in terms of three structural analyses: 'Verb with Object' (e.g.*She ate a peach*), 'Verb with Complement' (e.g.*She is a peach*) and 'Verb with Adjunct' (e.g.*Don't talk that way*). This decision committed us to the task of analysing each pattern that we had identified, considering not only those questions that have long been the stuff of grammatical debate (is *I remember him stealing the money* the same in constituent terms as *I caught him stealing the money*?) but also questions that have tended to be overlooked by less comprehensive surveys of verbs (is *She is looking into the gang* the same as *She has infiltrated into the gang*?).

This task proved both fascinating and frustrating. We began with two principles:

1. We would aim to have an explicit and consistent policy for each decision regarding the categories used, so that the system of analysis would be both internally consistent and defendable.
2. We would, as far as this was compatible with our first aim, reflect the traditional consensus of grammarians (and language teachers) regarding the categories of Object, Complement and so on.

As time went on, however, we became increasingly disenchanted with our self-imposed task, not merely because it turned out to be difficult to the point of impossibility, but because it seemed to be more and more futile. In a handful of cases, the structural analysis added an insight that was missing from our pattern description. In most cases, however, the structural analysis added nothing, and all that was important to say about a verb could be said in terms of its pattern and its meaning group, irrespective of the structural interpretation. Our conclusion was that structural analysis is a pointless exercise, a conclusion that we hope to bring evidence for in this chapter.

In this first section, however, we confine ourselves to statements of policy, explaining aspects of the system of analysis that we have used. We restrict ourselves in this section to the relatively straightforward cases: we will consider the more problematic cases later in this chapter. Our intention here is to convince the reader that our rejection of structural analysis is not the result of a lack of thought or commitment. Although the reader may disagree with some or all of the decisions discussed below, we hope at least that he/she may agree that we have made a reasonable attempt to achieve consistency.

6.1.2   *Objects, Complements, Adjuncts and Object Complements*

Our policy with regard to Objects, Complements, Adjuncts and Object Complements is very much in line with traditional thought. The following explanations are adapted from the Glossary of terms in Francis et al. (1996: xix–xxii):

> An **Object** (in an active clause) realises a person or thing involved the action but not responsible for the action. It may be a noun group or a non-finite clause. When an active clause has a passive equivalent, the Object of the active clause is equivalent to the Subject of the passive clause.

> A **Complement** provides further information about the Subject of a clause. It may be a noun group, adjective group, or an amount. Clauses with Complements typically have no passive equivalent. Complements usually, though not always, follow link verbs.

> An **Adjunct** provides information about the circumstances of an action, event, or situation, such as time, place, or manner. Adjuncts may realise something that is part of the pattern of a verb, or something that is outside the pattern of the verb.

> An **Object Complement** provides further information about the Object of a clause. It may be a noun group, an adjective group or an '-ed' clause.

More controversial decisions are involved when a clause has two Objects. Traditional grammar distinguishes between Direct and Indirect Objects. In *She gave her son some cash*, for example, *some cash* would be analysed as a Direct Object, but *her son* would be the Indirect Object. Part of the argument for this is that the son is the recipient of the cash, and the use of the term 'Indirect Object' recognises this role. However, verb-Object pairs realise a wide variety of relationships, and it seems perhaps unnecessary to single out one for special coding. Passive equivalents are possible with either *her son* or *some cash* as Subject (*Her son was given some cash, Some cash was given to her son*). Another argument is that a transformational equivalent of *She gave her son some cash* is *She gave some cash to her son*. Only certain items (the Indirect Objects) are capable of being replaced by prepositional phrases in this way. However, the object of study here is *She gave her son some cash*, with the pattern **V n n**, not some potential equivalent. Both *her son* and *some cash* are involved in, but not responsible for, the action of giving, so both are termed Object by us. We do not use the category 'Indirect Object'. (See Section 6.2.4 below for our analysis of clauses of the type *She gave some cash to her son*.)

An Object may be a non-finite clause as well as a noun group. Where a pattern involves a noun group and a non-finite clause, comprising two clausal elements, we say that both of these elements are Objects in those cases where the person or thing realised by the noun group is responsible for the process realised in the clause. In the following examples, the noun group following the verb is one Object and the non-finite clause is another Object:

(1)   *Julia was assisting him to prepare his speech.* ('He prepared his speech')

(2)   *I'll show you what to watch out for.* ('You will watch out for something')

(3)   *She noticed a man sitting alone on the grass.* ('A man was sitting alone on the grass')

(4)   *She heard the man laugh.* ('The man laughed')

(5)   *They saw their father swept to his death.* ('Their father was swept to his death')

(In the final example above, 'their father' is not responsible for the process, but is the affected participant in a passive clause.)

Where the noun group and the non-finite clause do not have this 'Subject-Verb' relationship, the analysis is not 'Verb-Object-Object' but 'Verb-Object-Adjunct', as in this example:

(6)   *I spend the time reading.*

In some cases of the pattern **V n -ed**, the clause gives further information about the state of the person or thing realised by the Object and is therefore the Object Complement:

(7)   *They kept their hair cut short.* ('Their hair was short')

In most of the examples above (with the exception of the **V n -ed** examples, which will be discussed below), a passive equivalent is possible which separates the noun group from the non-finite clause of the pattern, such as *He was assisted to prepare his speech, You will be shown what to watch out for, A man was noticed sitting alone on the grass* and *The time is spent reading.* This is evidence for the noun group and the clause comprising two separate clause elements. In the case of other verbs with the same patterns, however, no such evidence exists, and we conclude, again in accordance with tradition, that in those cases the noun group and the clause together form a single element, which we classify as an Object. Here are some examples where the analysis is 'Verb with (single) Object':

(8)   *I'd love her to go into politics or on the stage.*

(9)   *I hope you don't mind me calling in like this, without an appointment.*

(10)   *We had the house done up just before Christmas.*

In other words, we use passivisation as a test to distinguish between examples where a noun group and a non-finite clause together comprise one element and those where the noun group and the non-finite clause comprise two elements (admittedly, this is an exception to our general avoidance of transformation tests). With the pattern **V n inf**, however, this test does not work, as the pattern has no true passive, except with the verb *let*, as in *He was let go.* With other verbs, such as *see*, there is a passive with a to-infinitive rather than a bare infinite, as in *He was seen to go*; with other verbs, such as *watch*, there is no passive at all. By our own criterion, then, examples such as *She watched him go* should be analysed as 'Verb with (single) Object', since there is no passive equivalent. This would have the unfortunate consequence of analysing *She watched the man go* differently from *She saw the man go* (Verb with two Objects, as there is a passive equivalent, though not with a bare infinitive). We therefore decided to analyse all our **V n inf** examples as 'Verb with two Objects', by analogy with other patterns.

6.1.3   *Patterns with finite clauses*

In many traditional grammars, finite clauses as well as non-finite clauses are analysed as clause elements. For example, Quirk et al. (1972: 832–834) offer the following as examples of 'Verb with Object':

   (11)   *Everybody hoped that he would sing.*

   (12)   *I regret that he should be so stubborn.*

   (13)   *He asked if they were coming.*

Similarly, the following are given as examples of ditransitive complementation, that is, where the verb has two Objects (Quirk et al. 1972: 849):

   (14)   *John convinced me he was right.*

   (15)   *John didn't ask me whether my wife was coming.*

It must be admitted that there are strong arguments in favour of this kind of analysis. In each case, the finite clause is a necessary part of the complementation pattern of the verb in question. If each example is to be analysed as a single clause, then the finite clause component must be analysed as a clause element, and Object is the most appropriate choice of category.

It is by no means apparent, however, that each example should be analysed as a single clause. The argument in favour of doing so is that, in the first set of examples, 'Everybody hoped', 'I regret' and 'He asked' are not by themselves complete clauses, so what follows them should be analysed as part of the same clause. The argument against is simply that the finite clause is a clause in its own right, much as a subordinate clause is, and it should therefore be allowed to stand by itself.

In analysing the patterns **V that, V wh, V n that** and **V n wh**, we do not use the label 'Object' for the finite clause. Instead, we use the analysis 'Verb with Clause' and 'Verb with Object and Clause'. Table 6.1 shows examples of our structural analysis from Francis et al. (1996: 97 and 299). In each case, the first line of the table shows the pattern and the second line shows the structural analysis.

Table 6.1a

	Verb group	that-clause
Subject	Verb	Clause
I	*agree*	*that the project has possibilities.*
The president	*ordered*	*that the conference be suspended.*
He	*said*	*the country was unstable.*

Table 6.1b

	Verb group	noun group	that-clause
Subject	Verb	Object	Clause
She	*told*	*me*	*he'd planned to be away all that night.*
I	*warned*	*her*	*that I might not last out my hours of duty.*

A valid objection to this analysis might be that we are not here offering a true structural analysis consistent with the analyses offered for other patterns. We are saying that the Verb in the first table, or the Verb and Object in the second table, is followed by a new clause that is not a subordinate clause or an embedded clause, and we leave completely unanswered the question of the status of the Subject+Verb or Subject+Verb+Object as clauses. Our argument against this objection is that the alternative analysis, which would downgraded the that-clause to a mere component of the initial clause, ignores the status of the that-clause as a complete, finite clause which encodes what is often the main information of the sentence. Following Sinclair (personal communication), we regard the that-clause as in a sense the 'main' clause of the sentence, with *He said* or *She told me* as a contextualising 'preface'.

In effect, what we are doing here is to move away from a structural analysis that in this case we find particularly misleading, towards a straightforward pattern analysis that we find more useful. This analysis has the additional advantage of presenting language as dynamic. It presents the speaker moving, metaphorically, from one clause (*He said* or *She told me*) into the next, new clause. In so doing, our analysis disregards the synoptic view of language which demands to know the constituency of the initial clause. We will return to and extend this dynamic view of grammar in Chapter 8.

6.1.4 *'Extraposed' subjects*

Another place where we part company with traditional grammar is in the context of so-called 'extraposed Subjects'. These are said to occur primarily in clauses that begin with an 'introductory' or 'anticipatory' *it*. In a clause such as

(16) *It seemed that he would keep his word,*

the Subject (called the 'extraposed Subject') is often taken to be *that he would keep his word*, with the *it* analysed as a 'dummy Subject' or 'formal Subject'. In other words, *it* occupies the place typically occupied by a grammatical Subject, but the that-clause contains the content of the Subject.

Much of the argument in favour of extraposed Subjects, however, is based on transformations. For example, if

(17)   *It is obvious he is right*

is indeed a transformation of

(18)   *That he is right is obvious,*

then it is reasonable to suggest that *(that) he is right* is the Subject of both versions. However, as Francis (1993) has noted, examples of the supposed pre-transformation type are extremely rare, and it makes a great deal more sense to accept *It is obvious he is right* as a pattern in its own right, and analyse it accordingly, rather than regarding it as a version of something that hardly ever occurs.

In patterns with introductory *it*, there is always a finite or non-finite clause occurring at the end of the pattern. We analyse these as new clauses, in the way that we treat any finite clause (see 6.1.3 above), and assign labels to other elements in the pattern in the usual way. Table 6.2 shows our analyses of two patterns with introductory *it*: *it* **V n -ing** (Francis et al. 1996: 536) and *it* **V n n to-inf** (Francis et al. 1996: 537):

Table 6.2a

it	Verb group	noun group	-ing clause
Subject	Verb	Complement	Clause
It	*is*	*no fun*	*doing things alone.*
It	*is*	*no use*	*complaining.*

Table 6.2b

it	Verb group	noun group	noun group	to-infinitive clause
Subject	Verb	Object	Object	Clause
It	*cost*	*me*	*a fortune*	*to renovate the house.*
It	*will do*	*me*	*good*	*to have a rest.*

6.1.5   *Structure and Meaning*

Part of the motive behind a structural analysis of clauses is that it reveals similarities and differences between elements of different clauses. For example, if we take two clauses with a Subject-Verb-Complement analysis, such as

(19)   *She became very depressed about Thomas* and

(20)   *She became an ardent supporter of the single European market.*

the Complement label identifies *very depressed about Thomas* and *an ardent supporter of the single European market* as similar in role, even though one is an adjective group and one is a noun group. Similarly, the argument for assigning the label 'Object' to a clause, as in

(21)   *I've never wanted to go to America.*

is that the clause *to go to America* plays the same role as *a Rolls Royce* in

(22)   *I've never wanted a Rolls Royce.*

Conversely, in offering three different analyses of the pattern **V n**, as follows:

Verb with Complement

(23)   *Paul Davies has proved a man of his word.*

Verb with Object

(24)   *For dinner I ate a fried steak.*

Verb with Adjunct

(25)   *I have a friend who thought that way.*

we take note of the fact that the noun groups following the verb play very different roles, in spite of being the same in terms of form. In fact, however, case or participant analysis, such as that proposed by Halliday, indicates that a term such as 'Object' can itself cover a wide range of roles, such as Goal, Experiencer, Range, and so on (see, for example, Halliday 1994: 106–149). We regard the meaning group, rather than the structural analysis, as the most appropriate site for representing this kind of insight.

Offering more than one structural analysis for a pattern can be useful, as in the case of **V n n**, where there is a clear distinction between examples of the *give* type, such as

(26)   *He gave her a card*, or

(27)   *Joyce cooked him a three-course breakfast,*

and examples of the *elect* type, such as

(28)   *His supporters elected him president in June* or

(29)   *Many people considered her an egomaniac.*

This distinction is captured by the difference in structural analysis. *(He) gave her a card* is analysed as 'Verb-Object-Object', whilst *(His supporters) elected him president* is analysed as 'Verb-Object-Object Complement'.

A similarly useful distinction occurs with the pattern *it* **V n -ing**, where in examples of the type

(30)   *It <u>is</u> no fun going to school in the dark,*

the noun group *no fun* is analysed as a Complement, whereas is in examples such as

(31)   *It <u>worries</u> me having her in the house,*

the noun group *me* is analysed as an Object. In cases such as these, the verbs with a particular pattern are usefully distinguished by the contrasting structural analyses.

In other cases, however, drawing structural distinctions seems much less useful. For example, the pattern **V n -ing** is analysable in three separate ways, as discussed in detail above. These are:

Verb with Object:

(32)   *I <u>remember</u> him ringing me up.*

Verb with two Objects:

(33)   *You <u>notice</u> women counting under their breaths.*

Verb with Object and Adjunct:

(34)   *You <u>don't have to waste</u> time pondering what to wear.*

Whilst this distinction may be valid, its usefulness is less apparent. One rationale for the analysis would be as a basis for prescription. It is argued, for example, that when a verb with the pattern **V n -ing** is followed by a single Object, an alternative way of expressing this is with a noun group beginning with a possessive. For example,

(35)   *I remember him ringing me up*

above might also be expressed

(36)   *I remember his ringing me up.*

When a verb with two Objects is used, however, this alternative expression is not possible:

(37)   **You notice women's counting under their breaths.*

These prescriptions are in a sense the grammarian's tests in reverse. For example, in 6.1.2, we cited passivisation as a test for the distinction between the 'one Object' and the 'two Objects' analyses of **V n -ing**. It follows that, for the learner, verbs classified as having one Object cannot be passivised, whereas those classified as having two Objects can be. The analysis, according to this argument, is useful as a pointer to what Swan (1994) calls 'Demarcation', that is, indicating what can and cannot be said, or rather, indicating what transformations can and cannot be made.

Such transformational information is of varying degrees of usefulness. For example, in the 300 million word Bank of English, examples of the pattern *I remember him ringing me up* are about ten times as frequent as those of the pattern *I remember his ringing me up*, with the verb *remember*. With other verbs, such as *hate*, the possessive pattern is very rare indeed. The passive is also variable. Whilst there are about 1500 instances of *be seen doing ...*, and 500 instances of *be heard doing ...*, there are only 10 instances of *be brought doing ...* and fewer than five instances of *be noticed doing ...* and *be watched doing ...* In the case of *have* in the **V n — ing** pattern (as in *The show had them cheering until they were hoarse*), there is no passive at all (Francis et al. 1996: 289).

In other words, we would argue that what it is helpful for a learner to know is not the structure of a clause, with its attendant transformational information, but the pattern that a verb has. This is, however, a purely pragmatic argument. It might be argued that structures may be unnecessary for a pedagogic grammar but that they are necessary for an academic one. In the following sections we consider two cases where the allocation of structural categories is not only of little value but also of little genuine validity. We refer to these as the problem of prepositional phrases and the problem of phase.

6.2　Problems with prepositional phrases

Our description of verb patterns (Francis et al. 1996) aims to be complete, in the sense that it seeks to account for every verb pattern recorded in CCED, and to translate each pattern, without exception, into structural terms. This comprehensive approach has thrown up a number of problems with relation to traditional views of structure, problems which led us ultimately to conclude that traditional structural descriptions of English were neither necessary not sufficient to account for actual language use. In this section and in Section 6.3 below, we discuss two of these problems.

The problem discussed in this section is that of how to analyse verbs followed by prepositional phrases, or verbs followed by noun groups and prepositional phrases. This is by no means a peripheral area of English grammar: in Francis et al. (1996), no fewer than 57 sections out of 87 deal with verbs followed by prepositional phrases, or by noun groups and prepositional phrases.

6.2.1   Example 1: **V for n/-ing**

Here are two examples of verbs with the pattern **V for n/-ing** (taken from Francis et al. 1996):

(38)   *I longed for a sister.*

(39)   *She could pass for a man.*

One possible analysis of these clauses would be Subject-Verb-Adjunct, on the grounds that a verb that is not immediately followed by a noun group is an intransitive verb, and that therefore any prepositional phrase following a verb is an Adjunct rather than an Object. There are two objections to this. Firstly, it implies a sharp distinction between, for example,

(38)   *I longed for a sister*

(analysed as Subject-Verb-Adjunct) and

(40)   *I wanted a sister*

(analysed as Subject-Verb-Object). The role of *a sister* is very similar in both examples, and an analysis should ideally reflect this. Similarly, the role of *a man* in

(39)   *She could pass for a man*

is very similar to its role in

(40)   *Jay was a man*

and an accurate analysis should reflect this.

Secondly, it implies a one-to-one relation between a phrase type (prepositional phrase) and a functional category (Adjunct). In other words, having identified a prepositional phrase, no further decision as to functional category needs to be made. Whereas this is simple to apply consistently, such unique identification of form and function is rare in language.

We propose, therefore, a set of functional categories such as 'prepositional Object' or 'prepositional Complement', which indicate that the noun group fulfils the role of an Object or a Complement but is preceded by a preposition. Using these terms, the clauses above are analysed as in Table 6.3.

Table 6.3a

Subject	Verb	Prepositional Object
I	longed	for a sister.

Table 6.3b

Subject	Verb	Prepositional Complement
She	could pass	for a man.

6.2.2 Example 2: V from n

In categorising prepositional phrases, therefore, we propose a system in which two main options are possible (there is a third option — phase — which will be discussed in Section 6.3 below):

a. the prepositional phrase may realise one of the functional categories 'prepositional Object', 'prepositional Complement', or 'prepositional Object Complement'; *or*
b. the prepositional phrase may realise the functional category 'Adjunct'.

Distinctions between each of the first set ('prepositional Object', 'prepositional Complement', and 'prepositional Object Complement') are easy to draw, as they follow the distinctions between Object, Complement and Object Complement. What is less easy is the distinction between Adjunct on the one hand, and one of the other categories, usually prepositional Object, on the other. This can be illustrated using the pattern **V from n**.

From intuition only, the prepositional phrases following some verbs, especially verbs of movement, seem to be clearly Adjuncts. These include examples such as:

(41)   *Smoke belched from the steelworks.*

(42)   *The service will depart from Inverness at 10:15...*

(43)   *He escaped from prison on Saturday.*

(44)   *He's run away from home twice.*

(45)   *She recently returned from an 18 month spell in Australia.*

Again from intuition, the prepositional phrases following other verbs seem to be clearly Objects, by analogy with other noun groups without prepositions. These include examples such as:

(46)   *The culture of the south <u>differs</u> from that of the north.*

(by analogy with 'resembles that of the north')

(47)   *Leeds never <u>recovered</u> from losing to Rangers.*

(by analogy with 'survived losing to Rangers')

(48)   *Many areas of the world <u>would</u> actually <u>benefit</u> from global warming.*

(by analogy with 'would welcome global warming')

(49)   *They <u>abstained</u> from meat...*

(by analogy with 'they avoided meat')
There are also examples where there is no clear analogy but where, intuitively, the prepositional phrase is 'Object-like', such as the following:

(50)   *The hatred <u>sprang</u> from fear.*

(51)   *She <u>digressed</u> from her prepared speech.*

(52)   *... bad presentation <u>can detract</u> from your message.*

(53)   *You <u>haven't heard</u> from Mona, have you?*

In these examples, it seems to us that constituent analysis would divide 'sprang from' from 'fear', 'digress from' from 'her prepared speech', 'detract from' from 'your message' and 'heard from' from 'Mona'.

In addition, there are examples where intuition offers no firm guidance, as in the following:

(54)   *She <u>comes</u> from Wiltshire.*

(55)   *He <u>quoted</u> from a medieval lament.*

(56)   *The mechanic <u>drank</u> from the bottle with enthusiasm.*

(57)   *I continued to <u>recoil</u> from the prospect of returning home.*

(58)   *I could feel <u>emanating</u> from her the enjoyment she derived from being centre stage.*

In the final set of examples above, arguments could be made for the prepositional phrase 'feeling' more like an Object or like an Adjunct. Clearly, a more decisive criterion for distinguishing prepositional Object from Adjunct than intuition is needed. Passivisation, the traditional test of an Object, cannot be relied on in these circumstances. For example, whilst the 300 million word Bank of English does offer one example each of *have been quoted from* and *cannot be escaped from*, it offers no evidence at all for the existence of the passive forms

be abstained from, be differed from, be recovered from or *be benefited from*
(although some speakers of English might consider such passives to be acceptable), even though we have suggested that these verbs might be followed by an
Object. In short, the existence or otherwise of a passive equivalent is an uncertain guide to the analysis of the clause. As Elizabeth Manning has pointed out
(personal communication), using a passive clause in itself retrospectively
analyses the active equivalent as Verb+Object, whatever the analysis of the
active clause itself might be. Thus, whereas

(59)   *They escaped from prison on two occasions*

may suggest an interpretation which classifies *prison* as a place, and as a
circumstance in the escape, the passive clause

(60)   *This prison has been escaped from on two occasions*

forces an interpretation which classifies *prison* as an institution, and as a
participant in the process of escaping.

As an alternative to the criterion of transformation, then, we considered the
possibility of using questions to distinguish between Adjuncts and prepositional
Objects. Adjuncts are considered to answer the questions When? Where? How?
and Why? whilst prepositional Objects answer the questions What? and Who(m)?
The following examples shows the questions they might be considered to answer:

(61)   *The service will depart from Inverness.* (Where?)

(62)   *Tito's portrait has vanished from the dilapidated waiting room.*
        (Where?)

(63)   *...the party would not deviate from the course outlined...* (What?)

(64)   *...bad presentation can detract from your message.* (What?)

(65)   *I'm sure our players would benefit from having fewer matches.*
        (What?)

There are also, however, examples, where the relevant question is not particularly
obvious. For example, in

(66)   *Restlessness radiated from him,*

the relevant question might be 'Where did restlessness radiate from?' or 'Whom
did restlessness radiate from?' Similarly,

(67)   *The mechanic drank from the bottle*

might equally well answer the question 'Where did the mechanic drink from?' or the question 'What did the mechanic drink from?'. Many verbs with the pattern **V** *from* **n** illustrate this dilemma.

The problem, then, is that we have two categories — a Where? category and a What? category — but that individual examples cannot uncontroversially be placed in one or the other category. One possible solution would be to propose 'fuzzy categories', that is, to suggest that there are 'prototypical Adjuncts' and 'prototypical prepositional Objects', and that other examples are more or less like Adjuncts or more or less like Objects. Unfortunately, a functional analysis does not permit such a solution. Although we might end up by admitting that some prepositional Objects are more centrally 'Object-like' than others, we do have to have an absolute boundary between the Objects and the Adjuncts. This type of grammatical analysis does not permit a cline.

A better solution, therefore, is to propose a default. That is, instead of seeking to define Adjunct and prepositional Object in absolute terms, one of them is defined as clearly as possible, and then all other items are said to belong in the other class. We have found Where? When? and Why? questions easier to identify than What? or Who? questions, and we therefore establish the category of Adjunct as the defined category, and the category of prepositional Object as the default category. In the pattern **V** *from* **n**, for example, we say that all verbs where the prepositional phrase answers the question Where? fall into the Verb+Adjunct class, and all other verbs fall into the Verb+prepositional Object class.

There is one further condition, however. As far as possible, we propose that verbs belonging to the same meaning group have the same analysis. This occasionally leads us to analyses that may seem strange even according to our own criteria. For example, *radiate* (from) belongs in a meaning group concerned with "leaving or coming from a place, group, thing, person, or position" (Francis et al. 1996: 191), even though the meaning of *radiate* is metaphorical. The verbs in this meaning group on the whole belong in the question Where? class, and as a result all of them, including *radiate*, have the Verb+Adjunct analysis even though, as we commented above, the question eliciting the clause

(66)   *Restlessness radiated from him*

is not clearly fixed. The same argument can be used for the verb *part*, as in

(68)   *I have parted from my wife.*

Similarly, there is a meaning group concerned with 'getting something from a source' (Francis et al. 1996: 188), which includes verbs such as *borrow, crib, generalize, plagiarize, copy, extrapolate* and *quote*. With these verbs, the question

Where? is not clearly relevant, so the verbs are classified as Verb+prepositional Object. However, the verb *import* is also included in this group, and so also has the analysis Verb+prepositional Object, even though the question Where? is relevant here.

In the description of the pattern **V *from* n** in Francis et al. (1996), only verbs 'concerned with leaving or coming from a place, group, thing, person, or position' (Francis et al. 1996: 191) are analysed as Verb with Adjunct. These include: *abscond, ascend, belch, commute, defect, depart, desert, diverge, drain, emanate, emerge, escape, fall, part, radiate, recede, recoil, separate, transfer, vanish* and *withdraw*.

All other verbs belong to the category 'Verb with prepositional Object'. Here is a list of the meaning groups identified:

The 'result' group

> (69)   *Alzheimer's is a complex disease and is probably unlikely to result from a defect in a single human gene.*

The 'derive' group

> (70)   *The term 'cannibalism' derives from the Spanish 'canibal', meaning 'savage'.*

The 'borrow' group

> (71)   *That's why it's so expensive to borrow from finance companies.*

The 'drink' group

> (72)   *The mechanic drank from the bottle with enthusiasm.*

The 'benefit' group

> (73)   *I'm sure our players would benefit from having fewer matches.*

The 'suffer' and 'recover' group

> (74)   *He's been suffering from a niggling shoulder injury.*

The 'differ' group

> (75)   *The culture of the south differs from that of the north in many ways.*

The 'abstain' and 'withdraw' group

> (76)   *They abstained from meat because they believed that killing life injured the spirit within.*

The 'backtrack' group

(77)   *Lufthansa's decision to* <u>*backtrack*</u> *from the imposition of a new pay structure means that its staff will continue to enjoy among the highest salaries paid in the airline business.*

The 'detract' group

(78)   *...bad presentation* <u>*can detract*</u> *from your message.*

Verbs with other meanings

(79)   *You* <u>*haven't heard*</u> *from Mona, have you?*

6.2.3   *Example 3:* **V n *as* n**

The functional categories 'prepositional Object', 'prepositional Complement' and 'prepositional Object Complement' apply also when the prepositional phrase follows a verb and a noun group. For example, the pattern **V n *as* n** has examples of the following structures (Francis et al. 1996: 348):

Verb with Object and prepositional Object Complement
Verb with Object and prepositional Complement

In the first analysis, the noun group in the prepositional phrase has an equivalence with the noun group immediately following the verb. This is analogous to verbs that are followed by two noun groups, such as *We named her Elfreda*, where *her* realises an Object and *Elfreda* realises an Object Complement, and where *her* has an equivalence to *Elfreda*. Examples include:

(80)   *I* <u>*consider*</u> *him as a friend.*
        ('him' = 'a friend')

(81)   *It was a performance that* <u>*stamped*</u> *him as the star we had been searching for.*
        ('him' = 'the star we had been searching for')

(82)   *People* <u>*have been keeping*</u> *parrots as indoor pets since Egyptian times.*
        ('parrots' = 'indoor pets')

If the passive version of the pattern occurs, the analysis is Verb+prepositional Complement, as in:

(83)   *He* <u>*was deposed*</u> *as president.*
        (He = 'president')

In the second analysis of Verb with Object and prepositional Complement, the noun group in the prepositional phrase has an equivalence with the noun group that realises the Subject of the clause. There are few examples of the analogous 'Verb with Object and Complement' structure:

(84) *She made him a good wife*

is one. Examples of Verb with Object and prepositional Complement include:

(85) *He always struck me as a very dispassionate and calculating sort of man.*
      ('He' = 'a very dispassionate and calculating sort of man')

(86) *Lloyd Wright began his career as a landscape architect.*
      ('Lloyd Wright' = 'a landscape architect')

(87) *Turkish replaced Arabic as the language of the ruling elite.*
      ('Turkish' = 'the language of the ruling elite')

6.2.4 *Example 4: V n to n*

The final pattern to be discussed in this section is **V n *to* n**. We have analysed one set of verbs with this pattern 'Verb with Object and prepositional Object'. These are the verbs such as *give, show* and *sell* which also have the pattern **V n n**, and the structure 'Verb with two Objects'. For example, we analyse

(88) *He gave his mother the money*

as 'Verb-Object-Object' and

(89) *He gave the money to his mother*

as 'Verb-Object-Prepositional Object'. In this we concur with the traditional view that the role of 'his mother' and 'the money' remains constant in the two examples. (Our reasons for avoiding the terminology 'Indirect Object' have been given in Section 6.1.2 above.)

In general, then, we are using the potentiality of another pattern (**V n n**) to identify the structure 'Verb with Object and prepositional Object'. However, we also keep to the principle, mentioned above, that words with the same meaning should belong to the same meaning group and therefore should have the same structural analysis. Thus the 'give' group (Francis et al. 1996: 419) includes verbs that have both the pattern **V n n** and the pattern **V n *to* n**, such as *accord, allocate, award, bequeath, give, grant, hand, lend* and *vouchsafe*, but it also includes verbs that have a similar meaning but which only have the pattern **V n *to* n**, such as *contribute, donate, restore* and *transfer*. Thus, we argue, if in the example

(89)   *He gave the money to his mother,*

'the money' and 'his mother' both have the role of Object, by analogy with

(88)   *He gave his mother the money,*

then in the example

(90)   *He donated the money to the church,*

'the money' and 'the church' have the same roles of Object, even though no analogous clause such as

(91)   **He donated the church the money*

exists.

The second structure associated with the pattern **V n *to* n** is less problematic. Examples such as

(92)   *He changed his name to Adam*

are analysed as 'Verb-Object-prepositional Object Complement', on the grounds that there is equivalence between 'his name' and 'Adam'.

All other verbs, that is, those which are not clearly of the *give* type or the *change* type, are categorised as 'Verb with Object and Adjunct'. Here, then, the default has changed. We regard those prepositional phrases that follow noun groups as being more 'Adjunct-like' than the prepositional phrases that follow verbs. Therefore, prepositional phrases in patterns such as **V n *to* n** will be analysed as Adjuncts unless there is good reason for an alternative analysis. In many of the sections in Francis et al. (1996) where the pattern consists of a verb followed by a noun group and a prepositional phrase, the prepositional phrase is always analysed as an Adjunct and the only structure for the pattern is 'Verb-Object-Adjunct'.

6.3 Problems with phase

The second problem to be considered here is that of 'phase'. The argument for phase is that when one verb follows another, the two verbs together might constitute a single verb phrase. Thus, in

(93)   *He seems to be an intelligent person,*

the verb phrase is argued to be *seems to be* rather than just *seems*. The rationale for this is that it allows the noun group *an intelligent person* to be analysed as the Complement, whilst the alternative analysis would make *to be an intelligent person* the Complement. This alternative is unsatisfactory because it reduces the status of the verb *be* and makes the main verb of the clause *seems*. However, the clause answers the question 'What does he seem to be?' or 'What is he, in your opinion?' rather than the question 'What does he seem?' This suggests that *be* is the main carrier of information.

Two verbs are considered to be in phase if they constitute one single verb phrase. For example, in

(94)   *He started to sing a ballad,*

the verb phrase might be considered to be *started to sing,* rather than only *started*. In that case, the next element, the Object, would consist of *a ballad* rather than *to sing a ballad*. We originally considered two verbs to be in phase only if there was nothing between them, or if the only item between them was the *to* particle in a to-infinitive. Thus the candidate patterns for an 'in phase' analysis were **V to-inf, V -ing** and **V inf**. Later other patterns were considered, as we shall describe below. First, though, we had to consider each of the candidate patterns to determine whether all the verbs with that pattern could be analysed in terms of phase, or if not, what the distinguishing criteria were to be.

6.3.1   *V to-inf*

The motivation for considering two verbs to be in phase is that they constitute a single process rather than two processes. The first verb acts on the second verb rather in the way that a modal auxiliary or an adverb does, altering an aspect of the meaning of the second verb but not constituting a separate activity (Downing and Locke 1992). This 'modal-' or 'adverb-like' meaning is illustrated in the following examples, in which the two verbs in phase are underlined.

(95)   … a breakthrough in the trade talks <u>seems to be ruled out</u>. (= 'must be ruled out' or 'is probably ruled out')

(96)   *The police <u>managed to close down</u> the party.* (= 'closed down the party with difficulty')

(97)   *I <u>regret to say</u> that over the weekend Mr Bunn has been taken ill.* (= 'have to say', or 'say regretfully')

(98)   *Mrs Hardie <u>hurried to make up for</u> her tactlessness by asking her guest to describe the other houses his father had designed.* (= 'quickly made up for')

(99)   *Toads tend to lay their string of eggs in deeper water.* (= 'usually lay their eggs')

(100)   *Last week I attempted to buy a Saver ticket on the train and was told this was against the rules.* (= 'did not buy')

(101)   *I absolutely refuse to believe he did it.* (= 'will not believe')

Some of these are more uncontroversially modal-like than others. Examples of very clear modal meaning include *seems to* and *tend to*, which realise the typical modal meanings of probability and usuality. Less clear are examples such as *managed to* and *hurried to*, where the meaning may be encoded as an adverb or prepositional phrase rather than as a modal. Finally, whereas *refuse to* clearly indicates a negative, *attempted to* only implies one.

We then have to consider whether *all* verbs with this pattern should be regarded as one verb phrase rather than two. Here are some examples of other verbs with the pattern **V to-inf**.

(102)   *He remembered to buy his wife chocolates.*

(103)   *You forgot to go to the chemist.*

(104)   *The soldiers promised to restore order.*

(105)   *I hate to be slow at anything.*

(106)   *I wanted to start a magazine.*

(107)   *They claim to have been cured.*

(108)   *I didn't ask to look at the engine.*

It seems a simple matter to count all of these examples as 'in phase', with a verb group made up of two verbs. However, there are two implications of the 'in phase' analysis which may prove to be unfortunate in some cases. Firstly, the 'in phase' analysis suggests that the second verb (the verb in the to-infinitive) is the 'main verb' of the clause. This seems a reasonable suggestion in the case of *The police managed to close down the party* or *Mrs Hardie hurried to make up for her tactlessness...* where a reasonable answer to the question 'What happened?' would be 'The police closed down the party' or 'Mrs Hardie made up for her tactlessness'. On the other hand, in the example *I wanted to start a magazine*, *start* is not the main verb in the clause. A question-answer sequence 'What happened? — I started a magazine' does not reflect in any way the meaning of the original clause.

Secondly, we have to consider that this decision affects the analysis of the other items in the clause. For example, in *Toads tend to lay their string of eggs in deeper water*, our phase analysis means that *their string of eggs* is analysed as the Object of the clause, with the main verb of the clause being *lay*. The question with relation to the other examples, then, is what the logical Object is. In *The soldiers have promised to restore order*, for example, is *order* the logical Object of *have promised to restore*, or is *to restore order* the logical Object of *have promised*? This is not an easy question to answer, although we may say that intuitively the second alternative seems most reasonable.

Our solution to this problem is to propose two analyses of the pattern **V to-inf**: one in which the two verbs are in phase, another in which the to-infinitive clause is the Object of the verb. The first analysis will apply only to those instances where the meaning of the pattern is that the action realised by the second verb either is or is not done. The second analysis will apply to those instances where the pattern does not indicate whether or not the action realised by the second verb is done. Thus these verbs and phrasal verbs with the pattern **V to-inf** are among those analysed with the 'in phase' analysis:

begin	*commence*	*proceed*
cease	*continue*	*start*
appear	*pretend*	*seem*
feign	*prove*	*turn out*
attempt	*fight*	*struggle*
endeavour	*labour*	*try*
contrive	*remember*	*suffice*
manage	*serve*	
decline	*forget*	*omit*
fail	*neglect*	*refuse*
choose (to believe)	*hate (to say/to be rude)*	*presume*
condescend	*hesitate*	*regret*
dare	*opt*	*venture*
hasten	*hurry*	*rush*
chance	*happen*	
incline	*stand*	*shape up*
promise	*tend*	
conspire	*live*	
help	*stop*	

These verbs are among those analysed with the 'Verb with Object' analysis:

agree	*decide*	*opt*
arrange	*guarantee*	*promise*
choose (to go home)	*intend*	*propose*
consent	*offer*	*threaten*
ask	*campaign*	*petition*
beg	*demand*	*plead*
aim	*dread*	*long*
aspire	*expect*	*seek*
crave	*fear*	*want*
desire	*hope*	*wish*
hate (to be interrupted)	*like*	*prefer*
claim	*profess*	*purport*
deserve	*need*	
afford	*learn*	

It should be noted in passing that these analyses involve different interpretations of the coding **V to-inf**. Where the two verbs are in phase, '**to-inf**' means 'the to-infinitive form of a verb'. What follows that verb is not itself part of the pattern. On the other hand, where the verbs are not in phase, '**to-inf**' means 'the to-infinitive clause', the whole clause being the Object. Tables 6.4a and 6.4b follow the tables that appear in Francis et al. (1996: 87, 91) which illustrate this. The term 'Completive' is a portmanteau term for 'Object', 'Complement' or other structural label, the choice of which is dependent on the second verb in the verb group, not the first verb.

Table 6.4a. *Structure 1: Verbs in phase*

	Verb group	to-infinitive	
Subject		Verb	Completive
The arrangements	*appeared*	*to be*	*satisfactory.*
Prison officers	*continued*	*to patrol*	*the grounds.*
He	*refused*	*to comment.*	

Table 6.4b. *Structure 2: Verb with Object*

	Verb group	to-infinitive clause
Subject	Verb	Object
The President	*agreed*	*to be interviewed.*
Turkish airlines	*has offered*	*to lay on a dozen flights.*
He	*pleaded*	*to speak with me privately.*

So far, we have spoken of two analyses of this pattern. There is, however, a third analysis, which accounts for cases where the to-infinitive clause has the meaning of 'in order to', 'for the purpose of' or 'at that time'. We have said in Chapter 2 that to-infinitive clauses meaning 'in order to' are not normally shown in verb patterns. However, there are some cases where the to-infinitive is particularly frequent following a given verb, or where the meaning of that verb is incomplete without the to-infinitive, yet where the to-infinitive clause cannot reasonably be said to be the Object. Here are some examples:

(109) *The women <u>had collaborated</u> to bring charges against Eckersley.*

(110) *We <u>hurried</u> to catch our bus.*

(111) *Newspapers <u>competed</u> to attract more readers.*

(112) *We <u>waited</u> to see if the birds would return.*

(113) *I <u>trained</u> to be an actress.*

(114) *I <u>paid</u> to see the movie three times.*

(115) *I <u>awoke</u> to find the sun streaming into the bedroom.*

(116) *We <u>sat back</u> to wait for the phone to ring.*

These examples are analysed as 'Verb with Adjunct'.

In some cases, the distinction between analyses is a subtle one, and depends on the second verb as well as the first one. For example, when *hurry* means 'move quickly', as in *hurried to catch the bus*, the to-infinitive clause following is analysed as an Adjunct. When it means 'do something quickly', as in *hurried to reassure her*, the two verbs are analysed as in phase. Similarly, when *hate* is part of a phrase such as *hate to tell you*, where the main verb is *tell* and *hate* simply indicates an attitude, the two verbs are in phase, but when *hate* is followed by a to-infinitive with another kind of verb, as in *hated to be beaten*, the to-infinitive is the Object.

Our principle, then, is that two verbs are in phase only when they indicate that the action realised by the second verb is or is not done. We carry this principle over to other patterns in which the verb is followed by a non-finite clause. The pattern **V -ing**, for example, has three possible analyses: 'Verbs in phase', as in *She started walking*, 'Verb with Object', as in *He liked dancing with her* and 'Verb with Adjunct', as in *They ended up fighting*. The pattern **V inf**, which is used with only five verbs: *dare, need, help, come* and *go*, always has the analysis 'Verbs in phase'. The pattern **V *and* v** has the analysis 'Verbs in phase' only in respect of the verbs *go, try* and *up*, and the phrasal verbs *go ahead, go on* and *turn around*. (See Francis et al. 1996 for examples.)

6.3.2   *Verbs followed by prepositions*

In treating some but not all of verbs with the patterns **V to-inf**, **V inf** and **V -ing** as 'in phase', we are in keeping with traditional analyses, in essence if not in detail. When we extended our structural analyses to verbs followed by a preposi- tional phrase, however, we found it necessary to extend the 'in phase' analysis to other instances. For example, in *They told me to forget about running*, where the preposition *about* is followed by an '-ing' clause, the meaning of *forget* is that the action realised in the '-ing' clause is not done. This is very similar to *She was told to avoid smoking*. If *avoid doing* is analysed as verbs in phase, why should *forget about doing* be analysed any differently? This argument led us to an 'in phase' analysis in the following cases:

V *about* -ing

(117)   *They told me to forget about running.*

V *from* -ing

(118)   *Hannah forbore from pointing out that she would be put out very little.*

V *in* -ing

(119)   *I don't know whether they'll succeed in banning boxing.*

V *on* -ing

(120)   *He insisted on driving me home.*

V *out of* -ing

(121)   *Many farmers are dropping out of retailing their crops.*

V *with* -ing

(122)   *I helped with making the fudge.*

Whereas these analyses are reasonable in themselves, they do have an unfortunate consequence. Only two verbs can, logically, be in phase: a verb group cannot consist of a verb and a noun. Therefore, the verbs exemplified above have a different analysis depending on whether the preposition is followed by a noun group or an '-ing' clause. For example, in

(123) *She succeeded in becoming President,*

succeeded in becoming is analysed as one verb group, with *President* as the Complement. In

(124) *She succeeded in her bid to become President,*

however, *succeeded* comprises the verb group, with *in her bid to become President* being analysed as a prepositional Object. Thus two clauses with very similar role relationships have to be analysed very differently. This is the consequence of following structural analyses to their logical conclusions.

6.4 Conclusion to Chapter 6

In this chapter we have presented some details of our attempt to apply traditional structural analyses to clauses comprising all patterns of all verbs. Our aim has been that of all analysts: to achieve in every instance an analysis that is explicitly justifiable in terms of criteria, and to achieve a set of analyses that are consistent with each other. In addition, in Francis et al. (1996), we attempted to be comprehensive, that is, to give an analysis, not for selected examples only, but for all verbs in all their patterns. In doing so, we ran into many problems, particularly in the areas of verbs with prepositions and of phase. We readily acknowledge that our resulting analyses have in them many problems and points of contention. We would, however, claim that they are consistent and explicit.

The conclusion that we draw from our attempt to present a consistent and comprehensive analysis is that, with nearly every verb pattern, distinctions have to be drawn between one analysis and another, and that whereas in a few cases these distinctions are revealing, in most cases they are trivial. If these distinctions are not drawn, however (for example, if all prepositional phrases are analysed as Adjuncts, or if all verb-verb combinations are analysed as in phase), the result is an inconsistent analytical system or, in effect, no analytical system at all. In other words, as soon as one starts to use structural terms, such as Object, Complement and so on, the exercise of analysis inevitably becomes both complex and of minimal usefulness in terms of the information it adds to the clauses under analysis.

The logical outcome of this conclusion is to replace a structural analysis with a pattern analysis, that is, to allow the pattern analysis to stand by itself, without attempting to relate the elements of the pattern to other, more abstract, categories. In those cases where the abstract categories reflect a useful distinction, as in

(125)   *They elected him President* versus

(126)   *They sent him a letter*,

a description of meaning groups would have to carry this distinction. The result, of course, would be a description of English that was less abstract, more lexical and 'surface' in orientation.

There are at least four advantages to a pattern analysis of English in the place of a structural analysis:

a. Consistency is unlikely to be a problem, as the analysis is relatively easy to do with a minimum of training.

b. The analysis allows meaningful, surface distinctions to be made, while avoiding meaningless distinctions.

c. The analysis is truly comprehensive in that as well as being applicable to all verbs it allows analysis of other word classes using the same system.

d. The analysis is flexible and does not pre-judge the type of pattern a word may have. This in turn allows the analysis to be comprehensive, as no pattern is beyond its scope.

We believe that these advantages outweigh the relative unfamiliarity of pattern descriptions.

CHAPTER 7

Word class and pattern

7.1 The word class as pattern set

There are two alternative ways of identifying word class: meaning (e.g. a noun denotes a person, place or thing), and pattern.

In this chapter we will argue that word classes can be most easily identified on the basis of the behaviour of the words that constitute them. Each word class has a set of patterns that are associated with it, and pattern is the most consistent way of determining class. Although the words in a class do often have semantic and morphological features in common, for example nouns do name things, and adverbs are very often formed by adding *ly* to an adjective, we argue that environment is a more reliable guide than meaning or form. This approach is not without its problems: for example there is the question of how many sets of behaviours have to overlap for a word class to be identified. This question will be discussed below; in this section we present some straightforward cases.

The first example concerns the distinction between count and uncount nouns. In the case of count nouns, their major characteristic is that they have a plural form, usually formed by adding 's' or 'es'. In addition, they are associated with particular patterns: that is, they are often preceded by *a* or *an* or *the* in the singular, or a possessive determiner, and by *some* or a number in the plural. They are often preceded by adjectives or noun modifiers. They may also function as noun modifiers themselves. Examples such as *book* and *cat* occur in lines like these:

```
ht. Well, you can't cure a cat of its natural territorial insti
honse, pointing to a white cat on the bench beside me, 'that is
predatory animal, a jungle cat stalking her prey. And at the en
on't let you keep dogs and cats. They appeal to people otherwis
. The back door also had a cat flap set into thin plywood which
```

The uncount noun is the most frequent sort of noun after the count noun. These have no plural, and they differ from uncount nouns in terms of their immediate patterning: they are not used with the article *a*, (with some exceptions — see below) though they may be preceded by *the, some, any* etc. Like count nouns, they are often preceded by adjectives and noun modifiers, and may function as noun modifiers themselves. *Blood* and *assistance* are typical of this sub-class, and occur in examples such as:

```
should have found even more blood at his house and fingerprints
d he was given contaminated blood during surgery at a Californi
iously shown that the donor blood given to Mr Clegg was not inf
eveloping potentially fatal blood clots and should be treated w
e out, am I entitled to any assistance such as unemployment ben
ht much-needed humanitarian assistance to many victims of the w
sentials such as food, rent assistance and access to cultural a
ttle over the bus transport assistance scheme resulted in the S
```

Some uncount nouns, however, are associated with a slightly different pattern of behaviour which differentiates them from the typical members of the class. These are nouns which often have the article *a* or *an* when they are modified or qualified. Examples are *happiness* and *admiration*:

```
del Davies a deep untroubled happiness, which was one source of
ut of unending pictures of a happiness that is often what a chi
s. Nouvel admits to a strong admiration for Foster's work-whi
ouvel, 'Johnson expresses an admiration for those fellow studen
```

In cases such as this, it is difficult to decide on criteria for identifying a class. One can either say that *happiness* and *admiration* are uncount nouns which share some of the behaviour of count nouns, or that they form a class of their own. In Collins COBUILD English Dictionary (CCED), they were called uncount nouns, and the ability to occur with an article was listed as one of the features of uncount nouns. This is true of a wide range of uncount nouns, though there are some, like *furniture* and *information*, which never occur with an article.

The second example concerns the difference between graded and ungraded adjectives. When adjectives are graded they have clear patterns of behaviour. They may be used in comparative patterns, with the *-er* ending or with the adverbs *more* and *less*. One typical pattern is the use of a comparative graded adjective, *than*, and another element, such as a noun group, an -ing clause, or a finite clause:

(1)   *Though chess is infinitely <u>more civilised than war</u>, I had no appetite for chess.* (noun group)

(2)   *It'll be <u>nicer than being at home</u>, in some ways.* (-ing clause)

(3)   *His face seemed <u>slightly narrower than she had remembered</u>.* (finite clause)

(4)   *They're increasingly frustrated and <u>more willing than ever</u> to take their business elsewhere.* (adverb)

(5)   *The response has been <u>better than expected</u>.* (-ed form)

(6)   *Though the average temperature was only about one degree <u>colder than usual</u>, severe effects followed.* (adjective)

(7)   *We look after our creatures so well that, arguably, they're <u>better off than in the wild</u>.* (prepositional phrase)

Other patterns involving *than* have a noun before *than* and the element that follows it:

(8)   *Dietrich belonged to a far different and far <u>more fascinating industry than the</u> movie world of 1992.*

(9)   *The President has said that if war breaks out they will suffer <u>bigger losses than in Vietnam</u>.*

(10) *I'm a much <u>better father than I was 25 years ago</u>.*

In addition, graded adjectives are associated with a pattern consisting of *the* followed by a graded comparative adjective, *the* again, and another graded comparative adjective. This may or may not be followed by another noun:

(11) *The <u>more indebted</u> a company, the <u>bigger</u> the change in its cost of capital.*

(12) *The <u>more outrageous</u> the bid, the <u>more likely</u> its chances of success.*

(13) *The press generally is wrong, and the <u>more wrong</u> the <u>more unanimous</u>.*

In short, a word is assigned to a word-class based on its patterns of behaviour. This leaves the question as to what groups of behaviours can be taken to identify or create a word-class or sub-class.

7.2 Some 'new' word classes

7.2.1 *Classes of nouns*

In our work on CCED, we proposed some 'new' word classes, mostly sub-classes of the main classes 'noun' and 'verb'. For example, we identified other patterns of nouns than those traditionally recognised. In particular, there are a large number of nouns which have a wider range of patterns than either count and uncount nouns. They occur without determiners, when the writer or speaker is making reference to something as a general phenomenon, but they often occur with an indefinite article when it is an instance that is being referred to. One solution would be to refer to these nouns as count/uncount nouns. However, this does not capture the fact that they are a large sub-class of noun with their own patterns of behaviour, deserving of being described in their own right rather than as a sort of hybrid. In CCED the term N-VAR (variable noun) was coined to describe them. Here are some examples:

```
crusade against poverty and injustice, and if the Labour Party could it
           would have been an injustice for, by the end Nottingha
t acitly acknowledging the injustices suffered by a Maori trib
ed into the realm of casual atrocity, routine destruction and v
their imagination. After an atrocity, people clutch at any stra
ght to book for its alleged atrocities and massacres during its
ree Conservative people had lunch with her to discuss ideas, bu
he was talking to. During a lunch, he would be speaking about t
erful traditional Irish pub lunches. Pick up the tourist board
```

There is another sub-class of noun with similar behaviour to that of N-VAR. These are nouns that refer to substances, and when they are used with an indefinite article, or in the plural, they refer to brands or types of a substance. For these we have used the term N-MASS (mass noun). It should be pointed out that this is the only word-class categorisation that depends on a semantic distinction rather than a pattern one: in CCED we could have called these N-VAR too, as the pattern is the same. The reason we called them N-MASS is largely because of the distinction between instance, in the case of N-VAR, and brand or type in the case of N-MASS. N-MASS is also a traditional sub-class of noun, and seemed worth maintaining on those grounds. There is a pattern difference in terms of frequency, however. In the case of N-VARs the instance use (*an atrocity*) is as frequent as its other uses, whereas with mass nouns the brand or type (*a metal*) is far less frequent than its other uses. Here are some examples of mass nouns:

```
m the reprocessing of spent fuel has reportedly contaminated ai
t of the area and used as a fuel. They also commissioned a com
emissions and saving fossil fuels. It's a very good thing to d
the mud are sheets of rusty metal, mountains of corrugated iron
 this gas compressed into a metal. Another mystery is Jupiter's
es experience wind. Why are metals better thermal conductors th
```

Having established four main sub-classes of noun — count, uncount, variable and mass — it is perhaps surprising to note the large number of nouns that do not fit precisely into any of these classes in terms of their pattern behaviour. Potentially, then, many more sub-classes of noun could be identified and named. The alternative is to describe each noun in terms of the class it most nearly fits, and to note the additional behaviour patterns. For example, there are some nouns, like *discontent* and *oppression*, which behave like uncount nouns but which also occur in the plural. They cannot be coded as N-VAR because they do not occur with an indefinite article:

```
in 14 states. There is clear discontent over the way economic p
forces and to change and to discontents real and imagined, bot
```
```
are working again, there is oppression and it is very difficul
s a thriller set against the oppressions of a truly totalitari
```

In CCED these are coded as **N-UNCOUNT: also N in pl.**

Similarly, there are some nouns which behave like uncount nouns but which are also used with the indefinite article. They cannot be labelled N-VAR or N-COUNT because they have no plural form:

```
t interest rates and yet more gloom in the housing market. But
ife and I together can cast a gloom over an entire evening, not
```

In CCED these are coded as **N-UNCOUNT: also *a* N.**

As is to be expected, nouns which share meanings also share patterns of behaviour. Words referring to wild animals, birds or plants, for example, share the feature that the singular form is sometimes used with a plural verb to refer to the entity collectively, as in *Deer are not declining in number*; *Pheasant are challenging to shoot.*

Similarly, words referring to members of a family share a range of behaviour in that they are used as a vocative, they are also proper nouns, and they often occur after a possessive determiner:

```
and the new rules. You see, Dad, I'm confused, and I wanted yo
ldren — Mum loved babies and Dad liked the idea of a large fami
aid. 'As a matter of fact my dad owns it, but property is worth
```

In CCED these are coded as **N-FAMILY**.

The final example is words referring to colours. These words are traditionally identified as adjectives, but in fact they also behave like nouns, and have a plural form. In the first two examples, below, *red* is an adjective, and in the second two it is a noun:

```
e convoy, unfurling green, red and blue flags of the Mindanao
ms which cause people to go red, how to tone the colour down or
tectors. Tony is dressed in red; Trudy wears black — sounds of
is anachronistically bright reds jar with the soft colours l
```

For the sake of brevity, in CCED we coined a new term, **COLOUR**, to cover both adjective-like and noun-like behaviour.

7.2.2   *Ergative verbs*

Ergative verbs can be defined as verbs which have two major patterns, one in which they are intransitive and have the pattern **V**, and one in which they are transitive and have the pattern **V n**. The **V** pattern indicates that something happens to the Subject, or that the Subject does something, as in *The car stopped.*

The **V n** pattern indicates that someone or something causes something to happen, as in *The driver stopped the car.* In other words, the Subject in the **V** pattern is the Object in the **V n** pattern. Ergative verbs can, however, be classified into sub-classes depending on the patterns they have. In fact, on this basis there are ten sub-classes of ergative verb. The first six are symmetrical, that is, the only difference between the two patterns is that one has a noun group following the verb and the other does not, as in *The stick broke* and *She broke the stick.* The other four are asymmetrical — that is, the patterns are different in more ways than the presence or absence of a noun group. For example, the verb *puff* has the patterns **V n** and **V prep/adv**, as in *The chimney puffed smoke* and *Smoke puffed out of the chimney.*

The ten sub-classes are identified in terms of the following patterns:

Symmetrical

1. **V, V n**
    The vase broke.
    John broke the vase.
2. **V prep/adv, V n prep/adv**
    The boat sailed up the river.
    We sailed the boat up the river.
3. **V adj, V n adj**
    The door slammed shut.
    She slammed the door shut.
4. **V *as* adj, V n *as* adj**
    That score counts as successful.
    We count that score as successful.
5. **V to-inf, V n to-inf**
    She trained to compete.
    They trained her to compete.
6. **V ord prep, V n ord prep**
    They rank sixth in the world.
    Most people rank them sixth in the world.
    Note: ord = ordinal number

Asymmetrical

7. **V prep/adv, V n, V n prep/adv**
    Light reflects on the water.
    The mirror reflects light.
    The glass reflected light onto the wall.

8. **V prep/adv, V n**
   Smoke puffed out of the chimney.
   The chimney puffed smoke
9. **V adv, V n**
   This carpet cleans easily.
   We cleaned the carpet.
10. **V adj, V n**
    The chair folds flat.
    He folded the chair.

There is another class of ergative verb in which the verb is reciprocal as well as ergative. In the four examples which follow, (14) and (15) are standard reciprocal verb patterns (see Section 2.4). That is, the verb has a plural subject indicating that two or more things or people are interacting with each other. It also occurs with a singular Subject and is followed by a prepositional phrase, usually introduced by *with,* indicating that one thing or person is interacting with another. Examples (15), (16) and (17) are typical of the behaviour of ergative verbs, with the patterns **V *with* n** and **V n**.

(14)   *The liquids will blend to make a rich sauce.*

(15)   *The chocolate blends with the coffee.*

(16)   *Blend the remaining ingredients.*

(17)   *Blend the butter with the sugar.*

Again, we are arguing that this behaviour justified the identification of a new class of verb: the ergative reciprocal verb. In CCED these are coded as **V-RECIP-ERG**.

7.2.3   *Shell nouns*

Another proposed 'new' class may be 'shell' nouns, arguably another class of nouns which could be identified on the basis of their behaviour. Basically these are nouns which require lexicalisation in their immediate context. The term *lexicalisation* is also termed *lexical realisation,* for example in Winter (1977). It means that a word such as *allegation, theory* or *fact* is not used without some kind of expansion in the surrounding text, indicating what the allegation, theory, or fact is. Often the lexicalisation occurs in a that-clause following the noun:

(18)   *I deny your allegation that he 'bullied staff and inmates, who all feared him'.*

(19)   *The discovery of twin pandas in Sichuan province has refuted the theory that only one of any pair of giant panda twins could survive.*

(20)   *He had an unshakable premonition that he would die.*

(21)   *David wanted an underktaking that Shirley would leave him alone in peace to get on with his life.*

(22)   *The motto that one's home is one's castle is engraved on my heart.*

(23)   *Which French leader made famous the remark that the British are a nation of shopkeepers?*

(24)   *There's a belief that saving for private education should start on the day the child is born.*

Using the Bank of English corpus, it is possible to list fairly exhaustively all the nouns that have this particular pattern of behaviour. The idea that they are a distinct and definable group — arguably a class of their own — is reinforced by the discovery that all these nouns have features of meaning in common. They fall into two major groups. The first group consists of nouns which refer to something that is written or spoken; the that-clause lexicalises what it is that is written or spoken. The second group consists of nouns which refer to beliefs, ideas, wishes, and thought processes. Again, the that-clause lexicalises what it is that is thought or believed.

The nouns which are listed below are those which a) need lexicalisation in their immediate context and b) have the behaviour pattern in which they are followed by a that-clause in a significant number of their occurrences in the corpus. They are divided into two groups on the semantic grounds suggested above. Note that the criteria may not apply to all the senses of the nouns listed, but they apply to at least one:

Nouns referring to something that is written or spoken:

accusation, acknowledgment, adage, admission, advice, affirmation, allegation, announcement, aphorism, appeal, argument, assertion, assurance, axiom, boast, caveat, charge, claim, cliché, comment, complaint, condition, confirmation, contention, criticism, declaration, decree, defence, demand, denial, dictum, directive, disclosure, edict, equation, excuse, explanation, forecast, generalisation, gossip, guarantee, guess, hint, implication, information, insinuation, insistence, jibe, legend, maxim, message, motto, myth, news, notification, oath, objection, observation, order, plea, pledge, point, prediction, proclamation, promise, prophecy, proposal, proposition, protest, proverb, provision, proviso, question, reassurance, recommendation, remark, reminder, report, request, resolution, retort, revelation, rule, ruling, rumour, saying, slogan, speculation, statement, stipulation, story, suggestion, tale, teaching, testimony, threat, truism, undertaking, verdict, vow, warning, whisper

Nouns referring to something that is thought or believed:

acceptance, agreement, analysis, anticipation, appreciation, assessment, assumption, attitude, awareness, belief, calculation, certainty, certitude, concept, conception, conclusion, consensus, conviction, credo, decision, delusion, desire, determination, doctrine, dogma, doubt, dream, expectation, faith, fallacy, fantasy, fear, feeling, finding, hope, hunch, hypothesis, idea, ideal, illusion, impression, inference, inkling, interpretation, intuition, judgement, knowledge, misapprehension, misconception, notion, opinion, perception, persuasion, philosophy, position, postulate, precept, premise, presentiment, presumption, presupposition, principle, projection, rationale, rationalisation, realisation, reasoning, recognition, recollection, reflection, resolution, resolve, scepticism, sense, sentiment, speculation, stance, standpoint, superstition, supposition, suspicion, tenet, theory, thesis, thinking, thought, understanding, view, viewpoint, vision, wisdom, wish, worry

In addition, there are a few nouns which similarly need lexicalisation in a that-clause but do not fit into either of the above groups. The most frequent of these is *fact*:

(25)   *The <u>fact</u> that the earthquake hit so early in the morning probably saved tens of thousands of workers.*

Arguably, then, this is a distinct class of nouns, with its own pattern of behaviour. Moreover, there are other behavioural patterns associated with these words. For example, they often function as advance or retrospective labels (Francis 1994). Again, the feature that sets them apart from the majority of nouns is the fact that they require lexicalisation in their immediate co-text. Where the label precedes its lexicalisation it can be termed an advance label, and where it follows the lexicalisation, it can be termed a retrospective label. Labels very often operate across clause boundaries. In this example (ibid 84) *reason* operates as an advance label, and *question* is a retrospective label:

(26)   *I understand that approximately 12 per cent of the population is left-handed. Why, then, should there be such a preponderance of right-handed golfers, which extends, I am informed, to club level? In reply to that <u>question</u> a golfing colleague of mine offered two <u>reasons</u>.*

    The first was that beginners usually start with handed-down clubs, which are usually right-handed. The second was that, for technical reasons, left-handed individuals make good right-handed golfers.

These labels have an important organising function which stretches over two paragraphs of this text. Note that they do not refer to any single stretch of text; they are not repetitions of any other noun, and nor do they have any other cohesive link with another noun such as synonymy, antonymy etc. Instead the nouns *questions* and *reasons* refer to stretches of text with which they are presented as equivalent.

In the next example, *details* is an advance label, requiring lexicalization in what follows (*two* and *salacious* also require lexicalization, of course) and *allegation* is a retrospective label, summing up the *Post*'s claim:

(27)   *The New York Post, which has been leading the tabloid pack, has added two salacious <u>details</u> to this bare outline. It reported that the alleged attack took place on a concrete staircase that runs from the Kennedy house to the beach. More sensationally, the Post claimed on Friday that Ted Kennedy, half naked, was romping round the estate with a second woman while the alleged attack was taking place. This <u>allegation</u> was at best dubious and at worst an outright fabrication.*

This capacity to encapsulate previous or ensuing text is a characteristic of many of the nouns listed above as being followed by lexicalising that-clauses. There are some nouns which are often followed by that-clauses but are not used as labels, and some nouns which are not typically followed by that-clauses but are used as labels, but there are a large number of nouns that do both. Arguably, we could identify a new class of noun based on these criteria.

7.2.4   Evaluative adjectives

We referred above to graded adjectives, pointing out that there are typical patterns associated with them, notably patterns using *than*. What we would like to suggest here is that there is a sub-set of graded adjectives which have a number of patterns of their own and are candidates for class-hood and that this class can be labelled 'evaluative adjectives'.

One pattern typically associated with evaluative adjectives begins with *there* and the verb *be*, and is followed by an indefinite pronoun — *something, anything, nothing* — then a graded adjective and finally a prepositional phrase beginning with *about* (Hunston and Sinclair 2000):

(28)   *There is something <u>oddly noble</u> about Charles.*

(29)   *I still think there's something <u>not quite</u> right about celebrities writing books.*

(30)   *There was something <u>alluring</u> about the idea of a great inland sea.*

(31)   *There is something <u>peculiarly exciting</u> about the arrival of a new company on the Stock Exchange.*

(32)   *There was nothing <u>malicious</u> about anything he did.*

(33)   *There was something <u>profoundly disturbing</u> about his pale, ghostlike face.*

(34)   *There was something <u>familiar</u> about his voice.*

(35)   *I began to think there must be something <u>very strange</u> about the way I was singing.*

(36)   *All available evidence suggests that there is nothing <u>abnormal</u> about the way fat people eat.*

(37)   *There was something <u>boyish</u> about her build and she was handsome in a hard-featured way.*

(38)   *Was there not also something <u>addictive</u> about his branch of the banking business?*

(39)   *There's something <u>very English</u> about the tradition of watercolour.*

(40)   *Mr Hannah insisted there was nothing <u>Machiavellian</u> about the control of information from the ship.*

All the adjectives in these examples are graded, but also qualify as being evaluative in some way — they evaluate the situation that follows them as being strange, abnormal etc. Notice that it is not usual to classify nationality adjectives like *English* as evaluative or even graded, but this serves to make a point about meaning and pattern. This pattern is so strongly associated with evaluative adjectives that as soon as it is used, the adjective within it is seen as evaluative.

Another adjective pattern involving evaluative adjectives is the pattern *it* followed by the verb *be* (or another link verb), followed by an adjective or adjective group, and a that-clause:

(41)   *It's <u>arguable</u> that Patrick and Sally's marriage could have been saved if he'd voiced his problems earlier.*

(42)   *Our correspondent says that it is <u>improbable</u> that the Prime Minister will be forced to resign.*

(43)   *I felt it was <u>logical</u> that I should finish my career with the club where it began.*

(44)   It's _reassuring_ that only seven per cent of you have had an accident in
         your home in the last two years.

(45)   It is _awful_ that it should end like this.

(46)   I sometimes think it's _so sad_ you and Patrick have no children of your
         own.

(47)   At home, it is sometimes _necessary_ that children have to share rooms.

(48)   It's _interesting_ that she's never asked what he looks like.

(49)   Isn't it _a bit odd_ that she lives with two husbands?

All the adjectives used in this group are evaluative. They fall into groups
according to their meaning (see Francis et al. 1998), but all the meanings
involved are within evaluative scales such as _good/bad, easy/difficult, proba-
ble/impossible_ and so on.

The same applies to the pattern _it_ + _be_ (or other link verb), adjective or
adjective group + to-infinitive clause:

(50)   Anita did not take much notice of the types of people present. It would
         be _more accurate_ to say that she did not see them.

(51)   If you are in a new country it is always _difficult_ to get work; people
         don't know you and you don't have contacts.

(52)   It would be _easy_ to lose heart, but to lose heart would serve no pur-
         pose, other than to ruin our lives.

(53)   It is always _a little dangerous_ to let a child loose in an action play-
         ground on his own while he is very young.

(54)   It's _more expensive_ to live alone and it can be very isolating.

(55)   I thought it was _best_ to announce my decision now.

(56)   When Japanese people visit friends, it's _customary_ to bring a gift.

(57)   It is _important_ to check the success of a university's graduates on the
         job market.

As seen in relation to the previous pattern, the effect of using the pattern is so
strong that the appearance of an adjective at this point is enough to identify it as
evaluative. Take this example:

(58)   In this climate of success-driven theatre, it is _shimmering_ to find work
         that reflects just passion.

The use of _shimmering_ is an unusual choice in this pattern, but it is interpretable simply because we have a mental stereotype of this *it* pattern and we know the common currency of evaluation from which it deviates. The pattern is basically a chunk of meaning, involving the co-selection of items in a predictable way. But this example shows the productivity of such patterns: we always have recourse to the paradigms of the possible as an alternative to relying on the syntagms of the typical.

All these patterns, and many more, are typically associated with evaluative adjectives. The point we have been making here is that all word-classes can be identified in terms of their patterns — we know for example what an evaluative adjective is by looking at its immediate environment. Word classes cannot be identified in isolation — their identification rests crucially on their context.

7.2.5 *Reciprocal adjectives and nouns*

We have long recognised reciprocal verbs as being a distinct class of verb, but some adjectives function in a similar way. Reciprocal adjectives are defined as follows in Francis et al. (1998: xv):

> A reciprocal adjective indicates that a feeling or situation applies to two or more people or things equally and reciprocally. When a reciprocal adjective is used in the pattern **v-link ADJ**, the Subject of the clause is normally a plural noun group, or another noun group that indicates two or more people or things. For example, *Tristram and Sophie are well-matched* indicates that Tristram is well-matched to Sophie and that Sophie is well-matched to Tristram, and *The jury was unanimous* indicates that all the members of the jury agreed with each other. Reciprocal adjectives may also have patterns with *to* or *with,* in which one person or thing is indicated by the Subject and the other person or thing is indicated by the noun group following the preposition, for example *Men need to learn to be intimate with their children.*

There are several adjectives which behave in this way:

agreed, alone, apart, betrothed, close, comparable, compatible, concurrent, congruent, deadlocked, different, divided, engaged, equal, friendly, identical, incompatible, inseparable, interchangeable, interdependent, interlaced, intimate, irreconcilable, locked, married, neck-and-neck, opposed, the same, similar, split, suited, synonymous, unanimous, unconnected, well-matched

It would also be possible to propose a class of reciprocal nouns, defined in Francis et al. (1998: xv) as follows:

> A reciprocal noun indicates that a feeling or situation applies to two or more people or things equally and reciprocally. A reciprocal noun is often used in

a prepositional phrase following a link verb. The Subject of the clause is normally a plural noun group. For example, *Belinda and Coral are at logger-heads* indicates that Belinda disagrees with Coral and that Coral disagrees with Belinda. Reciprocal nouns may also have patterns with *with*, in which one person or thing is indicated by the Subject and the other person or thing is indicated by the noun group following the preposition, for example *Insulin release is out of phase with blood sugar levels.*

Little work has been done on reciprocal nouns, but some of those identified in Francis et al. (1998) are:

at...with
cross-purposes, loggerheads, odds, variance, war

in...with
accord, agreement, alliance, cahoots, collusion, communication, competition, conference, conflict, consultation, contact, conversation, disagreement, dispute, harmony, league, negotiation, partnership, step, touch

in/out of...with
phase, sync

There may be other definable word-classes, or sub-categories of word-class other than those recognised in CCED and suggested here.

7.3 Some problematic word classes

Some word classes are particularly difficult to identify, and raise important questions as to the very nature of word class itself. Either we can say that each type of behaviour corresponds to one word-class, or that a word-class comprises words which have a cluster of behaviours. Nouns tend to be identified on the second principle, but we have already seen that this can create problems because there are nouns whose cluster of behaviour does not fit neatly into the categories N-COUNT, N-VAR etc.

This problem is particularly difficult in the case of function words. For example, the range of words which constitute the class 'determiner' also occur with different patterns. For example, *many* and *both* are followed by *of* and a noun group: *many of the children, both of the boys.* They also occur before a determiner: *many a time, both the boys.* Some determiners also function pronominally: *I want some, I liked both.*

A typical example is the word *all*, which occurs in the following types of sentence:

(59)   *There is built-in storage space in <u>all</u> bedrooms.*

(60)   *He felt betrayed by his mother, and this anger twisted <u>all</u> his later relationships.*

(61)   *He was told to pack up <u>all</u> of his letters and personal belongings.*

(62)   *As you'll have read in our news pages <u>all</u> has not been well of late.*

(63)   *He came over <u>all</u> dizzy as he stood up.*

There is a clear choice here. *All* may be said to be a member of a particular word-class in spite of the different ways in which it behaves, or it may be said that in each aspect of its behaviour it belongs to a different class.

In the first case, the result would be that a wide range of function words would be in a class of one, since they all have a different cluster of behaviours. For example, *all* and *both* share some patterns but not others; they are different in a variety of ways. In the second case, it would be necessary to propose a different word-class for each of the uses exemplified above. In the first example it is a determiner, in the second a predeterminer, in the third a quantifier, in the fourth a pronoun, and in the fifth an adverb. In the course of the compilation of CCED, then, we took that second option and came to the decision that *all* should not be seen as belonging to a single word class; instead it can be considered to belong to five different word-classes according to its behaviour. In many ways this is more satisfactory and certainly easier, since we do not have to say that *all* is 'basically' a determiner or anything else. The problem is that function words are being identified in a different way from the other word classes — nouns for example — where a cluster of behaviour determined a word-class.

The word *both* is another example. In the following examples it is a determiner, a quantifier, a pronoun, an emphatic pronoun, a predeterminer, and part of the co-ordinating conjunction *both...and.* (We use the term *emphatic pronoun* to refer to a pronoun used after a noun group for emphasis.)

(64)   *She cried out in fear and flung <u>both</u> arms up to protect her face.*

(65)   *<u>Both</u> of these women have strong memories of the Vietnam War.*

(66)   *Miss Brown and her friend, <u>both</u> from Stoke, were arrested on the 8th of June.*

(67)   *He visited the Institute of Neurology in Havana where they <u>both</u> worked.*

(68)   *<u>Both</u> the band's writers are fascinating lyricists.*

(69)   *Now women work <u>both</u> before and after having their children.*

What and other 'question words' are further examples of words which span a number of classes. In the following examples *what* is a question word, a subordinating conjunction (71 and 72), a determiner (73 and 74), a predeterminer, and an adverb.

(70)   *What are you doing?*

(71)   *He drinks what is left in his glass as if it were water.*

(72)   *What she does possess is the ability to get straight to the core of a problem.*

(73)   *They had to use what money they had.*

(74)   *What ugly things; throw them away.*

(75)   *What a horrible thing to do.*

(76)   *It's, what, eleven years or more since she's seen him.*

When is a question word, a subordinating conjunction, and a relative pronoun:

(78)   *When is the press conference?*

(79)   *Mustard is grown in the field when weeds are there.*

(80)   *He could remember a time when he had worked like that himself.*

Another area where this sort of problem arises is in the assigning of word classes to words which typically precede a noun and can therefore be seen to be either noun modifiers or adjectives. Take the word *key*. In CCED this has seven senses, six of which are nouns. The seventh, however, is an adjective, defined as follows: 'The **key** person or thing in a group is the most important one.' Examples are: *He is expected to be the key witness at the trial; Education is likely to be a key issue in the next election.* Here too different word-classes were assigned where the behaviour was different. In the case of a noun/adjective like *key*, the decision was that if in any of its various senses a word always precedes a noun, then it is an adjective. Again this is in keeping with the view that pattern should determine class.

A similar case is the word *dairy*. This has four senses, the first two being definitely nominal, referring to a company, shop, or building. The next two senses are adjectival. The first is '**Dairy** is used to refer to foods such as butter and cheeses that are made from milk' e.g.*dairy produce; vitamins found in eggs, meat, and dairy produce.* The second is '**Dairy** is used to refer to the use of cattle to produce milk rather than meat' e.g.*a small vegetable and dairy farm; the feeding of dairy cows.* Again, it could be argued that *dairy*, here, is a noun used as a modifier. Again, however, we have decided that since in these two senses

it always comes before a noun, then it is an adjective. There are a large number
of nouns which have adjectival senses; a few of them are:

satellite (TV)
armchair (critic, traveller)
world (statesman, power)
embryo (idea, party)
mercy (mission)
iron (hand, discipline)
vintage (wine)

7.4 Words without classes

Finally, there are some words which seem to defy classification altogether. A
notable one is *worth*. It is interesting to see that even Quirk et al. (1985) have
trouble with this word. *Worth* is defined as a 'marginal preposition' in sentences
like *Two gold-hilted swords, each <u>worth</u> 10,000, were sold at Sotheby's last
Monday* (1985: 667). They also say "The prepositional status of *worth* is confirmed by the fact that it can govern a noun phrase, a nominal *-ing* clause with
a genitive subject, and a nominal relative clause (but not a *that*-clause or a
to-infinitive clause):
> *San Francisco is worth frequent visits / your visiting frequently.*
> *The bicycle is not worth what you paid for it.*" (p. 1064)
Later, however, (p. 1230) *worth* is treated as an adjective in a section concerned
with adjective complementation, in the sentence *It is scarcely <u>worth</u>(while) you /
your going home.*
 Here are some examples of how *worth* is used:

Before a noun, pronoun, or amount:

```
ut Rennes is still well worth a visit to see its Palais de Just
aders to a cash jackpot worth about $350. Entry costs a little
ed-up guys'. But it was worth it. His letters, like his poetry,
e ragged and it will be worth nothing. At the moment it is very
seems to think it'll be worth our while, but he's so damn crypti
ounds that they are now worth rather less than when they were va
he battle is simply not worth so much effort. In that case, perh
saying. You got it. Not worth the trouble. We ever had a hassle
he certificates are not worth the paper they are written on. The
 'People with ideas are worth their weight in gold,' he sums up.
```

Before an -ing clause:

```
't know whether it's worth bothering on the phone about. You e
 was something there worth discussing, Baker suggested, erta
ase stop, she is not worth going to prison for. We have alrea
```

```
estments, then it is worth looking outside the UK. Take umbr
urage sex. It may be worth noting that the Puritans approved
he possibilities are worth pursuing. Our choice falls on him
nting ban, but it is worth remembering the problems that the
d foolproof and well worth risking in daylight, Walker caugh
t for a living. It's worth seeing if only for the special ef
 delights, it may be worth trying to cheat the tide at the R
```

Before a prepositional phrase introduced by *of*:

```
search and 12 million worth of engineering, the space shuttle
seven-million pounds' worth of gold recovered from HMS Edinbu
f a quarter-century's worth of songs; they take a delight in
to provide a dollar's worth of coverage. And America's Medic
on about $200 million worth of dual-use equipment, including
```

In the first two groups above, *worth* is functioning very much like a preposition, coming before a noun and an '-ing' clause respectively. Here pattern and meaning are at odds, however, as *worth* has an adjective-like meaning in spite of its preposition-like behaviour. In CCED we unusually did not assign a class to the first two uses, and got round the problem by putting *worth* in the grammar column to indicate that we consider it to be a class of one. In the case of its use in the third set above, we called this a COMB IN QUANT; that is, it combines with amounts of money or time (plus the possessive) to mean the quantity of something that you can buy for that amount, or the length of time that something lasts. Here the whole phrase is functioning like a quantifier such as *most of* or *all of*. In this use it can also be a pronoun: *How many do you want? I'll have a pound's worth* and *There's really not much food down there. About two weeks' worth*.

Quirk et al. (p. 667) identify a number of other 'marginal prepositions' with verbal affinities: *bar, barring, excepting, excluding, save, concerning, considering, regarding, respecting, touching, failing, wanting, following, pending, given, granted, including*. These are generally easier to classify than *worth*; with some misgivings they were labelled as prepositions in CCED.

Another word that seems to defy classification is *such*. There is no problem with the determiner or predeterminer use:

(81)　*We regard such methods as entirely unacceptable*

(82)　*We could not believe such a thing.*

But expressions like *such as* and *as such* resist classification entirely. So does *such* in examples like this:

(83)　*Such is the mood in Congress that it could muster the two-thirds support required to override the certain veto from Bill Clinton.*

It is also difficult to classify in sentences like

(84)   *Children do not use inflections <u>such</u> as are used in mature adult speech* and

(85)   *His confessions to the two killings did reveal special knowledge <u>such</u> as could only have been known by the killer.*

The only class that could conceivably be used here is adverb; but *such* in the above examples does not behave like any other adverb, and there is a danger of making adverbs a rag-bag category into which all troublesome words are thrown.

7.5 Are word classes necessary?

It is clear that words do not 'have' classes as something intrinsic to them. Instead we create classes for them, based on their behaviour. Sometimes we fail to allocate them to classes at all, as in the case of *worth* and *such* above. If, as we have argued, word class is determined by pattern, then in theory it should be possible to describe patterns without recourse to pre-determined word classes. The notion of class is just a convenient short-hand: it is easier to say that a word is a count noun than to say it is preceded by *a* or *some* and or by other 'open-set' words which typically occur at that position in a pattern. Similarly, the words that typically precede it could be described in terms of their patterns rather than put into the class of adjectives. Although such a description is possible it would be cumbersome in practice. The point of word class nomenclature is to accord a label to words which behave in the same way: we know that *cat* and *dog, blood* and *assistance, injustice* and *atrocity, fuel* and *metal* have the same behaviour and therefore can be said to 'belong to' the same class.

So word-classes are necessary in order to make sense of the huge range of behaviour that words have. The basic problem, as mentioned above, is to create the right number of classes: too few mean that some words fit badly into a class, as in the case of some nouns, and too many would lead to the situation where the map tends to be as large as the area of land it represents.

CHAPTER 8

Text and Pattern

8.1 Patterns in running text

The focus in this chapter is on continuous text, rather than on concordance lines. We ask what a grammatical analysis of the text using patterns would look like and, in Section 8.5 below, we ask what such an analysis can show about the text it analyses.

The first text is short, reasonably self-contained, and not unusual in terms of vocabulary. The text, reproduced below, is a brief account of a soldier who was executed for desertion during the First World War. It was printed in The Guardian (28th May 1997) as part of a story about calls to have men such as this posthumously pardoned. The sentences have been numbered for convenience.

(1)   *The 'Joseph Byers' text*

[1]Private Joseph Byers was the first Kitchener volunteer to be executed. [2]He was 17 and under age when he enlisted in the 1st Royal Scots Fusiliers in November 1914, and was sent to France with two weeks training. [3]By January 1915, his inexperience and the horrors he witnessed caused him to go absent without leave with another private, Andrew Evans. [4]Byers pleaded guilty, believing his candour would save him from the death sentence. [5]Despite being under age, he was given no representation at his trial and he and Evans faced a firing squad at Locre on February 6.

[6]According to rumours, one of them did not die until the third volley, leading to speculation that the firing squad had fired wide to avoid killing the youth.

The patterns in this text include (numbers refer to sentences in the text):

[1] The ordinal *first* occurs in a pattern with a to-infinitive ***the* ORD n to-inf**: *the first Kitchener volunteer to be executed;*

[2] The verb *enlist* occurs in the pattern **V *in* n**: *enlisted in the 1st Royal Scots Fusiliers;*

[2] The verb *send* occurs in the pattern ***be* V-ed *to* n** (the passive of **V n *to* n**): *was sent to France*;

[3] The verb *cause* occurs in the pattern **V n to-inf**: *caused him to go absent without leave*;

[4] The verb *plead* occurs in the pattern **V adj**: *pleaded guilty*;

[4] The verb *save* occurs in the pattern **V n *from* n**: *would save him from the death sentence*;

[5] The verb *give* occurs in the pattern ***be* V-ed n** (the passive of **V n n**): *was given no representation*;

[6] The verb *lead* occurs in the pattern **V *to* n**: *leading to speculation that the firing squad had fired wide to avoid killing the youth*;

[6] The noun *speculation* occurs in the pattern **N that**: *speculation that the firing squad had fired wide to avoid killing the youth*;

[6] The verb *fire* occurs in the pattern **V adj**: *fired wide*;

[6] The verb *avoid* occurs in the pattern **V -ing**: *avoid killing the youth*.

In addition to these, there are several more mundane verb patterns used in the text, mainly **V n**. These are listed below, again in sentence order.

[1] The verb *be* occurs in the pattern **V n**: *was the first Kitchener volunteer to be executed*;

[1] The verb *execute* occurs in the pattern ***be* V-ed** (the passive of **V n**): *be executed*;

[2] The verb *be* occurs twice in the pattern **V adj**: *was 17 and under age*;

[3] The verb *witness* occurs in the pattern **V n**, but the verb group is in a relative clause modifying the noun group (see Chapter 2 for 'different forms of the pattern'): *the horrors he witnessed*;

[3]The verb *go* occurs in the pattern **V adj**: *go absent without leave*;

[4] The verb *believe* occurs in the pattern **V that**, though on this occasion the that-clause does not begin with *that*: *believing his candour would save him from the death sentence*;

[5] The verb *be* occurs in the pattern **V adj**: *being under age*;

[5] The verb *face* occurs in the pattern **V n**: *faced a firing squad*;

[6] The verb *die* occurs in the pattern **V**: *did not die*;

[6] The verb *kill* occurs in the pattern **V n**: *killing the youth*.

Analysing the second sentence of the text, for example, in terms of these patterns, gives the analysis shown in Table 8.1.

Table 8.1

	V	**adj**	**+**	**adj**
He	*was*	*17*	*and*	*under age*

	V	***in***	**n**	
when he	*enlisted*	*in*	*the 1ˢᵗ Royal Scots Fusiliers in November 1914*	

	***be* V-ed**	***to***	**n**	
and	*was sent*	*to*	*France*	*with two weeks training.*

In this representation of the analysis parts of the sentence that do not form part of a pattern (*in November 1914* etc.) are not labelled.

As was discussed in Chapter 2, however, a pattern may be represented as 'belonging to' the lexical item that constitutes any one of the elements in it. The point of this may be illustrated by sentence 1 of the text. The verb *be* has the pattern **V n**, but the noun group itself is patterned according to one of the typical uses of an ordinal such as *first*: ***the* ORD n to-inf**. In addition, the verb *execute* has its own pattern. The representation of this needs several layers, as Table 8.2 shows.

Table 8.2

	V	**n**				
		the	**ORD**	**n**	**to-inf**	
						***be* V-ed**
Pte Joseph Byers	*was*	*the*	*first*	*Kitchener volunteer to*		*be executed*

This analysis is in essence no different from any grammatical analysis, in that it analyses in turn each component of the larger components. We can, however, take this principle further. Consider sentence 4 from the text:

[4]*Byers pleaded guilty, believing his candour would save him from the death sentence.*

This has already been discussed in terms of the patterns of *plead, believe* and *save*. In addition, the adjective *guilty* occurs after a verb that is not a link verb,

in the pattern **ADJ after v**; the noun group *death sentence* is treated in the
Collins COBUILD English Dictionary as a single lexical item, but we might also
describe this as the noun *sentence* with the pattern **n N**. The noun *candour*, like
most nouns, sometimes occurs after a possessive determiner, as it does here (in
the pattern **poss N**). The determiners *his* and *the*, like all determiners, are
positioned at the beginning of a noun group and are therefore followed by a
noun, in the pattern **DET n**. The pronoun *him* is what is traditionally known as
an 'object pronoun', that is, it occurs after rather than before a verb, in the
pattern **v PRON**. The modal *would*, like all modals, occurs before the bare
infinitive form of a verb, in the pattern **MODAL inf**. The preposition *from*, like
all prepositions, occurs before a noun group, in the pattern **PREP n**. An analysis
which showed all this information would look quite complex. Table 8.3 is an
attempt to represent it.

Table 8.3

			V				**adj**			
			v				**ADJ**			
Byers			*pleaded*				*guilty*			
V					**that**					
			V	**n**	*from*			**n**		
					PREP			**n**		
	poss	**N**	**v**	**PRON**			**n**	**N**		
	DET	**n**	**MODAL**	**inf**			**DET**	**n**		
believing	*his*	*candour*	*would*	*save*	*him*	*from*	*the*	*death*	*sentence.*	

It should be noted that here we are using the word 'pattern' in two different ways:

1. Firstly, we are using it to indicate a sequence of elements that occur with
(usually after) a particular lexical item in this text, which typically occur with
this lexical item, and whose occurrence goes some way to distinguishing this
lexical item from others. For example, the verb *plead* occurs in this text with the
pattern **V adj**; this is a typical use of this verb which distinguishes it from other
verbs such as *claim* or *say*.

2. Secondly, we are using it to indicate the behaviour of words that is typical of
their word class (see Chapter 7). For example, *would* has the pattern **MODAL**

inf simply because it belongs to the word-class 'modal', and *from* has the pattern **PREP n** because that is a pattern that all prepositions have.

In addition, we use the word 'pattern' in a third way, though there is no example in sentence 4:

3. Thirdly, we use it to indicate a sequence of elements that occur with a particular lexical item in this text, whether or not such a sequence is typical. For example, we show the verb *fire* (sentence 6) with the pattern **V adj**, even though that pattern is productive, is not particularly frequent with this verb, and does not distinguish this verb from others. This decision not to be limited to the typical in our analysis allows us to identify patterns in a particular text that are unusual with a particular lexical item.

To return to the analysis of sentence 4, it is clear that such a comprehensive analysis is of little use, other than to make the point that every lexical item used in a text occurs in a pattern, and to allow the further observation that most patterning is typical. In general, though, more would be learnt about the text if the analysis were restricted to those patterns that distinguish one lexical item from another. (It must be emphasised that this restriction is purely pragmatic and does not reflect a theoretical distinction between patterns.) Patterns such as **V n from n** (*save him from the death sentence*) would be included, but patterns such as **DET n** (*his candour*) would be excluded. Behaviours that are typical of a sub-group of word-class would also be excluded. For example, the pattern **v PRON** does not occur with every pronoun, but it does occur with every 'object pronoun'. We would, however, include patterns which, even though they are associated with a word class, comprise a number of elements and so play a major role in organising the sentence. For example, even though all ordinals have the pattern *the* **ORD n to-inf**, we would include the pattern because it is interesting in itself.

Following these pragmatic guidelines, a complete list of the lexical items in the 'Joseph Byers' text that have patterns which will be represented in our analysis is as follows:

[1] *was; first; executed*
[2] *was; 17; under age; enlisted; was sent*
[3] *witnessed; caused; go; absent*
[4] *pleaded; guilty; believing; would save; sentence*
[5] *being; under age; was given; faced*
[6] *did not die; leading; speculation; had fired; wide; avoid; killing*

Table 8.4 shows an analysis of the 'Joseph Byers' text.

Table 8.4

Sentence 1

	V	n				
		the	ORD	n		to-inf
						be V-ed
Pte Joseph Byers	was	the	first	Kitchener volunteer	to	be executed.

Sentence 2

	V	adj	+	adj
	v-link	ADJ		
	v-link			ADJ
He	was	17	and	under age

		V	*in*	n	
when	he	enlisted	in	the 1st Royal Scots Fusiliers	in November 1914

	be V-ed	*to*	n	
and	was sent	to	France	with two weeks training.

Sentence 3

		n		V
By January 1915	his inexperience and	the horrors	he	witnessed

V	n	to-inf	
		V	adj
		v-link	ADJ
caused	him	to go	absent without leave	with another private, Andrew Evans.

Sentence 4

	V	adj
	v	ADJ
Byers	pleaded	guilty

V	that					
		V	n	from	n	
					n	N
believing	his candour	would save	him	from	the death	sentence.

Sentence 5

	V	adj
	v-link	ADJ
Despite	being	under age

	be V-ed	n	
he	was given	no representation	at the trial

+		V	n	
and	he and Evans	faced	a firing squad	at Locre on February 6.

Sentence 6

		V	
According to rumours	one of them	did not die	until the third volley

V	to	n	
		N	that
leading	to	speculation	that...

(…n)					
(…that)					
	V	adj			
	v	ADJ			
			V	-ing	
				V	n
...the firing squad	had fired	wide	to avoid	killing	the youth.

A notable feature of this type of analysis is that although it deals with traditional clause and group structure, it prioritises the lexical choices made in the text, seeing the structures or patterns as dependent on the lexical choices. For example, in sentence 3, the occurrence of the pattern **V n to-inf** is dependent on the choice of *cause* as the verb. The analysis enables us to see how much of the text is dependent on these choices. The empty boxes in the analysis (e.g.*in November 1914* in sentence 2, *By January 1915* in sentence 3) show groups and phrases that are not dependent on other lexical items. This includes clause Subjects such as *Private Joseph Byers* in sentence 1. In some parts of the text, there is very low dependency. For example, in the first clause in sentence 6 (*According to rumours, one of them did not die until the third volley*), no part of that clause is dependent on any other part (though we will discuss this clause again below). On the other hand, the second clause in sentence 6 (*leading to speculation that the firing squad had fired wide to avoid killing the youth*) shows a very high degree of dependency. Taking the text as a whole there are relatively few empty boxes, suggesting that a great deal of it is dependent on lexical choices and the patterning of specific lexical items.

What this analysis omits is collocation, although it is quite possible to take this into account. Returning to the first clause of sentence 6 —

(2)   *According to rumours one of them did not die until the third volley*

— which, as argued above, shows very little lexical dependency, it is possible to show that *according to rumours* counts as a significant collocation. In the 300 million word Bank of English, *according to rumour(s)* occurs 20 times. Taking *rumour(s)* as the node, the occurrence of *according to* in the Bank of English has a t-score significance of 4.1132. Furthermore, if we consider only those instances of *rumour(s)* that occur in a prepositional phrase or a clause that realises the Adjunct of a clause, as happens in sentence 6, there are 139 occurrences, comprising only the phrases *according to* and *contrary to* and clauses of the type *as rumour has it*. Thus, *according to rumours* is a more-or-less fixed phraseology.

Now consider the verb group *did not die*, which occurs 162 times in the Bank of English, 5 of them followed by *until*. This is not in itself a high frequency, but *until* is the eighth most significant word occurring immediately to the right of *did not die*, with a t-score significance of 2.2070. If we consider only those instances where *did not die* is followed by an indication of time, there are around one dozen occurrences, almost half of these comprising a clause or phrase beginning with *until*.

In short, we can show that those parts of the text that show little pattern dependency do depend to a large extent on the co-occurrence of significant collocations. Sinclair's (1991) concept of 'the idiom principle' would include both our notion of pattern and the collocational co-occurrences mentioned here.

In many ways, of course, our analysis is similar to any constituent analysis. In our analysis of sentence 1, for example, first, by implication, the clause is analysed (Subject — Verb — Complement), then the noun group that realises the Complement is analysed (pre-modifiers — head — post-modifiers), finally the embedded to-infinitive clause is analysed. Our analysis, like any constituent analysis, can be used to demonstrate the degree of complexity in the text. The analysis of sentence 1 shows a degree of layering (or embedding) that is missing from the subordinate clause (*when...*) in sentence 2, for instance. The analysis of sentence 1 comprises three lines, while the analysis of the subordinate clause in sentence 2 comprises only one line. This difference occurs because the noun group *the first Kitchener volunteer to be executed* is more complex than the noun groups *the 1st Royal Scots Fusiliers* and *France*. However, in other cases, the increased number of layers of analysis is caused by the fact that a pattern must be seen from the point of view of two lexical items, something that would not happen in a traditional constituent analysis. For example, in the first clause in sentence 2 (*He was 17 and under age*), three lines of analysis are necessitated by the fact that three items (*was, 17* and *under age*) have patterns. Clearly, the two kinds of complexity must be distinguished, and this is done in the following section (8.2). The analysis shows complexity in another way also. In the first clause of sentence 4 (*Byers pleaded guilty*) for example, only three columns are needed to show the analysis. In the second clause of the same sentence, seven columns are needed. This is partly explained by the degree of embedding, but a second cause is the number of elements in the pattern **V n** *from* **n**.

Before we continue this discussion of complexity and how an analysis may represent it, we shall consider an alternative way of representing a pattern analysis, which we call 'pattern flow'.

8.2 Pattern flow

8.2.1 *Patterns as linear grammar*

In the analysis of the 'Joseph Byers' text above, each element of each pattern was treated as a self-contained component. Each component was then, if appropriate, further analysed. For example, the first sentence of the text —

(3) *Private Joseph Byers was the first Kitchener volunteer to be executed.*

— was analysed first as an utterance whose pattern was dependent on the verb *was*. This analysis was precisely compatible with a view of the sentence as a clause comprising Subject — Verb — Complement. The to-infinitive clause (*to be executed*) was treated as part of the noun group realising the Complement. Thus the constituent analysis is consistent with, though not identical to, most traditional approaches to grammar, which treat sentences and clauses as finished products to be divided into constituent parts.

Some recent approaches to grammar, however, prefer to treat utterances as examples of process rather than of product. Brazil (1995), for example, proposes a grammar of spoken English which is linear rather than hierarchical. Comparing his approach with that of immediate constituent analysts (who commonly use brackets or tree diagrams to display their analyses), he comments:

> When analysing a piece of language we can, if we wish, assume — and most often grammarians *do* assume — that the object we are analysing already exists in its entirety. ... To insert brackets or draw the tree diagram, one needs to have everything there in place beforehand. ... What we [propose] in this book is something different. ... We are trying to think of discourse as something that is now-happening, bit by bit, in time, with the language being assembled as the speaker goes along. This means that we can no longer use the essentially static concept of 'constituent structure', because the function of one structure with the organization of larger structures can be explored only if everything is present simultaneously. (Brazil 1995: 37–38)

A constituent analysis preserves the integrity of the clauses and groups that comprise the sentence. However, it fails to represent how the sentence is written, or how the utterance is spoken. The speaking or writing process does not follow the analysis line by line, progressively 'filling in' each constituent with more detail. If we consider utterances (written or spoken) as a process, that is, something occurring word by word, we need a different analysis. This would have to draw, as Brazil does, upon the notion of 'prospection' (Sinclair 1995), and interpret a pattern as something prospected by the selection of a particular lexical item. Each word that has a pattern might be said to prospect the elements of that pattern. A speaker or writer fulfills that prospection and in doing so may use another patterned word which sets up new prospections to be filled, and so on.

A linear grammar would treat the first sentence of the 'Joseph Byers' text in this way. Selection of *be* prospects a noun, because one of the possible patterns belonging to *be* is **V n**. *Be* therefore prospects *volunteer*. On the way to the fulfilment of the prospection, however, the ordinal *first* occurs. The ordinal prospects, among other possibilities, a noun and a to-infinitive. The verb *be executed* does not prospect anything more, because the requirements of the pattern **V n**, in the passive, have been met.

8.2.2   *Representing patterns linearly*

To continue the discussion of patterns as linear grammar, let us consider another written text, this one from a letter written to a newspaper (The Guardian, 28.5.97).

(4)   *The 'Young MPs' text*

[1]Christopher Leslie is wrong to say that he is the youngest MP since Bernadette Devlin. [2]I was elected as a Liberal Democrat in 1987 at 24; [3]my colleague, Charles Kennedy, was 23 when he was elected in 1983. [4]I held the title of 'Baby of the House' for over 10 years (a record, at least this century).

[5]The Commons needs more young people in it — though it is not always a particularly pleasant experience. [6]Many MPs are patronising, the hours make a normal life for any twentysomething impossible, and Parliament is both undemocratic and a poor overseer of government.

[7]On the other hand, if you know what you believe in, and use your position to campaign for change, being the youngest MP can be rewarding and sometimes even fun.

Taking a hierarchical, constituent view of grammar, the first sentence of this letter can be analysed as in Table 8.5.

Table 8.5

	V		adj			
	v-link	ADJ	to-inf			
		V	that			
			V	n		
				the **ADJ-SUPERL**	n	*since* n
Chris... Leslie	*is*	*wrong*	*to say*	*that he is*	*the youngest*	*MP*	*since Bern... Devlin.*

This analysis shows the following patterns:

a. **V adj**: The verb *be* is followed by an adjective group *wrong to say that he is the youngest MP since Bernadette Devlin.*
b. **v-link ADJ to-inf**: The adjective *wrong* follows a link verb and is followed by a to-infinitive clause *to say that he is the youngest MP since Bernadette Devlin.*

c. **V that**: The verb *say* is followed by a that-clause *that he is the youngest MP since Bernadette Devlin.*

d. **V n**: The verb *be* is followed by a noun group *the youngest MP since Bernadette Devlin.*

e. *the* **ADJ-SUPERL n** *since* **n**: The superlative adjective *youngest* follows *the* and is followed by a noun group *MP*, the preposition *since* and a noun group *Bernadette Devlin.*

A linear representation of the same patterns might look like Table 8.6.

Table 8.6

Christopher Leslie is wrong	
V.. adj	
wrong to say	
ADJ...to-inf	
say that he is	
V...that	
is the youngest MP	
V.................n	
the youngest MP since B. Devlin	
the ADJ-SUPERL..n....since....n	

Or like Table 8.7.

Table 8.7

Chris Leslie is wrong to say that he is the youngest	*MP since*	*Bernadette Devlin*
V.adj		
ADJ...to-inf		
V...that		
V.........................n		
the ADJ-SUPERL...n... *since*...n		

Each representation is an attempt to show how each lexical item sets up its own prospections, so that the patterns flow from one lexical item to the next. It is important to recognise, however, that representing the analysis in a linear manner implies a more radical reinterpretation than at first glance appears to be the case. In the constituent analysis, **V adj** meant 'verb followed by (the whole of) an adjective group' and **ADJ to-inf** meant 'adjective followed by (the whole of) a to-infinitive clause'. **V n** meant 'verb followed by (the whole of) a noun group' and **V that** meant 'verb followed by (the whole of) a that-clause'.

In the linear analysis, however, **V adj** means 'verb followed by (anything up to and including) an adjective', and **ADJ to-inf** means 'adjective followed by (anything up to and including) the to-infinitive form of a verb'. **V n** means 'verb followed by (anything up to and including) a noun'. **V that** means 'verb followed by the start of a new clause, or by *that* and the start of a new clause'. In other words, the prospection of the pattern ends (is fulfilled) as soon as the minimum requirement of the pattern has been met, that is, as soon as an adjective, a to-infinitive verb, a noun, or a new clause has occurred. It is irrelevant where the group or clause of which that adjective, verb or noun is a part comes to an end. This is consistent with a point that Sinclair has made (personal communication) that the beginnings of units are important, but the ends are not.

8.2.3 *Pattern flow*

For some sentences, a hierarchical and a linear analysis will not be very different. One example is this part of sentence 5 of the 'Young MPs' text:

(5)   *The Commons needs more young people in it*

The verb pattern here is **V n prep**. We can interpret **V n prep** as 'verb followed by (the whole of) a noun group followed by (the whole of) a prepositional phrase', in which case the analysis looks like Table 8.8.

Table 8.8

	V	n	prep
The Commons	*needs*	*more young people*	*in it.*

Alternatively, we can interpret it as 'verb followed by (anything up to and including) a noun, followed by a preposition, followed by (anything up to and including) a noun'. In this case, the analysis looks like Table 8.9, and is not very different from that in Table 8.8.

Table 8.9

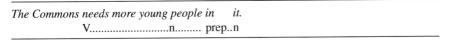

The first sentences of both the 'Joseph Byers' text and the 'Young MPs' text, however, look very different in the two analyses, as has been shown above. This is because both sentences demonstrate a phenomenon that we call 'pattern flow'. Pattern flow occurs whenever a word that occurs as part of the pattern of another word has a pattern of its own. The advantage of a linear representation of a pattern analysis is that it shows pattern flow as flow, rather than disguising it as constituent analysis.

Pattern flow is an extremely common phenomenon and can be found in all kinds of speech and writing. It is not restricted to any one mode or genre, though we will discuss below whether it is likely to be more commonly found in some genres than others. First, here are some more examples of pattern flow, taken from a range of sources.

First, some examples from spoken English. The first is part of a recording of a telephone call to a Local Government office from a member of the public (from the Bank of English corpus). The pattern words are *want, ensure* and *send*. The utterance and its analysis are shown in Table 8.10.

Table 8.10

I wanted to ensure that you could send me a university award form.
  V......... to-inf
       V.. ..... that
                   V.... n................................. n

---

The next example (Table 8.11) is from Brazil's transcription of a story being re-told by an actor Brazil 1995: 25). The pattern words are *be, good* and *sort*.

Table 8.11

I'm not very good at this sort of   thing
  V.............. adj
         ADJ. *at*....... n
              N....*of*... n

Next, some examples from a novel: *Eureka Street* by Robert McLiam Wilson (QPD edition, pp 107, 178, 181), shown in Table 8.12.

Table 8.12a

I'd made her feel bad   that I wasn't getting my feet under her table that night.
  V...... n....inf
       V... adj
           ADJ.. that

Table 8.12b

Slat had asked the poet whether it was entirely nice   to kill soldiers
V..............n..... wh
it.v.................. ADJ...to-inf
V... n

Table 8.12c

Don't you prefer your dates to at least look like they might have had some hair once?
V...,,...........n............. to-inf.........
V.....like
V............. n

The next example is from a published diary: *Writing Home* by the playwright Alan Bennett (QPD edition p189). Here is the whole sentence:

(6)   *Then I realize, absurdly, that what made me think of him as somehow more sensitive, a creature of conviction, even, was that little knot of hair at the back.*

To simplify layout, only part of the sentence is analysed, in Table 8.13. The pattern words are *realise, made, think* and *knot*, and there is also a pattern with *what*, normally described as a pseudo-cleft sentence.

Table 8.13

Then I realize that what made me think of him as more sensitive was that knot of hair.
V.........that
what.v.. *be*.......... n
V...... n... inf
V......*of*.n.....*as*..........adj
N.....*of*.n

Next, some examples from academic books. The first is from Janet Holmes, Women Men and Politeness (1996:68). The pattern words are *be, concerned, easy, see, tend* and *talk*. The sentences and its analysis are shown in Table 8.14.

Table 8.14

If women are concerned with solidarity and connection,
    V... adj
       ADJ..........*with*.n
it is easy to see why they tend to talk least in formal and public contexts...
it.v..ADJ.to-inf
    V... wh
          V.....to-inf
         V

The next example (in Table 8.15) is from Michael Stubbs' *Text and Corpus Analysis* (1996: 129). The pattern words are *focus, methods* and *analysing.*

Table 8.15

The main focus in this chapter is on   methods of analysing long texts.
    N............................ *be.on*...n
              N........... *of.*-ing
                  V..................... n

The final example comes from a film review in the Birmingham listings magazine *What's On* (31 May-13 June 1997, p. 7). The whole sentence is quoted here:

(7)   *People familiar with Ballard's novel may be surprised, and perhaps a little disturbed, to discover that, whereas the author, at least at the time, described it as a 'cautionary' tale, Cronenberg sees the perverse possibilities that it opens up as ones that might be embraced in a more positive way.*

In the analysis shown in Table 8.16, a few parts of the sentence have been omitted for clarity of layout. The pattern words are *familiar, be, surprised, discover, describe, see* and *embrace.*

Table 8.16

People familiar with Ballard's novel may be surprised to discover that
  ADJ...... *with*................n   V. adj
                                    ADJ........ to-inf
                                                  V.......... that

whereas the author described it as a cautionary tale
        V............. n.*as*.....................n

Cr. sees the possibilities as ones that might be embraced in a more positive way.
      V......... n..................*as*.n
                                    be V-ed

These examples show that pattern flow is not restricted to spoken or to written English, or to formal or informal genres. Such random examples, however, do not indicate what the relative frequency of the phenomenon in different genres might be. This will be considered in the next section.

8.3 Pattern configurations

It has been established that naturally-occurring discourse, written or spoken, occurs as a sequence of patterns. In the previous section it was argued that one way that these patterns may follow on from each other is by overlapping, a phenomenon that we called 'pattern flow'. Pattern flow is one possible configuration of pattern and text. If patterns do not overlap, a different configuration occurs, which we will call 'pattern strings'. To illustrate these two configurations, here is another text, a letter to the Guardian newspaper (11th June 1997). In this text, the start of each pattern is indicated by a number.

(8)   *The 'Space Agency' Text*

       While the European Space Agency and NASA [1]are spending public money on [2]trips to Mars [3]to look for [4]evidence of life, [5]much of [6]the rest of the ...scientific community [7]is struggling for funds. [8]I only wish that [9]I could persuade the research funding bodies to [10]divert [11]billions of pounds [12]to fund our research [13]on the strength of such tenuous evidence.

The patterns are as follows:

[1] *spend*: **V n *on* n**

[2] *trips*: **N prep**
[3] *look*: **V** *for* **n**
[4] *evidence*: **N** *of* **n**
[5] *much*: **QUANT** *of* **def-n**
[6] *the rest*: **QUANT** *of* **def-n**
[7] *is struggling*: **V** *for* **n**
[8] *wish*: **V that**
[9] *persuade*: **V n to-inf**
[10] *divert*: **V n**
[11] *billions*: **QUANT** *of* **pl-n**
[12] *fund*: **V n**
[13] *on the strength of*: **PHR n**

Notes: **QUANT** = quantifier
      def-n = definite noun group, beginning with a definite article
      PHR = phrase (treated as such in the Collins COBUILD English Dictionary)

A linear analysis of the text, based on these patterns, looks like Table 8.17.

Table 8.17

While the ESA and NASA are spending public money on trips to   Mars
          [1]   V...................... n.........*on*.n
                         [2] N..... prep..n

to look for evidence of life
[3] V.... *for*.n
      [4] N............*of*.n

    much   *of the rest*   *of the scientific community is struggling for funds*
[5] QUANT...*of*.def-n
        [6] QUANT...*of*...................... n
                    [7] V................ *for*.n

I only wish that I could persuade the res... funding bodies to divert billions of pounds
    [8] V..... that
          [9] V...................................... n.........to-inf
                 [10] V........................... n
                       [11] QUANT.*of*...pl-n

to fund our research
[12] V........... n

on the strength of such tenuous evidence
[13] PHR.................................n

The following patterns are related by a flow configuration (where the beginning of one pattern overlaps with part of another pattern):

[1] — [2]
[3] — [4]
[5] — [6]
[8] — [9]
[9] — [10]

The following are related by a string configuration (where there is no such overlap):

[2] — [3]
[4] — [5]
[6] — [7]
[11] — [12]
[12] — [13]

Patterns [10] and [11] are related in a different way again. The prospection that is set up by the verb *divert*, based on the pattern **V n**, is not fulfilled until the noun *pounds* is met. Before that prospection is met, there is another pattern with the quantifier *billions*. There are two possible ways of dealing with this. One is to treat it as another pattern-text configuration. The other way would be to argue that as the pattern **QUANT** *of* **n** is a normal pattern for the word it can be ignored, in the same way that patterns of determiners and so on are ignored (see Section 8.1 above). However, when the quantifier patterns come first in the clause, as in *much of the rest of the scientific community is struggling for funds*, it seems helpful to include it as a pattern. A possible solution would be to include quantifier patterns when the noun that they modify is not prospected by another pattern (as in *much of the rest of the scientific community*) but not when the noun that they modify is prospected by another pattern (as in *divert billions of pounds*). In this case, then, we shall ignore pattern [11].

Another part of this text which deserves further discussion is the pattern **V that** (*I only wish that I could persuade...*). We have included this above in the list of pattern sequences that have a flow configuration. This implies that we interpret the prospection of the pattern **V that** as fulfilled only when the verb in the that-clause has been met. If it were argued that the prospection has been met as soon as the clause has begun, that is, when the word *that* occurs, or when the noun that is the subject of the clause occurs, then we would have to interpret this configuration as the string type. To do so would be to treat the word *that* as something like a conjunction and to treat a verb followed by a that-clause without *that* as two clauses in apposition. At the moment, this is a matter of opinion. Whatever the argument, the same would apply to wh-clauses and to 'quote' clauses.

It is difficult to represent both pattern flow and pattern strings in a single diagram, partly because a whole sentence must be shown on a single line, partly because it is not easy to show the difference between flow and string diagrammatically. Table 8.18 is an attempt to show the two sentences of the 'Space Agency' text, somewhat shortened, with patterns in the flow configuration shown overlapping, and patterns in the string configuration shown with vertical lines between them.

Table 8.18

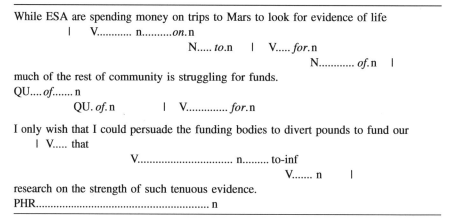

While ESA are spending money on trips to Mars to look for evidence of life
   | V............ n..........*on*. n
                              N..... *to*.n | V..... *for*.n
                                        N............ *of*. n |
much of the rest of community is struggling for funds.
QU.... *of*....... n
        QU. *of*. n | V.............. *for*.n
I only wish that I could persuade the funding bodies to divert pounds to fund our
   | V..... that
                        V.............................. n......... to-inf
                                        V....... n |
research on the strength of such tenuous evidence.
PHR... n

This analysis shows a combination of pattern flow and pattern string, but it would also be true to say that the first sentence is predominantly string, while the second sentence is predominantly flow. This conclusion is based on two observations about the second sentence which are not true of the first sentence. One is that there is greater 'depth' of flow, that is, the analysis runs to three lines instead of two. This is because there are three words in succession which have a pattern — *wish, persuade* and *divert*–instead of two. The second observation is that the patterns are based on verbs and are more central to the organisation of the sentence than are the noun patterns in the first sentence.

We would hypothesise that a string configuration is more typical of certain genres, notably narrative, whereas a flow configuration is more typical of other genres, notably academic and political argument. Testing such a hypothesis, however, involves a number of imponderables, such as finding a measurement of pattern string and pattern flow, so that different texts may be compared statistically.

We are not in a position at the present time to offer answers to these problems, but we can illustrate the issue by considering some extracts from narrative and argument to illustrate the hypotheses. The following four paragraphs have been selected at random on the basis of suitable length. They have not been selected to fit a predetermined idea. In some cases, so that the analyses will fit on to a single line, part of a sentence has been omitted.

Example of spoken narrative. This example is taken from Brazil (1995: 24). Punctuation has been added, and some false starts omitted.

(9)   *A friend of mine told me this amazing story the other day. She'd been shopping and she came back to this multi-story car park that she's been in and it was kind of deserted. And as she was walking towards her car she saw this figure sitting in the passenger seat. She thought 'What's that I've been burgled'. And as she walked towards the car feeling a bit scared this person got out of the car and it was a little old lady.*

Table 8.19

A friend of mine told me this amazing story the other day.
　N........*of*...n | V.... n..........................n |

She'd been shopping and she came back to this multi-story car park that she's
　　V......-ing | V...... adv...prep............................ n | n
been in and it was kind of deserted.
V......prep# | V................. adj |

And as she was walking towards her car she saw this figure sitting in the passenger seat.
　　　　V..........prep.............n | V..........n........ -ing
　　　　　　　　　　　　　　　　V........prep.................... n |

She thought 'What's   that I've been burgled'.
　V.......... quote
　　　　　　V..n | *be*.....V-ed |

And as she walked towards the car feeling a bit scared this person got out of the car
　　　　V..........prep.............n | V................. adj | V...P....*of*....... n

and it was a little old lady.
　　V..................... n

Note that the symbol # is used to indicate that a pattern appears to be incomplete because one element in it has already occurred. In this case, the pattern is **V prep n**, but the noun occurs before the rest of the pattern because it is a relative pronoun (*that*).

This extract shows very little pattern flow. It is almost entirely composed of pattern strings.

Example of written narrative. This example is taken from Wilson's *Eureka Street* (84). The analysis is in Table 8.20.

(10)   *But for now the important thing was to catch my cat and kill him. I'd nearly cornered him between a bookshelf and a sofa when my doorbell rang loudly. I froze. I thought the Pet Protection League were on my case. I looked at the big clock on my wall. It was after midnight. Belfast isn't the best town for those after-midnight social calls and, as I walked to my front door, I had the familiar fifteen-second feeling that there were two men in bomber jackets and balaclavas with Browning automatics standing at my door with some sincere political objectives. I shucked through it, as I always did, and opened up.*

Again there is little pattern flow, except in the clause beginning *I had the familiar feeling...*, which has a considerable amount of flow.

Example of academic argument. This example is taken from Thomas's *Meaning in Interaction* (1995: 58). The analysis is in Table 8.21.

(11)   *Before I go further into Grice's theory of conversational implicature, I want to interpolate a discussion of the difference between implicature and inference, implying and inferring. There are two reasons for doing this. The most important is that it is the confusion of these two levels of interpretation which is at the root of some misunderstandings of Grice's theory. The second is that in Britain, if not in other parts of the English-speaking world, there is widespread misuse of the terms themselves — people frequently say 'inferring' when they really mean 'implying'.*

In this extract, the main configuration is pattern flow, with pattern strings being something of a rarity.

Table 8.20

But for now the important thing was   to catch my cat and kill him.
            the..ADJ......... n....... v-link..to-inf
                                V............. n | V.. n |

I'd nearly cornered him between a bookshelf and a sofa when my doorbell rang loudly.
            V........... n | PREP........ n...............and..n | V |

I froze.
   V |

I thought the Pet Protection League were on my case.
   V......... that
                            V...... prep.... n |

I looked at the big clock on my wall.
   V......... *at*............. n |

It was after midnight.
it..V.... prep..n |

Belfast isn't the best   town for those after-midnight social calls and, as I walked to my front door,
         V.........................n
            ADJ-S..n......*for*..n. | V.........prep...........n |

I had the familiar feeling that there were two men in balaclavas standing at my door with
   V.......................n
            N..........that
                      there..V.............n...........................-ing
                                V...........prep...n |

some sincere political objectives.

I shucked through it, as I always did, and opened up.
   V........... *through*..n | V | V......... P |

Table 8.21

Before I go further into Grice's theory of conversational implicature,
     V............. P.................. n
             N........ *of*......................... n |

I want to interpolate a discussion of the difference between implicature and inference.
  V...... to-inf
     V................. n
          N.............. *of*....... n
                 N.............. *between*..n................. *and*..n |

There are two reasons for doing this.
there...v........... n
      N.......... *for*.-ing
           V....... n |

The most important [reason] is that
             N..............that
it is the confusion of these levels of interpretation which
it..v....... n... which
     N.............. *of*...........n
           N....... *of*..n |
is at root of misunderstandings of G's theory.
V.pr.n
   N.... *of*..n
       N........................... *of*........ n |

The second [reason] is that in Britain, there is widespread misuse of the terms themselves —
       N............. that
             there..v.................... n
                N........ *of*....... n |

people frequently say 'inferring' when they really mean 'implying'.
       V... quote | V....... quote |

Note that the words *first* and *second* are used as pro-forms for the noun *reason* and have the pattern that normally belongs to *reason*. In the analysis, the noun is inserted to enable the pattern to be shown.

Example of journalistic argument. The next example is taken from an article by Nick Sparrow in The Guardian (11.6.97) with an analysis in Table 8.22.

(12)   *Whether or not history repeats itself, 2001–2 could easily provide the*
       pollsters with a much tougher test of their methods. This makes an
       honest review of the different methods used in 1997 not only desirable
       but essential. We should avoid the temptation to bask in the perceived
       glory of success and learn instead from the experience. For example,
       every poll asks people what they voted in the previous election. Such
       data, potentially, offers the perfect way of ensuring the political
       balance of any sample. But received wisdom ran that some people
       forget how they voted last time and some others apparently prefer to
       reconcile their past votes with their present intentions.

Table 8.22

Whether or not history repeats itself, 201 could provide the pollsters with a tough test of the methods.
        V......... pronrefl | V............... n........... *with*..............n
                                               N... *of*.......n |

This makes an honest review of the different methods used in 1997 not only desirable but essential.
   V....................... n...adj.......... &...adj |
        N.........*of*......................n |

We should avoid the temptation to bask in the glory of success and learn instead from the experience.
      V.............n
         N...............to-inf
              V..... *in*.......n
                     N......*of*.n | V................. *from*.......n |

For example, every poll asks people what they voted in the previous election.
            V..... n..........wh
                   n   V# |

Such data, potentially, offers the perfect way of   ensuring the political balance of any sample.
          V...........................n
            N.....*of*...-ing
                V................................n
                     N.......... *of*........n |

But received wisdom ran that some people forget how they voted last time
        V... that
                  V........wh
                  adv   V# |

and some others apparently prefer to reconcile their past votes with their present intentions.
         V........to-inf
             V...........................n.......*with*......................n

---

Note that the symbol & is used to indicate that coordination has been used within a pattern.

Again, pattern flow is the predominant configuration here. This extract also demonstrates a third configuration in the sentence

(13)   *This makes an honest review of the different methods used in 1997 not only desirable but essential,*

where the pattern **V n adj** (*makes a review desirable*) is interrupted by another pattern: **N *of* n** (*a review of the different methods used in 1997*). In other words, the writer begins one pattern, flows into another, then loops back to the final element of the first pattern. We call this configuration 'pattern loop' (see also Section 8.4).

There is not enough data here to draw definite conclusions about the interaction of genre and pattern configuration. However, we perhaps have enough to formulate an observation and some hypotheses. The observation is that:

a. all kinds of discourse exhibit both *pattern string* and pattern flow.

In other words, there is no kind of discourse that precludes either pattern flow or pattern string. The same could probably be said of pattern loop, though we have insufficient evidence at the moment to be certain of this.

The first hypothesis is that

b. different genres prioritise different configurations, with narrative and argument at opposite ends of the spectrum.

Extensive analysis of these and other genres would be necessary to confirm or disconfirm this hypothesis. Although we would expect the hypothesis to be confirmed in broad terms, we also suspect that the picture is somewhat more complex. In the extract from *Eureka Street* (example 10) above, for example, pattern string predominates, except in the sentence that represents the emotional climax of the paragraph, which comprises several examples of pattern flow. From this and other examples of the same kind, we derive our second hypothesis:

c. in a discourse made up predominantly of pattern strings, an episode of pattern flow may indicate a kind of climax.

In the next section we look at the kinds of discourse patterning that our discussion so far has overlooked.

8.4 Collocation and clause collocation

8.4.1 *Introduction*

The kind of patterning that has been discussed so far in this chapter is not, of course, the only kind of patterning that is exhibited in naturally-occurring discourse. At least three further contributing factors to the patterns of discourse need to be taken into account:

1. Coordinating and subordinating conjunctions both occur with clauses and might therefore be said to have the pattern **CONJ cl**. Where a subordinating conjunction occurs at the beginning of a sentence, it might be said to have the pattern **CONJ cl cl**, indicating that two clauses follow the conjunction, one being a subordinate clause, the other the main clause of the sentence.
2. Clauses with certain lexical items in them are closely associated with other clauses of a particular kind. For example, a clause containing the lexical item *not quite* is typically followed by a clause beginning with *but* (unless *not quite* itself occurs in the phrase *but not quite*). We might say that *not quite* has a pattern ***not quite...but***, as in the example

> (14)   *The Grand is probably not quite as luxurious as it was, but it has been agreeably restored.*

3. Individual lexical items collocate with one another to varying degrees, sometimes to the extent that a group of words might be considered a single phrase. This was discussed briefly in Section 8.1. The importance of collocation, and how collocates are calculated, has been widely discussed in the literature on corpus linguistics (see, for example, Sinclair 1991: 109–121; Barnbrook 1996: 87–106; McEnery and Wilson 1996: 71; Stubbs 1996: 157–193).

8.4.2 *Subordinating conjunctions*

The first of these phenomena — subordinating conjunctions — has not appeared in our discussion so far because those patterns which define a word class have been omitted. Subordinating conjunctions are always associated with two clauses, either in the pattern **cl CONJ cl** or in the pattern **CONJ cl cl**, so the information has not been included. However, to illustrate the difference inclusion of these patterns would make to an analysis, consider two sentences from texts that have appeared before in this chapter. The first is from the final example in Section 8.3, and is analysed in Table 8.23.

Table 8.23

Whether or not history repeats itself, 2001–2 could provide the pollsters with a test...	
CONJ..............cl..............................cl	
V......... pr-refl |	V................ n............ with....n

The second is from the 'Space Agency' text from Section 8.2, and is analysed in Table 8.24.

Table 8.24

While the ESA are spending money on trips...the scientific community is struggling for funds.	
CONJ.cl... cl	
V.......... n.........on..n |	V............ for..n

The addition of the new patterns alters the pattern-text configuration. Patterns which we previously saw as entering into string or flow relations now seem to be nested inside the overarching conjunction pattern. This is another example of the 'loop' configuration. At a certain point (the end of the first clause), the original pattern of the subordinating conjunction is reasserted.

8.4.3   Clause collocation

To illustrate the other phenomena that we have described above, here is another text. This is a book review from the journal *New Scientist,* 18th November 1995. The first three paragraphs of the review are reproduced here:

(15)   *The 'Sunken Kingdom' Text*

As a rule, books proclaiming the solution of a mystery deal with something that isn't mysterious (Thor Heyerdahl's Easter Island comes to mind) or fail to deliver. The Sunken Kingdom falls into both categories: Plato's Atlantis is a mystery only to those who care; and the 'solution', offered in a readable and well-argued fashion, is not conclusive. Peter James distinguishes between 'believers', chasing the real Atlantis, and 'sceptics' who are hostile to the very idea; but I fear he is omitting a far larger category — those who find this a waste of time.

He assesses the traditional ideas about the site of Atlantis — the Atlantic Ocean, and the supposed link with the volcanic Aegean island of Thera. James then adds an interesting account of Plato's life and work, sometimes heavy-handed in his idolisation of Plato and denigration of Aristotle.

> *So far so good. Previous ideas about Atlantis are shown to be*
> *unsatisfactory, because they all begin by taking some of Plato's state-*
> *ments as gospel, but then discard one or another of them to make a*
> *theory work. Aristotle dismissed Atlantis as a fabrication — after all,*
> *he should know, being a pupil of Plato — so you might expect James*
> *to agree and write it off as an elaborate allegory. But he cannot resist*
> *building up his case for sticking another pin in an overcrowded map.*
> Paul Bahn: 'Trouble with Atlantis' *New Scientist* 18.11.95

There are no subordinating conjunctions in this extract, but there are examples of other clauses that seem to be associated with each other. Using the notion of clause relations (Winter 1977; Hoey 1983), it can be observed that the text is built on contrasts, between what is usual (*As a rule*) and this case, between the good (*So far so good*) and the bad (*But he cannot resist*), between how something begins (*they all begin by taking...*) and how it continues (*but then discard...*), between what might be the case (*you might expect*) and what is the case (*But he cannot resist*). These observations can be expressed as a set of intuitions about how particular lexical items prospect others. Intuitively, we might suppose that

As a rule	prospects	*The Sunken Kingdom [falls into both categories]*
So far so good	prospects	*but [he cannot resist]*
begin by –ing	prospects	*but [then discard one or another...]*
you might expect	prospects	*but [he cannot resist]*

The phrase *as a rule* is intuited to predict information about a specific instance, which may or may not contradict the general information which follows *as a rule*. This hypothesis was tested in the Bank of English corpus (323 million words). One hundred lines, randomly selected, of *as a rule* were taken (out of 664 altogether), from which only those which began a sentence (*As a rule*) were selected. Instances of *As a rule of thumb* were omitted, leaving 36 lines. Of these, 16, just under half, supported the hypothesis in that general information was followed by specific information, usually contradictory. In the other 20 lines, the general information was not followed by specific information. If we were to adopt our 'pattern grammar' terms to describe this, we would have to say that the most frequent pattern with *as a rule* was **PHRASE general** and another common pattern was **PHRASE general specific**.

There are 315 occurrences of *so far so good* in the Bank of English. Looking at a random 50 lines, it was found that in most cases — 31 out of the 50 — the phrase was followed by something that contradicted it, often introduced by *but* or *however*. In another 15 cases, there was no such contradiction. In the remaining lines, the phrase followed *but* and therefore itself constituted the contradiction. Again looking at this in pattern terms, we might note the existence of the pattern: **PHRASE contradiction**.

The phrase *begin by taking* led to the hypothesis that using the verb *begin* with the pattern **V** *by* **-ing** would prospect a contrary action. However, examination of the Bank of English fails to support this hypothesis. Of 50 lines selected from a total of 1401 instances of this pattern, only a handful were followed by an indication of a contrary action, and it was not felt that this constituted a pattern.

Turning now to the phrase *you might expect*, which was hypothesised to prospect a contradiction, evidence from the Bank of English overwhelmingly supports this. Looking at those instances where the phrase begins a sentence (*You might expect*) — 41 lines — all but two fit the hypothesis. The pattern again is **PHRASE contradiction**.

The next step is to map these patterns on to the text itself. As we are now dealing with longer stretches of discourse within each pattern, the single line representation has to be abandoned. The first phrase is *as a rule*, which has the pattern **PHRASE general specific** (the phrase is followed by a general clause and then by a specific clause). The mapping is shown in Table 8.25.

Table 8.25

As a rule, books proclaiming the solution	*of a mystery deal with something that*
PHRASE...general...	
V...................... n V.....*with*..n	
N..................*of*....n	
isn't mysterious or fail to deliver. <u>*The Sunken Kingdom*</u> *falls into both categories.*	
....specific	
V..... adj V... *to-inf* V.....*into*......... n	

In this case the phrase *as a rule* is operating rather like a subordinating conjunction, except for two things. Firstly, the pattern extends across two sentences instead of one and the relation between the two clauses (the general and the specific) is paratactic rather than hypotactic. Secondly, the pattern is expressed in terms of meanings ('general' and 'specific') instead of the group, phrase or clause types that we normally associate with patterns. *As a rule* is certainly not a subordinating conjunction, but it is associated with the same kind of pattern configuration i.e. pattern loop.

A similar configuration arises in the case of the phrase *you might expect*, as shown in Table 8.26.

Table 8.26

---

you might expect James to agree and write it off as an elaborate allegory.
...... PHRASE...
      V........ n.........to -inf....&...inf
         V | V....... n..P... *as*......................n

But he cannot resist building up his case for sticking another pin in an overcrowded map.
   contradiction
        V...... -ing
         V.......... P........ n
             N.....*for*..-ing
                 V...................... n....*in*.......................... n

---

There is a complicating factor here in that the verb *expect* has a pattern itself which is independent of the pattern associated with the phrase *you might expect*. Because of this, there is a discontinuity in the pattern, in that given the pattern **PHRASE contradiction**, the 'contradiction' element does not immediately follow the 'phrase' element, but follows the patterns prospected by a word in the phrase. We might want to represent this discontinuity in the pattern, for example in this way — **PHRASE...contradiction** — but in any case the pattern configuration is the same: pattern loop.

A more dramatic case of discontinuity occurs in relation to the phrase *So far so good*. Although this phrase is sometimes followed immediately by the contradiction, in the *Sunken Kingdom* text, two sentences intervene. These sentences are not prospected by *so far so good*. The pattern loop therefore begins with *so far so good*, is suspended for two sentences while other patterns intervene, and is taken up again at *but he cannot resist...*.

Thus the utterance *But he cannot resist...* is prospected by two items: *you might expect* and *So far so good*. This prospection by two items illustrates another phenomenon, that of two (or more) patterns accumulating, so that a single clause (or other group of words) represents an element of the same type in both patterns. This is illustrated in Table 8.27, in a simplified representation that ignores a large amount of other patterning present.

Table 8.27

So far so good. Previous ideas about Atlantis are shown to be unsatisfactory, PHRASE...
because they all begin by taking some of Plato's statements as gospel, ...
but then discard one or another of them to make a theory work. ....
Aristotle dismissed Atlantis as a fabrication — after all, he should know, being a pupil of Plato — ....
so you might expect James to agree and write it off as an elaborate allegory ....
...PHRASE...
But he cannot resist building up his case for sticking another pin in an overcrowded map. contradiction contradiction

To conclude, then, there are two major pattern configurations — pattern string and pattern flow — a third which is associated largely with subordinating conjunctions and clause collocation — pattern loop — and a fourth which may also be associated with clause collocation — pattern accumulation. It will be interesting to discover whether further research confirms or adds to these configurations.

8.4.4   *Collocation*

In the discussion above, certain word sequences, *as a rule, so far so good* and *you might expect,* have been treated as 'phrases'. That is, they have been treated as single, multi-word items which have patterns in the same way as single-word items do. There is a long tradition of research on phrases in lexicography and in second language acquisition (see Chapter 1), much of which assumes that phrases can be unambiguously identified as different in kind from ordinary word associations.

Another concept which is traditional in linguistics is that of collocation. Firth (1957: 11) famously commented that "You shall know a word by the company it keeps", and the study of words and their 'company' has been greatly aided by the development of computer technology (see, for example Barnbrook 1996 and Stubbs 1996). Sinclair (e.g.1991) has extended the notion of collocation into the 'idiom principle', which states that certain groups of lexical items commonly occur together and therefore, for the language user, constitute a single

language choice rather than a series of choices. One of the important consequences of the idiom principle, and of collocational studies in general, is that it
breaks down the artificial barrier between the phrase and the non-phrase. It is
replaced by a concept of more and less, that is, two or more lexical items
collocate with each other more or less strongly, leading to a phraseology that is
more or less fixed, more or less in conformation with the idiom principle.

Again responding intuitively to the *Sunken Kingdom* text, we isolated from
the first paragraph the following groups of words as worthy of investigation
using the resources of the Bank of English:

as a rule
books proclaiming
books...deal with
solution of a mystery
fail to deliver
comes to mind
falls into both categories
a mystery... to
hostile to...idea
waste of time
find ... waste of time

To identify the extent of the idiom principle involved in each case, we ask, 'how
frequent is this combination of words in the Bank of English?' and 'how much
stronger than random is each combination?' To answer the second question, we
use the t-score software used with the Bank of English (for a discussion of
statistical work on corpora, see Stubbs 1996; for a critique of t-score, see Stubbs
1995). Briefly, t-scores measures the degree of certainty that two words co-occur
with greater than a chance probability. It therefore gives a measure of significance of the co-occurrence. A t-score of 2 or more is held to be significant. Here
are the results for each of the word sequences mentioned above. In each case the
calculations have been performed on the 323 million word Bank of English.

As a rule

There are 664 occurrences of *as a rule*. Taking *rule* as the node (26874 occurrences), '*a + rule*' has a t-score of 23.1, and '*as + x + rule*' has a t-score of 21.2
(where '+' means 'is followed by' and '*x*' means 'any single orthographic
word'). These t-scores are very high, and with the frequency information indicate
that *as a rule* is a strong collocation.

books proclaiming

There are only 6 occurrences of *book/books* followed immediately or with one word intervening by any form of the verb *proclaim*. Taking all forms of the verb *proclaim* as the node (5016 occurrences), the word *book* is not found among the most significant collocates. There are 15 instances of *book/books* occurring within about seven words preceding a form of *proclaim*. Therefore, '*book+proclaim*' is not frequent enough to be a strong collocation. Our hypothesis in this case is not supported.

books...deal with

There are 229 occurrences of the noun *book/books* followed with up to five words intervening by any form of the verb *deal*, followed by *with*. The noun *book/books* is a very high-frequency item (123,442 occurrences) and because of this *deal with* is not significant, but 229 occurrences are enough to suggest that this is a collocation, nonetheless. A more accurate picture would be obtained if, instead of dealing with the numerical positions of words, we could ask for, say, all the verbs for which *book/books* is the subject. *Deal with* would probably be significant in that list.

solution of a mystery

There are only 4 occurrences of *solution of* followed with up to three words intervening by *mystery*. On the other hand, there are 24 lines of *solution to* and *mystery*. *The solution* is more frequently followed by *to* (514 occurrences) than by *of* (186 occurrences). Taking the sequence *the solution of*, with *solution* as the node, the significance of *mystery* occurring after *of* with one word intervening (as in *the solution of a mystery*) is only 1.4. Taking *mystery* as the node, the t-score of *solution* is 4.1, of *solve* is 12.5, of *solved* just over 12 and of *solving* 6.8. Thus, although *solution of a mystery* is by no means a phrase, there is a reasonably strong collocation between *solve/solution* and *mystery*.

fail to deliver

There are 477 occurrences of *fail to deliver*, in 132 of which the pattern for *deliver* is **V**. (The other occurrences are *fail to deliver a letter, fail to deliver on* something, and so on.) Taking the word-form *deliver,* the most significant item immediately preceding it is *to* (t-score 66.4). The most significant words immediately preceding *to,* with their t-scores, are as follows:

failed	16.5
able	13.4
can	11.3

ability	10.7
fails	8.5
expected	8.0
failing	7.9
fail	7.9
he	7.8
unable	7.5
failure	7.4

What is noticeable here is not only the high significance of forms of the verb *fail* and the noun *failure*, but the more general association of *deliver* with words to do with success and failure (*able, ability, unable*). Not only does the actual sequence *fail to deliver* have a relatively high significance, but the more general association between success or failure and *deliver* has a very high significance.

comes to mind

There are 726 occurrences of all forms of the verb *come* followed by *to mind*, indicating that this is a frequent phrase.

falls into both categories

This is an interesting case in that there is only one occurrence of any form of the verb *fall* followed by *into both categories* in the Bank of English, and that comes from this text. This sequence of words, then, is unique in 323 million words. However, if we check on the general profile of *categories*, we find that sequences of this type, if not this exact sequence, are common. Taking *category/ categories* as the node, the words that precede this most significantly are:

this	23.7
two	17.6
three	15.2
same	14.4
different	13.1
other	13.1
each	12.7
these	12.0

Both has a t-score of 5.7, which is reasonably high. What is more important, however, is that anaphoric reference items (including *both*), as well as numbers, are frequent in that position. Preceding that word, *into* (30.7) and *in* (26.7) are very significant. Among the words most significantly preceding these words are *fall* (17.6), *falls* (10.5) and *fell* (7.3). What is significant here, then, is the combination of the phraseology *fall into...categories* and the meaning 'fall into some category or categories already mentioned'.

a mystery to

There are approximately 300 occurrences of *'be a mystery to* someone'. The co-occurrence *'mystery + to'* has a t-score of 6.3, which is relatively high.

hostile to...idea

There are 1036 occurrences of *hostile to*. This would count as an adjective pattern, and is therefore dealt with in the other sections of this book and does not need special mention here. We hypothesised, however, that *idea* would collocate strongly with *hostile to*. Taking *hostile to* as a phrase with *hostile* as the node, the collocation of *idea* is relatively strong, with a t-score of 5.5.

waste of time, find...waste of time

There are 1123 occurrences of *waste of time*. Taking the noun occurrences of *waste* as the node, *time* is the most frequent collocate with one word intervening, with a t-score of 32.9, which is very high. Surprisingly, there were only 8 occurrences of any form of the verb *find* followed with up to five intervening words by *waste of time*.

In most of the cases above, with the exception of *books proclaiming*, a reasonably strong collocation between the intuited items was found. The levels of significance, however, ranged from very high (*as a rule, waste of time*) to relatively high (*comes to mind, be a mystery to*). In some cases (*solution of a mystery, fail to deliver, falls into both categories*) the general meaning seems to be more significant that the exact phraseology (as discussed in Section 4.2.6, Louw 1993 uses the term 'semantic prosody' to indicate this phenomenon). There is no sharp cut-off point between what we might want to call a 'phrase' and a non-phrase.

Although the evidence from the Bank of English suggests that this text is to a large extent built from more-or-less pre-existing 'chunks' (the idiom principle), the phrase 'more-or-less' here hides a multitude of different levels of significance, making it difficult to incorporate these findings into the pattern analysis. If we choose to represent strong collocates as unified items, this necessitates making a binary choice: a sequence of words does or does not represent an item, but the binary choice would mask the true situation. To illustrate what such an analysis might look like, however, Table 8.28 shows the first sentence of the *Sunken Kingdom* text, with an analysis that takes into account word-pattern, clause collocation, and strong word collocations.

Table 8.28

As a rule, books proclaiming the solution of a mystery deal with something
as a rule   *solve............ mystery*
                        books.................,.. deal with
PHRASE..general...
                        V...................... n
                                    N...........*of...* n | V.....*with*..n |

that isn't mysterious (Thor Heyerdahl's Easter Island comes to   mind)
                                                         come to mind

....
        V..... adj | V........ *to*..n |
or fail to deliver
        fail to deliver
....
        V... to -inf

8.5   The theory of a linear grammar

In this chapter it has been argued that a grammar of patterns can be viewed either as a constituent, hierarchic grammar or as a linear one. We have suggested that a linear interpretation may have certain advantages, in particular in allowing the demonstration of pattern flow. In this section we consider further the theory of a linear grammar, suggesting that there are some grammatical problems that it can solve, and asking whether it can be argued to be psychologically correct. We also consider our approach in the light of Brazil's work and that of Halliday.

8.5.1   *The problem of embedded clauses*

One of the paradoxes of traditional English grammar is that a unit at one rank of structure (to use Halliday's terminology) may occur as a component of a unit at the same or a lower rank. Most noticeably, a clause may occur as one of the elements in a clause, as in the following example from Quirk et al. (1972: 833) where the that-clause is traditionally analysed as the Object (though Francis et al. 1996 avoids this analysis; see Section 6.1.3):

(16)   *I regret that he should be so stubborn.*

or as the postmodifier of a noun group, as in the following example, again from Quirk et al. (1972: 874):

(17)   *The fact <u>that he wrote a letter to her</u> suggests that he knew her.*

Halliday (1994: 188, 267) has used the term 'rank-shift' to describe this phenomenon, and argues that it is a necessary feature of his theory of grammar
(1976: 70), but it is arguable that it represents an awkward anomaly in a constituent theory of grammar, and particular in one which is predicated on a concept of
rank. Viewing the grammar linearly and lexically, such problems are avoided.

In example (16) above, the that-clause might be termed an Object on three
grounds:

1. it is needed to 'complete' the verb: 'I regret' by itself does not occur;
2. by analogy with *I regret his attitude*;
3. the transformation 'That he should be so stubborn is regretted' is purportedly
acceptable (though rarely, if ever, found).

Looking at the example from the point of view of pattern, however, we can say
that the verb *regret* prospects either a noun (e.g.*attitude*) or the start of a that-
clause (e.g.*that he should be...*). (Other prospections are possible, of course, as in
'I regret killing him', 'I regret to tell you' and so on.) Once the verb in the that-
clause has been met, the patterns of that verb take over, and the original pattern
of *regret* is no longer relevant. Table 8.29 shows the analysis.

Table 8.29

I regret that he should be so stubborn.
  V........that
               V...... adj

In example (17), repeated here:

(17)   *The fact that he wrote a letter to her suggests that he knew her*

the noun group *the fact that he wrote a letter to her* is the Subject of the clause.
However, if we adopt a linear view, the result is two patterns in a 'string'
configuration, as in Table 8.30.

Table 8.30

The fact that he wrote a letter to her suggests that he knew her.
  N....that
        V.......... n.......*to*..n | V........... that
                   V...... n

This analysis assumes that *fact* predicts the that-clause but not the verb *suggests*. An alternative view will be discussed below in Section 8.5.3.

8.5.2 The problem of 'there'

Another problem that may be solved by the view of pattern as linear is that associated with patterns that begin with the 'dummy subject' *there*. Here are some sentences with clauses which begin with *there* (from Francis et al. 1996: 562–564):

(18)   *Granted <u>there are a great many who are extremely lean and wiry</u>, but others can certainly become overweight.*

(19)   *They get pleasure from the thought that <u>there are whales swimming freely about</u>.*

(20)   *And <u>there are signs that the richer nations are waking up to the broader problem</u>.*

(21)   *<u>There are only 100 places available</u>, so book now.*

(22)   *I just think <u>there are great sources of pain in everyone</u>.*

(23)   *<u>There seemed a note of venom in what he said</u>.*

In each of these examples, the subject *there* is followed by the verb *be* and a noun group. The noun group in each case consists of the following:

(18)   *a great many who are extremely lean and wiry*

(19)   *whales swimming freely about*

(20)   *signs that the richer nations are waking up to the broader problem*

(21)   *only 100 places available*

(22)   *great sources of pain*

(23)   *a note of venom*

In examples (22) and (23), the noun group is further followed by a prepositional phrase (*in everyone, in what he said*). In Francis et al. (1996), the pattern of examples (18)–(21) is given as **there V n** and the pattern of examples (22)–(23) is given as **there V n prep/adv**. This analysis of pattern is a necessary consequence of a constituent view of the pattern, where **n** indicates a whole noun group. However, Francis et al. (1996: 562) also comment that "In this pattern [**there V n**] the noun group often includes a clause such as a relative clause, a that-clause, or a to-infinitive clause, or an adjective group following the noun." The inclusion of this comment reflects an unease with the pattern **there V n**, a sense that this pattern coding does not give all the information it might. In addition, there is what may be seen as an inconsistency in the coding of examples (18)–(23) above. The general rule is that 'something usually follows the noun'. If that 'something' is an independent prepositional phrase or an adverb, it is represented in the coding, but if it is a clause that is part of the noun group, it is not represented. A more satisfactory coding might be something on the lines of ***there* V n cl/group/prep/adv**, indicating that the noun is followed by a clause, a group, a prepositional phrase, or an adverb, but this coding is impossible if **n** is interpreted as meaning 'noun group' rather than 'noun'.

A linear analysis, in which the **n** in the pattern ***there* V n** indicates only a noun, and not a noun group, makes it possible to remedy these problems. Given a linear analysis of this example —

(20)   *And there are signs that the richer nations are waking up to the broader problem.*

— pattern flow would allow us to express all the patterns in the sentence, as the that-clause is part of the pattern **N that** belonging to the noun *signs*. The analysis would look like Table 8.31.

Table 8.31

And there are signs that the richer nations are waking up to the broader problem.
  there..V... n
        N......that
                        V......... P...*to*.................... n

---

A similar analysis would account for sentences such as the one illustrated in Table 8.32, or for any other sentence where the noun itself has a pattern.

Table 8.32

There is a reason for every important thing that happens.
  there..V... n
      N........*for*...........................n

We might want to capture the fact that nouns of this kind — that is, nouns that have complementation patterns consisting of a clause or a prepositional phrase — are particularly frequent following *there* by expressing the pattern as ***there* V n-pat**, where **n-pat** indicates a noun with a complementation pattern.

Where there is a clause following the noun that is not prospected by the noun itself, the analysis would show a pattern string, as in the analysis of example (18), shown in Table 8.33.

Table 8.33

Granted there are a great many who are extremely lean and wiry, but others can certainly become overweight.
there.V...............n | V...................adj...&....adj | V......... adj |

In order to show that the relative clause is in a sense part of the pattern of (is prospected by) *there*, we might propose a new pattern, ***there* V n who/which**, where **who/which** indicates a relative clause. The analysis would then look like Table 8.34.

Table 8.34

Granted there are a great many who are extremely lean and wiry, but others can certainly become overweight.
there.V...............n........who
V...................adj...&... adj | V.........adj |

This would capture the unity of *there are a great many who are* while allowing for the fact that what occurs after *who are* is prospected by *are* and not by what has come before.

The similarly revised pattern for example (19) would be ***there* V n -ing**, and a revised analysis would look like Table 8.35.

Table 8.35

They get pleasure from the thought that there are whales swimming freely about.
V...n
N...........*from*.......n
N..........that
there..V... n...........-ing
V........................ adv

This analysis successfully captures the flowing nature of the patterns in this sentence.

Example (21) above would be accounted for by the pattern ***there* V n adj**, as shown in Table 8.36.

Table 8.36

There are only 100 places available, so book now.
there..V................. n.........adj | V

It is important to recognise that these revisions of the *there* patterns are possible only if one adopts a linear view of pattern, because it is only in that view of pattern that the noun group as a unit can be ignored.

8.5.3   *Linearity and prospection: Brazil's 'A Grammar of Speech'*

The interpretation of pattern that has been presented in this chapter owes much
to David Brazil's *A Grammar of Speech* (1995). In this book, Brazil offers a
view of grammar which is radical in many ways, three of which will be discussed below: it is entirely linear rather than hierarchic; it is based on the notion
of prospection; and it argues that what is and is not possible at any given
moment in an interactive sequence depends on the communicative situation at the
time rather than on an abstract system of grammar. We will here discuss each of
these points in relation to our own approach to grammar, taking the last one first.

Brazil argues that the 'grammar' of a language does not exist in abstract
terms, except as the broadest of generalisations. There are therefore few restrictions on what *might* be said, though some utterances are unlikely. For example,
Brazil (1995: 55) quotes *My friend told* as something that is unlikely to be
complete in itself, not because of an abstraction such as transitivity, but because
"[t]here are probably few situations where ... *My friend told* would satisfy a
conversational need". In a sense this contradicts our 'pattern' approach to
grammar, which is predicated on the supposition that words have some patterns
and do not have others. Our rules are lexical, while Brazil's are situational. We
would say, for example, that the verb *tell* has the patterns **V n** and **V n n** (among
others), but not the pattern **V** except in the sense 'give away a secret' (as in
Many children know who [the bullies] are but are not telling). On the other hand,
our rules do arise out of the observation of many situations. When we say that
the verb *tell* does not have the pattern **V**, we mean that there is corpus evidence
for the verb *tell* with the pattern **V n** but there is no (or very little) corpus
evidence for *tell* with the pattern **V**, except in the sense mentioned. In other
words, we give information about what has been observed to occur, what has not
been observed to occur, not about what, hypothetically, could or could not be
said. This approach is not the same as Brazil's, but it is not inconsistent with it.

Brazil (1995: 205) himself does cite several instances of what he calls 'constraints' that are dependent on specific lexical items. He comments that *She
agreed* may in the right circumstances be complete, but that *She found* or *She
piled* are very unlikely to be complete in themselves. We might rephrase this as
saying that whereas *agree* does have the pattern **V** (among other patterns), *find*
and *pile* do not have this pattern. Brazil's refusal to accept that certain patterns
of use can be ruled out completely (utterances are 'very unlikely', not 'impossible') finds an echo in our unwillingness to say that a particular word *never* has
a particular pattern, only that it does not, at this time, typically have a particular
pattern.

The second important feature of Brazil's work that relates to our own is the notion of grammar as prospection. The term 'prospection' is used to indicate that something that occurs in a discourse leads the reader or hearer to expect that some other thing will occur. For example, Sinclair and Coulthard (1975) argue that in a classroom exchange, a teacher's question predicts (or prospects) a response from a pupil, which in turn predicts (or prospects) an evaluation of that response by the teacher.

Brazil expresses the minimalistic syntactic requirements referred to above in terms of "chaining rules" (Brazil 1995: 47–56) which specify the kind of word that is expected to follow any other kind of word: the first element of a chain is a noun, which prospects a verb, which may in turn be followed by a noun, an adjective, an adjunct, or by nothing. Each of these choices in turn lead to further prospections. For example, a noun such as *Jemima* prospects a verb, which might be, say, *drove* or *felt*, and this in turn prospects nothing (meaning that the chain has come to an end), an Adjunct such as *quickly*, an epithet such as *ill* or a noun such as *the Rover*. Depending on the choices made, the speaker would say:

(24)   *Jemima drove* or

(25)   *Jemima drove quickly* or

(26)   *Jemima felt ill* or

(27)   *Jemima drove the Rover.*

Which utterance is actually used would depend on what had gone before in the discourse and what the purpose of the discourse was. We might in addition note that, as has been discussed above, the prospection is restricted by the lexical items involved. For example *Jemima felt* prospects an epithet but *Jemima drove* does not.

Sinclair and Coulthard talk about prospection in terms of a one-to-one match between a prospecting item and a prospected one (Tadros 1994 uses the term 'prediction' to indicate a similar one-to-one match in written discourse). Brazil's use of the concept is slightly different in that a single item, a verb, for example, prospects a choice from a limited range of possibilities. The match is not one-to-one but one-to-a few. Our use of the term 'prospection' is similar to Brazil's: a word such as *tell*, for example, prospects a range of possibilities, including 'tell someone', 'tell someone something', 'tell someone what to do', 'tell someone to do something' and so on. If we take an sequence such as *told me a story*, and argue that *told* prospects the two noun groups, we do not mean that this is the only prospection associated with *told*, but one of them.

The reason that the notion of prospection is a useful addition to the metalanguage of patterns is that it enables us to talk about a prospection being fulfilled, and this in turn allows us to deconstruct groups and clauses and to deal with patterns linearly. For example, if we take the pattern **V n n** and talk about it in terms of what it 'consists of', the only sensible way of describing the constituents is as a verb group and two noun groups. It would not be accurate to say that **V n n** 'consists of' a verb and two nouns. On the other hand, it is perfectly reasonable to talk about the verb prospecting two nouns. Even if the first noun is not followed immediately by the second noun, this does not present a problem for a linear description provided that the metalanguage of prospection is used. For example, a linear interpretation of

(28)   *I told an old friend of mine the story of Rumpelstiltskin*

might read thus:

'told'   prospects (among other possibilities) noun + noun
'an'   prospection not fulfilled yet, prospection still active
'old'   prospection not fulfilled yet, prospection still active
'friend'   first part of the prospection fulfilled, prospection still active
'of'   prospection not fulfilled yet, prospection still active
'mine'   prospection not fulfilled yet, prospection still active
'the'   prospection not fulfilled yet, prospection still active
'story'   prospection fulfilled; also prospects (among other possibilities) *of* + noun
'of'   first part of the prospection fulfilled, prospection still active
'Rumpelstiltskin'   prospection fulfilled.

Our linear analysis, shown in Table 8.37, is a visual representation of this.

Table 8.37

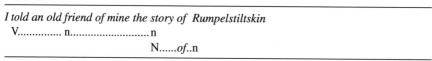

I told an old friend of mine the story of Rumpelstiltskin
    V............... n........................... n
                                N......*of*..n

Similarly, our linear treatment of clauses within patterns (e.g. **V that**) demands a notion of when a prospection has been fulfilled. The discussion in Section 8.2 about whether **V that** patterns should be interpreted as pattern flow or pattern string depends entirely upon a notion of prospection and its fulfilment.

Before we leave this discussion of prospection, let us return to the example from Quirk et al. that we quoted above:

(17)   *The fact that he wrote a letter to her suggests that he knew her.*

We argued above that *fact* prospects the that-clause but not the verb *suggests*. If we are operating within the parameters of what is prospected by a particular lexical item, this is undoubtedly true. However, Brazil's concept of 'chaining rules' suggests that there is also a general prospection that operates whenever a noun occurs at the beginning of a chain. The minimum chain proposed by Brazil is 'N V', that is, a noun followed by a verb. In general terms, then, we can say that *fact* does prospect a verb, though this is not determined by the nature of the lexical item *fact*, but simply by its word-class. *Fact*, then, prospects two things — the that-clause, and the following verb — and one prospection is put on hold while the other is fulfilled. This in turn would lead us to revise our analysis of the sentence as an exemplification of 'pattern string'. Instead, we have an example of 'pattern loop', as shown in Table 8.38.

Table 8.38

The fact that he wrote a letter to her suggests that he knew her.
N.. V
N....that   V........... that
V.......... n........ *to*..n   V...... n

Finally, we turn to Brazil's linear approach, which he works through more rigorously than we have done in this chapter. We have in this chapter come across many examples where a linear interpretation of a pattern leaves much of an utterance or sentence unanalysed. For example, in 'I told an old friend of mine the story of Rumpelstiltskin', the words 'an', 'old' and 'the' were described simply as not fulfilling the prospection of *told* represented by the pattern **V n n**, they were not analysed in themselves. A completely linear grammar demands that they be analysed, and this is what Brazil does. He notes, for example, that certain word-classes prospect other word-classes. A determiner, for instance, prospects a noun. We would express this in terms of a determiner having the pattern **DET n**. Similarly, for Brazil, an adjective (or epithet) prospects a noun. We have the pattern **ADJ n**. The advantage of Brazil's analysis is that it allows a completely linear representation. His analysis of

(28)   *I told an old friend of mine the story of Rumpelstiltskin,*

for example, would be as shown in Table 8.39.

Table 8.39

I	told	an	old	friend	of	mine	the	story	of	Rumpelstiltskin
N	V	d	e	N+	p	n	d	N	p	n

where small letters indicate the this element does not fulfill a prospection of the chaining rules, and the plus sign indicates that an element is reduplicated (the noun in this case). Our complete analysis of the same sentence (Table 8.40) would have to use separate lines, in order to express all the patterns, so that the appearance would be one of embedding or a hierarchy, even though the analysis is in fact linear.

Table 8.40

I told an old	friend	of mine the	story of Rumpelstiltskin			
N.V						
V................. n................................... n						
DET...... n		DET..n				
ADJ..n		N...... *of*..n				
N..............*of*..n						

8.5.4 *Halliday and the metaphor of metalanguage*

We have argued that patterns can be viewed in terms of constituency grammar or in terms of linear grammar. Constituency is in a sense the conventional view, and needs no further justification. Aitchison (1976: 22–24), for example, provides an entertaining and convincing argument for the necessity of constituent grammar. The view of grammar as linear is less obvious. In this chapter we have argued that a linear interpretation of patterns is plausible and that in some respects it is more satisfactory than a constituent interpretation. For theoretical support of this view we rely on Brazil (1995).

We now turn to the question: can these apparently inconsistent views of pattern be reconciled? Halliday (1982: 226; 1994: 35) talks of clauses, and texts, having different kinds of structures. While acknowledging that the term 'structure' normally implies "clearly defined boundaries", he goes on to argue:

> ...while this kind of segmental organization is characteristic of the clause as representation, the clause in its other guises — as message, and as exchange — departs somewhat from this prototype. In its status as an exchange, the clause depends also on prosodic features — continuous forms of expression, often with indeterminate boundaries; while in its status as message it tends to favour culminative patterns — peaks of prominence located at beginnings and endings. (Halliday 1994: 35)

To describe these structures — the segmental, the prosodic and the culminative — Halliday (1982: 226) uses the terms 'particle', 'field' and 'wave', which he borrows from Pike (1959), who in turn has borrowed them from science. Pike uses the terms to illustrate the fact that language, like physical phenomena such as light, may usefully be described in different ways for different purposes. Halliday systematises this by suggesting that different aspects of an instance of language (a clause or a text) are most satisfactorily viewed as either particle (the ideational metafunction), field (the interpersonal metafunction) or wave (the textual metafunction). We have suggested no such division of function, however, but have suggested that for some purposes, patterns are best seen in constituent terms, and for other purposes they are best seen linearly. We might adopt the term 'particle-like' for our constituent analysis, and the term 'wave-like' for our linear analysis. Pattern grammar, then, is both particle-like and wave-like.

This inconsistency can only be tolerated if the metalanguage of grammatical analysis is seen as a metaphor. Just as a writer or speaker may choose to talk about life as a container one moment and as a game of chance the next (Lakoff and Johnson 1980: 51), so a grammarian may find it useful sometimes to talk of the pattern **V n** as 'a verb group followed by a noun group' and sometimes to talk of it as 'a verb that prospects a noun'. The first view sees the components 'verb group' and 'noun group' as if they were a series of railway carriages, each one with a beginning and an end. The second view sees the verb pattern as a railway track along which the speaker-train proceeds until 'points' are reached in the form of a noun pattern, when the speaker-train transfers to this new track. Neither view is more 'correct' than the other, but each may have its uses.

Interestingly, Halliday (1993a: 116) also uses the analogy of particle and wave representations of light when discussing two contrasting ways which English uses to interpret states and processes. Halliday illustrates these with several examples, including the following:

(29)   *We now start experimenting mainly in order to test whether things happen regularly as we would expect if we were explaining in the right way.*

(30)   *Experimental emphasis becomes concentrated in testing the generalizations and consequences derived from the theories.*

Commenting on these two modes of expression, Halliday notes the following features:

The language represented by (29) is complex in the sense that it consists of several clauses, related to each other paratactically or hypotactically. It is grammatically 'congruent', typical of spoken or speech-like language. It views the world dynamically, as a world of process.

The language represented by (30) is complex in the sense that it uses complex noun groups and is lexically more dense. It is grammatically 'meta-phoric', typical of writing or writing-like language. It views the world synoptic-ally, as a world of things.

Halliday refers to the first mode of expression as 'doric' or 'choreographic' and to the second as 'attic' or 'crystalline'. Analyses of Halliday's examples using a linear approach to pattern grammar are shown in Table 8.41.

Table 8.41a

We now start experimenting mainly in order to test whether things happen regularly .
V..... -ing | V....wh
        V   V

as we would expect if we were explaining in the right way.
        V......#| V |

Table 8.41b

Experimental emphasis becomes concentrated in testing the generalizations and consequences derived from the theories.
        V.......................... adj
                        ADJ.............. *in.*-ing
                                V............. n...................... &... n | V-ed.....*from*.......n

---

We would describe the first example as characterised by pattern strings, the second by pattern flow. Viewed linearly, these strings act as a counterpoint to the choreographic clause complex identified by Halliday, while the pattern flow is a dynamic aspect of the predominantly crystalline character of the second example.

Halliday has identified two kinds of complexity here: complexity of clause complex, and complexity of group. We have added a third kind of complexity — complexity of pattern — that may run counter to the other two.

CHAPTER 9

Summing Up

9.1 Patterns and phraseologies

Put very generally, a pattern is a description of the behaviour of a lexical item, or one of the behaviours of that item, as evidenced in a record of large amounts of language use. This evidence is most readily obtained from a large, electronically-stored corpus. The term 'pattern' is sometimes used to describe everything about the phraseology of a word. For example, the pattern of *shred* in

(1)   *there was not a shred of evidence to support such remarks*

might be described as:

negative + *a* + *shred* + *of* + noun = abstract = assessment of certainty

This captures the fact that the phrase *a shred of* is typically followed by an abstract noun such as *evidence* or *truth*, which assesses certainty or truth, and that it typically occurs in a broadly negative clause (phrases such as *a shred of meat*, where the meaning is concrete rather than abstract, are found, but much less frequently). The pattern may be illustrated by a single example, but it can be observed as a pattern only when a large number of instances of *shred of* are seen together.

In this book, however, following the Collins COBUILD Grammar Patterns series (Francis et al. 1996; 1998), we use 'pattern' to describe a more generalised statement of behaviour. The pattern of *shred* as illustrated above is expressed as *a* **N** *of* **n**. That is, the noun *shred* follows the determiner *a* and is followed by a prepositional phrase beginning with *of*. The facts about the negative clause, and the nature of the noun in the prepositional phrase may be given separately, but they do not occur as part of the pattern statement.

Our use of 'pattern' has both advantages and disadvantages. As a description of the behaviour of an individual word (or sense of a word) it is clearly incomplete, and must be supplemented by other information (as is done, for example, in the definitions of the Collins COBUILD English Dictionary). On the other hand, it allows us to group together words which share pattern features, but which may differ in other respects in their phraseologies. For example, let us take the pattern **N** *as to* **wh**, where a noun is followed by *as to* and a clause beginning with a wh-word. A number of nouns have this pattern, including:

a. *debate, discussion, guess, question, speculation*
b. *confusion, doubt, uncertainty*
c. *answer, clue, explanation, evidence, indication*
d. *suggestion, advice*
e. *idea, opinion*

There is, however, a considerable amount of further information that can be given about each of these nouns. For example:

a. *answer* in this pattern is often used with a broad negative, as in *no one has come up with a definitive answer... nor was there any easy answer... there's no right or wrong answer... there are no cut and dried answers... there seem to be more questions than answers.* The wh-word following *as to* is often *why*, though a range of other words is also found.
b. *debate* in this pattern is often modified by an adjective or determiner indicating a large quantity, as in *much debate... a lot of debate... growing debate... considerable debate... full and fierce debate.* The wh-word following *as to* is often *whether*; *why* is not often found here.
c. *advice* in this pattern often follows a verb indicating having or obtaining, as in *have some advice... seek professional advice... I wanted your advice... give him some advice... obtaining legal advice.* A range of wh-words are found after *as to*, though rarely *why*.

In other words, each of these nouns has its own specific phraseology, but a useful generalisation can be made about the pattern that they share: **N** *as to* **wh**.

The patterns that we discuss in this book and in Francis et al. (1996; 1998) are for the most part complementation patterns. That is, they describe what follows the verb, noun or adjective under discussion. There are some exceptions, notably the patterns with *it* and *there*, but complementation is the norm. For verbs, this is an adequate description. Little additional information needs to be given, except that in some cases the verb is reciprocal and has a plural Subject, and in some cases the verb group is typically negative or includes a modal. In the pattern **V that**, for example, one sense of *agree* has a plural Subject, indicating reciprocity:

> (2)   *Scientists agree that these lumps of matter must originate in the asteroid belt*

mind is used in the negative:

(3)   *She tried not to mind that he was always late*

and *credit* is used with *cannot*

(4)   *I can't credit that he wouldn't tell me.*

In the case of nouns, however, the pattern may involve what comes before the noun rather than what follows it, and details of modification in the noun group itself may be part of the pattern. This is particularly true of patterns that begin with a preposition (*at* N, *by* N, *in* N and so on). For example, the pattern *at* N (Francis et al. 1998: 265–272) consists of the preposition *at* and noun group. That noun group sometimes has no determiner: *at church, at college, at home, at school, at sea, at university, at work* and so on. In some cases, the determiner can be specified: *at the airport, at the cinema, at the scene, at the station, at the supermarket; at an angle, at a distance, at a junction; at my elbow, at my heels, at my side*. Other nouns are found in any kind of noun group, that is with any determiner, adjective and so on, following the preposition *at*: *ball, banquet, barbecue, ceremony, concert, conference, dinner party, festival, funeral, hearing, match, matinee, meeting, news conference, party, press conference, rally, reception, summit, talks, trial* and *wedding* are the nouns from one meaning group that behave in this way. Yet other nouns are always or often followed by particular prepositions: *at cross-purposes with, at loggerheads with, at odds with, at variance with, at war with; at the bottom of, at the core of, at the heart of, at the root of*. Most complex of all are nouns which always occur in noun groups with pre- or post- modification. For example, *altitude, depth* and *distance* are used in noun groups following *at*, but not by themselves. Examples include: *at an altitude of twenty thousand feet, at a depth greater than that, at a greater distance*.

Where it is possible to reflect these details, we do so. Our coding, like any coding, is a compromise between the general and the specific, an attempt to describe the trees while keeping the forest in mind. The compromise for nouns appears to demand something that is closer to phraseology than that for verbs does.

9.2 Questions of theory

9.2.1   *Is theory necessary?*

In this book, we have argued that using a large corpus to study grammar will lead to observations about language that it has not been possible to make before.

In this section, we shall take some tentative steps towards considering the implications of this for theories of grammar and of language. First, though, we need to ask whether this discussion is necessary. Could we not simply present the evidence, without relating it explicitly to theory?

Halliday (1994: xii) considers a similar question with relation to his *Introduction to Functional Grammar* and concludes that "'facts' are constructed by theories; there can be no such thing as a theory-free description of grammar". He might have added that both facts and theories are, in a sense, constructed by methods; every description of grammar is dependent upon the method employed to arrive at it. Stubbs (1996: 231) suggests that, for linguistics since the development of corpora, "[t]he situation is similar to the period immediately following the invention of the microscope and the telescope, which suddenly allowed scientists to observe things that had never been seen before." He goes on to argue that new methods do more than simply confirm or deny previously-held beliefs: "When new quantitative methods are applied to very large amounts of data, they always do more than provide a mere summary. By transforming the data, they can generate insight" (Stubbs 1996: 232). New methods, in any field of enquiry, lead not only to more data, but to data of a different kind, and this in turn can inspire new theories.

The method of language investigation that has been described in this book is indeed theory driven, in that it is based upon two assumptions:

1. It is assumed that the behaviour of individual words is important. Because of this assumption, concordance lines for individual words are the raw material for investigation;

2. It is assumed that patterning that can only be observed when the researcher looks at large amounts of language is important. Because of this, concordance lines from a very large corpus are used.

Below we will summarise and discuss the two main theoretical statements, arising from this method, that have been made in this book — that lexis and grammar are not distinguishable, and that sense and syntax are associated — before returning to the question of what a theory of language based on a corpus is like.

9.2.2   *Lexis and grammar*

We have argued in this book, following Sinclair, that the observations of pattern and phraseology made using a large corpus blur the traditional distinction between lexis and grammar. Put simply, a description of a word and its patterns cannot be classified under the heading either of 'lexis' or of 'grammar'. For example, if we note that *want* is often followed by a to-infinitive clause, it is not possible to decide whether this is a fact about lexis (the collocation of *want* and *to*) or a fact about grammar (the distribution of to-infinitive clauses). Because, as we have argued (again following Sinclair), patterns are so central to the description of language, this cross-classification cannot be dismissed as a marginal peculiarity, but it must count as a challenge to the distinction between lexis and grammar itself, so that the word 'grammar', if it is used at all, must comprise information about lexis as well as information about syntax. Here we explore some of the consequences of this redefinition.

Before we do so, however, it is worth noting that our argument is somewhat different from that employed in Systemic-Functional Linguistics, which also unites lexis and grammar, but in a continuum, with lexis taken to be the most detailed ('delicate') level of grammatical description. Halliday (1994: xii) describes grammar and lexis as essentially the same phenomenon, which may be described from either perspective, hence the term 'lexicogrammar' (Halliday, 1994: xiv). Hasan (1987/1996) shows what this might mean in practice: system networks are presented, with each lexical item representing the end point of a unique set of choices. Hasan (1987/1996: 76) expresses it thus: "When the network reaches a point where further uniqueness cannot be postulated, this is the logical endpoint; and the total selection expression ... will, among other things, specify some formal structure(s) known as 'lexical item(s)'." There appear to be two problems here. Firstly, although Halliday notes that the lexicogrammar can be described from either end of the continuum, the use of networks does suggest directionality, with lexis downgraded to the end-point of grammar. Our own description suggests that taking lexis as the starting point leads to a very different kind of grammar. Secondly, there appears to be no place for what Sinclair calls the 'unit of meaning' (see Section 1.4), that is, the co-selection of a whole phraseology. For example, Johns (1995) uses an example of a pattern of co-occurrence in a corpus of economics texts which is exemplified by

(5)   *The dam is costing the government $2million dollars a month,*

which is used to evaluate rather than simply to describe, and which might be expressed as:

(noun = project) + *is costing* + (noun = organisation) + (noun = amount) + (noun = time period)

It is difficult to see how this pattern of co-occurrence, with its restrictions on noun-type and verb aspect, and with its implied meaning of negative judgement, could be expressed as a sequence of network choices. Butt (personal communication) suggests that it could be done if the end-point of networks were seen to be a 'bit of language' rather than necessarily a lexical item, but networks would probably have to be radically reinterpreted to allow this to happen.

Both Halliday and Sinclair, however, contradict the orthodoxy of structural linguistics, in which lexis and grammar have traditionally been seen as separate entities, with grammar being the most important, because the most easily generalisable, constituent. Joseph (1998: 93) argues that Saussure, for example, could have posited the idea of a common *langue* only if he conceived of grammatical structure being "the essential core of language", because he was "perfectly aware that words mean different things to different people". Joseph continues, mimicking Saussure's view: "Grammar is the girders, the 'real' structure, words merely the bricks which form the façade".

Taking a more specific example of the same phenomenon, Francis (1993: 140–141) points out that Quirk et al. (1985: 1393) describe the structures exemplified by

(6)   *You must find it exciting working here*

without indicating the necessary lexical restrictions: the verb occurring before *it* is most typically *find*, while the adjectives occurring after *it* belong to a limited set of meanings, most frequently *difficult, hard* and *easy*, but also a range of adjectives indicating other evaluations, such as *exciting*. Thus her criticism is two-fold:

1. Quirk et al. tend to downplay the lexical side of grammar; although they are primarily concerned with what 'can' and 'cannot' be said in English, they do not extend this concern for demarcation to lexis;

2. They do not distinguish between what is possible and what is typical; *find it difficult* is more frequent than *find it exciting*, but Quirk et al. either do not have access to this information or, more likely, do not consider it important.

Quirk et al. would, presumably, retort that the lexical restrictions and probabilities are both a logical consequence of the nature of the structure. If we begin with the clause *working here is exciting*, which clearly realises a reaction to a situation, and if we then make that clause an Object, it is bound to be the Object of a clause about such a reaction, with a relevant verb, such as *find*. It is a fact of life, rather than a fact about grammar, that we most typically talk about how easy or difficult a situation is for us. Francis herself argues the case that

> [t]hese lexical patterns [such as *find it difficult/exciting*] are closely connected with the communicative function of the structure, which is to present a

situation in terms of how it is evaluated, putting the evaluation straight after the verb... The ways in which we typically evaluate situations, using this particular structure, are stereotyped, showing our concerns tend very often to be with how difficult or easy life is made for us... (Francis 1993: 141)

But whereas Francis puts the functional meaning, and its associated vocabulary, at the centre of the description of the structure, Quirk et al. put the formal aspects of the structure (the relationship between *You must find it exciting working here* and *You must find working here exciting*) at the centre, with the lexis less important precisely because it is predictable from function.

This difference is not simply one of emphasis, but raises a question that is crucial to a consideration of the relation between lexis and grammar: what kind of account should be offered for particular language choices. If we agree that

(6)   *You must find it exciting working here*

represents a reasonably frequent pattern of use in English, there are then two possible rationales for why this is so. Those working in the Sinclair tradition argue that the explanation is phraseological: given the pattern **v** *it* **adj** **-ing**, *find* is a frequent realisation of the **v** element and *exciting* is a not infrequent realisation of the **adj** element. For those following Quirk et al. the explanation is structural: English allows an '-ing' clause occurring as Object to be extraposed, with *it* standing in as the dummy Object.

Once we have restored lexis to its rightful place at the centre of language description, the 'phraseology' account is a convincing one. It may not be particularly explanatory, but then neither is the alternative. Let us, however, consider a different, and more extreme, example. Sinclair (1991: 53–56) discusses the different senses of the lemma *yield*, pointing out that some word-forms are particularly associated with particular senses and their patterning. This contradicts the common-sense assumption that, with any given verb, choices of tense and aspect will be determined by context rather than by phraseology. For example, we might assume that the difference between

(7)   *They paint the wall green*

and

(8)   *They painted the wall green*

would be accountable in terms of specific or non-specific time reference, rather than in terms of the preference of this sense of the verb *paint* for one tense or the other. Gledhill (1996), however, takes Sinclair's example a stage further. Using a corpus of research articles in Pharmaceutical Science, he notes that past and present tenses of the verb *lead* followed by the preposition *to* are distinguished as follows (examples are Gledhill's):

Past tense is used with noun groups realising processes associated with the activity of research, as in:

(9)   These *observations* led to comparative *studies*

(10)   *Identification* of major cell response led to the *investigation* of radio-immunization

(11)   These *results* led to the *selection* of a battery of immune assays

Present tense is used with noun groups realising processes associated with biochemical activity, as in:

(12)   *response to DNA damage* leads to an *arrest of the cells*

(13)   This *process* leads to *inhibition* of intracellular concentrations

(14)   *altered membrane transport* leads to *degradation* of the extracellular matrix.

Gledhill comments that "[o]ne rationale for this intriguing difference is to argue that tense and aspect are 'phraseological'... That is, tense is not really optional but comes as 'part and parcel' of the whole expression". Alternatively, of course, it could be argued that the past tense in general is associated with sequences of research activities, as these are likely to be time specific, whereas the present tense might be expected to be associated with sequences of biochemical processes, because these are not likely to be time specific. The first account is phraseological, making the lexis (co-occurrence of noun and verb) the driving force behind grammar (choice of tense). (We could go further and say that tense is not being chosen at all, and that the word-form *leads to* is behaving as a completely separate lexical item from the word-form *led to*, both having different sets of collocations.) The second account is grammatical, making context (time reference) the driving force behind grammar (choice of tense). Both accounts are applicable only to this particular genre, of course.

If the first account seems less convincing, less explanatory, than the second, it is perhaps because we are accustomed to using phraseological accounts only when all else fails: there is no logical reason why we say *strong tea* rather than *powerful tea*, so we accept 'collocation' as an explanation (or in lieu of an explanation), but this remains an exception in our traditional grammatical system. This in turn affects our notion of what grammar is: it explains word-choice in terms of oppositions such as tense, and it is the logical consequence of looking at words in the context of running text. If we place phraseology at the centre of the description, however, we might start to see context-dependent accounts of tense-choice as the exception, to be used when phraseology does not help, for example if *get dressed* were found to be no more or less frequent than *got dressed*. Again, this affects our notion of what grammar is: it sets the specific example against the general norm, and it is the logical consequence of looking at words in concordance lines. Thus, a change in the method of observing something must lead ultimately to a change in theory.

9.2.3   *Pattern and meaning*

This book, and the research on which it is based (Francis et al. 1996; 1998), is in a sense an extended demonstration of Sinclair's assertion that "[t]here is ultimately no distinction between form and meaning" (1991: 7 and *passim*). We have argued, in chapters 4 and 5, that sense and syntax are associated, while raising the question of what exactly that association means. In this section, we will discuss two further issues: the lack of one-to-one correspondence between form and meaning, and the question of dictionary senses of words.

The argument that sense and syntax, or meaning and pattern, are associated, is based on two pieces of evidence. Firstly, when a word has more than one meaning, the meanings tend to be distinguished by having different patterns. For example, the verb *reflect* has three main meanings:

a. one has to do with light and surfaces, and is exemplified by

 (15)   *The sun reflected off the snow-covered mountains* and

 (16)   *The glass appears to reflect light naturally*;

b. another has to do with mirrors, and is exemplified by

 (17)   *His image seemed to be reflected many times in the mirror*;

c. the third has to do with thinking, and is exemplified by

 (18)   *We should all give ourselves time to reflect*

 (19)   *I reflected on the child's future*

 (20)   *Things were very much changed since before the war, he reflected.*

Examples are from the Collins COBUILD English Dictionary (1995: 1387).

Each of these meanings typically occurs in a particular phraseology, that is, collocating with different types of noun or pronoun (*the sun, the glass; the mirrors; we, I, he*) and with a different complementation pattern: **V prep, V n;** *be* **V-ed; V, V *on* n, V that**. Although this alignment between meaning and pattern is particularly neat, we must point out that these patterns indicate only the most typical uses of the verb. It might well be possible to invent utterances which do not conform to the patterns given above and yet which are not unacceptable English, such as *The mirror was so scratched it would no longer reflect*. Such invented (or genuine) examples do not invalidate the generality, but they remind us that the given patterns indicate typical usage and tell us when a usage is unusual; they do not set unbreakable parameters.

The second piece of evidence for the association of pattern and meaning is that words with the same pattern share aspects of meaning. This has been exemplified at length in Chapter 4. The argument will not be repeated here, but again we will draw attention to the limitations of this statement. A list of words that have the same pattern will be divisible in several ways, and different researchers would end up with different sets of groupings. The groupings will in most cases be of different sizes, including sometimes very small groups, and there may well be a 'ragbag' of words which do not fit into any other meaning group. We not believe that this indeterminacy in any way invalidates the assertion that words with the same pattern fall into groups based on meaning, but it does mean that the statement is not one that is provable in any objective way.

From the above we can see that a description of the pattern/meaning association in English is not rule-governed in the sense that subject-verb agreement is rule-governed. It is a grammatical statement of a very different kind.

We now turn to the first of the two issues we mentioned above: the lack of one-to-one correspondence between pattern and meaning. It is true that in many cases the meanings of polysemous words are distinguished by pattern, as in the example of *reflect* above. It is also true that a very few senses of words are identified by occurring in one pattern only. When the verb *eat*, for example, is used with an adverb such as *well* or *healthily* (in the pattern **V adv**), it has the meaning of 'habitually eat food that is good for you'. It is not possible to make this meaning of *eat* without using this pattern, or to use this pattern without making this meaning. (It is possible to use *eat* with an adverb but with a different sense, as in *She ate quickly*. In this case the occurrence of an adverb is not part of the pattern of the verb, because it is not typically associated with that sense of the verb. The pattern of *She ate quickly* is **V**, not **V adv**.) Such a one-to-one correspondence is rare, however. For example, the verb *dock* has two very different senses: it can refer to a ship coming into a dock, or to money or points being deducted. In the first sense, the verb has two complementation patterns: **V** and **V n** (the verb is ergative). Examples of these are:

(21)   *The vessel docked at Liverpool in April 1811* and

(22)   *Russian commanders docked a huge aircraft carrier in a Russian port.*

In the second sense, the verb also has two patterns: **V n** and **V n n**, as in

(23)   *He threatens to dock her fee* and

(24)   *She docked him two points for his mistake*

(Examples are from Collins COBUILD English Dictionary 1995:488). The pattern
V is exclusive to the first sense; thus,

(25)   *The vessel docked*

is correct, but

(26)   *Her boss docked*

is not. It appears that **V n n** is similarly exclusive to the second sense, so that

(27)   *She docked him two points*

is correct but

(28)   *He docked me my boat*

is not. However, because **V n n** has a productive use indicating that someone
does something for someone (Francis et al. 1996:274), *He docked me my boat*,
while unlikely, is not absolutely impossible. The remaining pattern, **V n**, does not
in itself distinguish between the senses (although the senses are, of course,
distinguished by their collocations): both

(29)   *He docked the ship* and

(30)   *He docked the money*

are equally acceptable. In pattern terms, then, the overall behaviour of the two
senses is different, but the behaviours do overlap.

Discussions of the relationship between meaning and pattern, such as that
above, tends to rely on the divisions between senses that are made in dictionaries. The descriptions of *reflect* and *dock* above are based, more or less, on the
divisions between senses that are made in the Collins COBUILD English Dictionary (1995). A statement such as 'If a word has several senses, each sense has
a different set of patterns' suggests that the identification of the sense is done
separately from, and prior to, the identification of theid3 patterns. And, indeed,
this is the case when lexicographers compile dictionaries: the decision as to how
many senses a word has, and where to draw the line between senses, is based on

all the evidence of word usage, of which patterning is a part but not the whole. The lexicographer may, however, distinguish senses in a different way from someone coming to the evidence from a different perspective. Consider, for example, the verb *recover*. The Collins COBUILD English Dictionary (1995: 1381) distinguishes six senses, shown here with their associated patterns:

1. When you recover from an illness or an injury, you become well again: **V from n/-ing, V**;
2. If you recover from an unhappy or unpleasant experience, you stop being upset by it: **V from n, V**;
3. If something recovers from a period of weakness or difficulty, it improves or gets stronger again: **V from n, V**;
4. If you recover something that has been lost or stolen, you find it or get it back: **V n**;
5. If you recover a mental or physical state, it comes back again. For example, if you recover consciousness, you become conscious again: **V n**;
6. If you recover money that you have spent, invested, or lent to someone, you get the same amount back: **V n**.

Clearly, two other divisions between senses are equally possible. One is made on the grounds of collocation and general meaning and might be expressed thus:

1. 'recover' means to become healthy or conscious after you have been ill, injured, or unconscious: the physical recovery sense (CCED senses 1 and 5);
2. 'recover' means to become happy or strong after a period of unhappiness or weakness: the metaphoric recovery sense (CCED senses 2 and 3);
3. 'recover' means to get back money or property that was lost, stolen, invested or lent: the re-obtaining sense (CCED senses 4 and 6).

The other is made on the grounds of pattern alone:

1. to recover (**V**) means to change from a poor state to a better state, either in terms of health, happiness, or weakness (CCED senses 1–3);
2. to recover from something (**V from n**) means to leave a poor state, either in terms of health, happiness, or weakness (CCED senses 1–3);
3. to recover something (**V n**) means to get it back, whether it is something physical such as money, or something abstract, such as health or consciousness (CCED senses 4–6).

Arguably, the CCED distinctions are the ones that are most useful to the learner, but if we ask the question 'Are the senses of *recover* distinguished by their patterns?', the answer must be 'It depends how you identify the senses'. As a hypothesis, then, it is not truly testable. A better question might be: 'If you distinguish between uses of the word *recover* based on its patterns alone, do the resulting categories make sense in terms of meaning?' In other words, is the third set of distinctions above at least as reasonable as the other two? This discussion is relevant to the practical problem of devising computer programmes that will distinguish between the senses of a word automatically. Such programmes tend to be written assuming the validity of dictionary sense-distinctions, and various parameters such as collocations or pattern are tested to see to what extent they fit the distinctions. It is worth pointing out, however, that a reverse procedure might be equally valid: that is, instances of the same word might be grouped according to pattern alone, with the sense distinctions following from that grouping. The idea of a dictionary in which, under each headword, there is a list of patterns and their associated meanings, rather than a list of senses with their associated patterns, remains an intriguing possibility.

9.2.4   *What kind of theory?*

We turn in this section to an important question to which we cannot provide definite answers, only possible pointers: what kind of grammatical theory does corpus investigation lead to?

It is relatively easy to point to traditional ideas about grammar which are challenged by the kind of work we have presented in this book. Some of these are:

a. word classes are challenged (see Chapter 7);
b. constituent units such as groups and clauses are challenged (see Chapter 8);
c. functional categories such as Object, Complement and so on are challenged (see Chapter 6);
d. the traditional distinction between lexis and grammar is challenged;
e. the traditional distinction between grammar and semantics is challenged;
f. the traditional role of grammar as specifying what can and cannot be said is challenged.

In place of these traditional concepts we have the following:

a. grammar includes both lexis and syntax: "any privileges of occurrence of morphemes ... whether these are lexical or syntactic" (Sinclair 1991: 104);
b. meaning and pattern are closely related: "the underlying unit of composition is an integrated sense-structure complex" (Sinclair 1991: 105);
c. grammar sets the individual utterance in the context of what is usually, typically, or often said.

The problem here is that we cannot be specific. We can say that the unit of meaning is important, but we cannot put boundaries to those units of meaning, because, by their very nature, they have fuzzy edges. We can say that sense and syntax tend to be associated, but we cannot specify the nature of that association or its limits. We can make generalisations about what is usually or often said, but we are less certain about what can or cannot be said. We could claim that such things will become clearer in the fullness of time, but it would be more fruitful to acknowledge that what we are looking at here is not simply a different grammar, but a different concept of what grammar is.

Traditionally, the role of a grammar has been to provide an explanation for instances of language use and to provide a unifying theory that will account for all language use. These roles suggest that there is an identifiable 'plot' which lies behind language, whether this plot is conceived of in terms of transformations, or metafunctions, or whatever. Doing grammar with a corpus encourages us to think of grammar differently. Sinclair, for example, comments that "[t]he new evidence suggests that grammatical generalisations do not rest on a rigid foundation, but are the accumulation of the patterns of hundreds of individual words and phrases" (1991: 100). This in turn suggests that a grammar cannot explain, it can only generalise, and that the unifying theories may be more-or-less useful metaphors, but nothing else. We could look for a metaphor that would capture what language, from the point of view of corpus-driven grammar, is like (we have done something like this in Chapter 8); alternatively we could insist that there is no plot, only sets of observations.

This brings us to our final question: Can corpus-driven grammar, that is, a description of language based on phraseology, co-exist with other theories, or must it seek to supplant them?

Stubbs suggests that the kind of grammar proposed by Sinclair might exist alongside other kinds. A corpus, he notes, consists, not of language *per se*, but of a record of language use. Like any record of behaviour, it encourages us to see broad patterns, but it is not the only way that that behaviour may be experienced. To continue the 'weather/climate' analogy developed by Halliday (1993a: 109–110) and adopted by Stubbs, a record of precipitation gives us very different information from that obtained by standing in a shower of rain. Stubbs proposes an "explicitly pluralist position":

> Language, depending on how we look at it, is utterances (unique events, realised by actual physical behaviour), subjective knowledge (individual, personal competence) or the patterns observable across the usage of many speakers, when their behaviour is recorded and made publicly accessible in corpora (1996: 234).

Martin (1998: 164), in a different context, implies an opposing view by arguing against eclecticism in applied linguistics. If a practical application (or, we might add, new evidence) is not served by an existing theory, it is better to encourage the theory to evolve (and absorb the new evidence?) than to reject it in favour of a new theory:

> theories which change through evolution in relation to practical concerns are probably a better investment than formal theories which change capriciously through revolution...

How the world of grammar will respond to the corpus revolution remains to be seen.

9.3 Questions of application to pedagogy

9.3.1 The 'COBUILD' approach

In this section we will consider the role that a 'pattern' approach to lexis and grammar might play in descriptions of English that are useful for teachers and learners of English as a second or foreign language. This aspect of the work is very much associated with the publications produced by COBUILD. The Collins COBUILD English Language Dictionary (1987) and the Collins COBUILD English Dictionary (1995) both incorporate information about the phraseology of individual words in their explanations of those words. For example, at sense 7 of *dim*, in the Collins COBUILD English Dictionary (1995: 459), we find the following explanation:

> (31)   *If you **dim** a light or if it **dims**, it becomes less bright.*

The explanation carries the information that this sense of *dim* collocates with *a light*, and that speakers say either that someone dims the light, or that the light dims. The grammatical coding for this sense of the word makes this information explicit. The word is described as an 'ergative verb' (see Chapter 2), with the patterns **V n** ('someone dims the light') and **V** ('the light dims'). The thinking behind the phraseological approach is described in Sinclair (1987) (and see Chapter 1 for more details).

  In 1990, the Collins COBUILD English Grammar extended the phraseological approach from dictionary to grammar reference book, by giving lists of words that are used in a particular way. It gives, for example, several lists of nouns and adjectives which are followed by that-clauses (p338–339). The adjectives, in particular, are grouped roughly according to their meaning: feelings (*afraid, angry, anxious, confident, frightened, glad, happy, pleased, proud, sad, sorry, surprised, upset* and *worried*); knowledge (*aware, certain, conscious, convinced, positive, sure* and *unaware*); and commenting on a fact (with *it*) (*apparent, appropriate, awful, bad, clear, essential, evident, extraordinary, fair, funny, good, important, inevitable, interesting, likely, lucky, natural, obvious, plain, possible, probable, sad, true* and *unlikely*). This approach was taken to its logical conclusion in the Collins COBUILD Grammar Patterns series (Francis et al. 1996; 1997; 1998). This series raises the question of how it might be used by teachers and how such concerns might fit into a language teaching syllabus.

Although in Francis et al. (1996: xvii-xviii) we suggested that a pattern approach to grammar could be adapted to any type of syllabus, we also pointed out that it is most readily incorporated into a lexical approach (Willis 1990; Lewis 1993). Our emphasis on the behaviour of individual words, which treats grammar as indistinguishable from lexis, corroborates the prioritising of lexis over structure as the organising principle in a language course. Furthermore, our approach is also consistent with the rejection of Presentation-Practice-Production as a model of language teaching (Willis and Willis eds. 1996). It is difficult to imagine a teacher building a lesson around the pattern **V** *on* **n** (or any other pattern), just as it is difficult to imagine a syllabus that consisted of a series of patterns. Rather, it seems that the role of patterns is as input and support to the concept of grammatical consciousness-raising. The role of reference books which detail patterns is to assist the teacher in designing materials to encourage such consciousness-raising.

In this section we consider in more depth the use that a teacher or course writer might make of materials such as those in the Grammar Patterns series. We also consider some objections to the approach under the heading 'Do patterns matter?'.

9.3.2   *Towards a pedagogic reference grammar*

Any reference grammar is designed to give the learner and the teacher information about what is or is not said in a given language or variety (or what can and cannot be said), when to use one word or structure rather than another, and what certain grammatical choices mean. A learner or teacher coming to a volume in the Grammar Patterns series might be surprised. Some expected information is not found at all, such as the meaning of certain tense choices. Some information is given in a very different form. Ditransitive verbs, for example, are treated as one pattern among many. Most of the information in these volumes is of a kind that is not found at all in other reference grammar books, or is touched upon only briefly in those books.

The learner or teacher may be disappointed in that the volumes do not state explicitly what cannot be said, only what is typically, often, or sometimes said. In Swan's (1994) terms, there is no 'demarcation' between the correct and the incorrect. (Owen 1993 objects to the lists in the Collins COBUILD English Grammar on very much these grounds, an objection countered in Francis and Sinclair 1994.) We have argued that, because of the diversity and changeability of language, it is rarely possible to state outright that something 'cannot' be said and that therefore it is justifiable to concentrate on showing what is said.

Although in many ways they are different from other reference grammars, the *Grammar Pattern* volumes are similar in that they provide a resource for teachers and other materials writers to exploit. How may this resource be used? There are probably two main uses, both utilising the potential of the *Grammar Patterns* books to organise vast amounts of information relating to lexis.

The primary use of the *Grammar Patterns* volumes is to give examples of words that behave in the same way and that share an aspect of meaning. This can be used to raise to consciousness information about words which a learner may already have, but in an implicit and unfocused way, as well as to fill in gaps in that information. For example, a learner may wish to express an idea about changing the topic of a conversation, and may have come across the verbs *turn* and *return* used in this context, as in *turn to the problem of... a theme all the writers return to*. Using the fact that these verbs are used with the pattern **V** *to* **n**, the learner can be directed to the relevant meaning group in Francis et al. (1996: 249), where the following verbs are listed and illustrated:

come	*keep*	*skip*
come back	*move*	*switch*
get back	*return*	*switch over*
go back	*revert*	*turn*

The learner can set his or her existing knowledge in the context of a more general observation, can also, perhaps, extend his or her vocabulary in the area of 'talking about topics', and perhaps can choose the most suitable word for the idea s/he wishes to express at this time.

Alternatively, a learner may be consciously directed towards researching a list of words, that list being motivated by meaning and phraseology. For example, if a learner comes across the word *spend* in a sentence such as *I spend most of my wages on food*, he or she may be asked to do a dictionary exercise using the following list (Francis et al. 1996: 409):

| *blow* | *save* | *spend* |
| *fork out* | *shell out* | *waste* |

The aim of the exercise would be to find the meanings of the words listed, bearing in mind that they are all used with the pattern **V n *on* n**. The kind of noun groups occurring after the verb and after the preposition could also be identified in each case, so that a more complete picture of the word use is built up.

A secondary use, and one that demands a little more on the part of the teacher or materials writer, is to identify 'different ways of saying similar things'. The teacher may wish to collect a small number of words and their patterns that can be used to express similar meanings. For example, the teacher may collect verbs, nouns and adjectives that are used with introductory *it* and with a that-clause in order to express a reaction to a fact or piece of news. Some examples are:

(32) *It <u>amuses</u> me that every 22-year-old now wants to own property.*

(33) *It <u>frightens</u> me that kids are now walking around with guns.*

(34) *It <u>puzzles</u> me that people are willing to pay any taxes at all to this Government.*

Verbs in this pattern/meaning group: *amaze, amuse, annoy, appal, astonish, bother, concern, disappoint, distress, disturb, embarrass, frighten, gall, hurt, infuriate, irk, irritate, pain, please, puzzle, sadden, shock, surprise, worry.* (Francis et al. 1996: 530–531)

(35) *It's a <u>pity</u> that we have to meet under such tragic circumstances.*

(36) *It's a <u>scandal</u> that charities like ours are being left out when the Government is making so much money.*

Nouns in this pattern/meaning group: *crime, disappointment, disaster, disgrace, farce, misfortune, mistake, outrage, pity, scandal, shame, shock, tragedy, travesty, worry* (Francis et al. 1998: 249).

(37) *In a way, it's a <u>blessing</u> that Michael is not alive to see what has happened.*

(38) *It was a <u>miracle</u> that no bones were broken.*

Nouns in this pattern/meaning group: *blessing, comfort, fluke, marvel, miracle, relief* (Francis et al. 1998: 249).

(39) *It's far <u>better</u> that you have a computer in the classroom.*

(40) *Isn't it <u>marvellous</u> that these buildings have survived.*

(41)   *It's <u>reassuring</u> that only seven per cent of you have had an accident in your home in the last two years.*

Adjectives in this pattern/meaning group (selection only): *acceptable, admirable, appropriate, beneficial, brilliant, convenient, desirable, fair, fantastic, fine, fortunate, good, helpful, lovely, marvellous, nice, preferable, reasonable, reassuring, right, sensible, terrific, useful, wonderful* (Francis et al. 1998: 482).

(42)   *It is <u>awful</u> that it should end like this.*

(43)   *I sometimes think it's so <u>sad</u> you and Patrick have no children of your own.*

(44)   *It seems extremely <u>unjust</u> that he has never had a starring role until now.*

Adjectives in this pattern/meaning group (selection only): *annoying, awful, crazy, depressing, disgusting, dreadful, horrific, infuriating, outrageous, ridiculous, sad, shocking, silly, terrible, unfair, unfortunate, unjust, worrying, wrong* (Francis et al. 1998: 482–183).

Whereas the reference book writer has a duty to be as complete as possible, the teacher has no such obligation and can select from the lists provided the most frequent or useful words. A curious learner can always be directed to the reference book for further examples.

A third, though more general, value of the reference book to the teacher lies in the change in perception of words and texts that emerges from simply browsing through lists of patterns and meaning groups. Once the teacher becomes aware of patterns and phraseologies in general, these are more easily observed in reading and listening passages in a coursebook, for example, and the teacher is then more able to draw learners' attention to this crucial aspect of English.

9.3.3   'Noticing' and using patterns

A reference grammar of patterns, then, is a resource which can be used in conjunction with other materials to increase learners' ability to recognise and use the words of English. Ideally, however, any work on pattern and meaning would build on and be motivated by a learner's own observations. Current theories of Second Language Acquisition and of methodology suggest that learners learn what they notice (e.g. Schmidt 1990), that they can be encourage to notice particular things (e.g. D. Willis and J. Willis 1996), and that lexis and its patterning is a useful aspect of language to notice (e.g. J. Willis 1997).

A view of language that prioritises patterning is likely to fit most comfortably into a teaching approach which favours consciousness-raising as a way of teaching grammar, and least comfortably with a PPP (Presentation, Practice, Production) methodology. The reason for this is that phraseologies are about detail, in that each lexical item has a unique set of behaviours. Although a pattern grammar can organise this detail in a helpful way, it does not reduce it. It is difficult to see how patterns could be 'presented' in the way that a tense, or a question form, is traditionally presented.

Below is a short reading passage. It is the text of a genuine leaflet, but it has been shortened slightly. Some of the verbs are underlined.

(45)   *Dear Sir or Madam,*

We would like to <u>introduce</u> ourselves to you. We are a group of skilled building tradesmen: carpenter, bricklayer, plasterer, plumber, electrician. We <u>have been made</u> redundant and have joined together to form a mobile workforce.

You the customer can now have first-class work carried out on your property by fully qualified tradesmen at prices you can afford. You do not have to <u>pay</u> for secretaries and other office overheads. We give free estimates. We <u>do not ask</u> for deposits before work starts. We can actually <u>show</u> you, the customer, how to <u>save</u> hundreds of pounds on materials — by employing us.

If you want us to <u>give</u> you a free quotation please telephone us on 0121 700 6000 anytime. We will be pleased to make an appointment to call and see you. If you do not require our services we <u>apologise</u> for troubling you. Just throw this leaflet away. We <u>will not knock</u> on your door.

It is our hope that we may be of service to you and <u>look forward to</u> giving you a free estimate.

There are many ways a teacher might want to exploit this leaflet: as a reading exercise, as a resource for an information-exchange task, as a prompt for role-play, or as a guide for a writing exercise. When these activities have been completed, learners might be asked to focus on the patterns of the verbs. This could be done quite simply, by asking questions such as 'What word comes after *pay, ask, apologise*?' or 'Underline the word that follows *apologise for* and *look forward to*'.

An approach that requires a more sophisticated awareness of patterns would be to ask students to match the pattern of a given sentence with a pattern in the passage. The given sentence would include a verb of the same pattern and similar meaning as the one in the passage. The reference grammar could be used as a source for these verbs. Here are some examples:

Can I present my partner to you?	matches	*introduce ourselves to you*
It was rendered useless	matches	*have been made redundant*
He coughed up for a new bike	matches	*pay for secretaries*
They prayed for rain	matches	*do not ask for deposits*
She taught me how to dance	matches	*can show you how to save money*
We spent a lot on food	matches	*save hundreds of pounds on materials*
He sent me a present	matches	*give you a free quotation*
We made up for insulting him	matches	*apologise for troubling you*
They hammered on the gate	matches	*will not knock on your door*

This matching exercise links what is known to what is unknown. A learner, for example, may be familiar with 'teach someone how to do something' but not 'show someone how to do something', or with 'spend a lot on something' but not 'save money on something', or with 'pay for something' but not 'cough up for something', or with 'apologise for doing something' but not 'make up for doing something'. It also reinforces the concept of pattern, and the link between pattern and meaning.

A potential problem with using authentic texts in this way is that they inevitably use a wide range of patterns; the examples above use seven different patterns, with only one pattern (**V *for* n/-ing**) repeated with three different verbs (*pay, ask* and *apologise*). The patterns have not been selected according to any principle: they are simply what happened to be in the text. A teacher who wishes to reduce the information load may choose to concentrate only on the repeated pattern **V *for* n/-ing**, giving short lists of other verbs with the same pattern:

like *pay: cough up, fork out, shell out*
like *ask: apply, beg, call, clamour, fight, negotiate, plead, pray, shout*
like *apologise: answer, atone, claim, retaliate, make up*

Alternatively, a teacher who has access to a corpus and a concordancing programme may use these to raise awareness of the various patterns of one of the verbs in the passage. For example, a teacher may select the following concordance lines and ask learners to identify the various uses of *save*:

```
      Investors will be able to save up to £9000 in a Tessa
                   You could save over £100 a year
   On average, Orange users save £20 per month
            She reckons she's saved £2000 so far
              Mind you I could save money that way, couldn't I?
```

```
                     the action saved taxpayers thousands of pounds a year
            it's designed to save you a lot of money
 sing custom-made machines could save them money
            they estimate it saved them around £24 million

                     Stella saved £491 on insurance costs
   You get 52 issues for £39 and save £2.60 on the usual price
an wear whatever you want and so save money on clothes
```

9.3.4   *Do patterns matter?*

Perhaps the most commonly quoted argument in favour of a focus on patterns for the learner is that this is what natural English, as produced by native speakers, is like. If the learner wishes to sound 'natural', 'idiomatic', or 'native-like', it is argued, he or she needs to use the collocations, the phraseologies and the patterns of English that native speakers automatically choose. Some writers, notably Prodroumou (1990) and Cook (1998), have argued, however, that many learners do not need to interact with native speakers of English and have no need or wish to sound natural or native-like. Instead, these learners need International English, as spoken by non-native speakers who do not share another language, such as the German tourist in Spain, or the Japanese businessperson in Sweden.

This argument raises two interesting issues, which we will deal with in turn below:

1. What is international English, as spoken by expert or near-expert speakers, like?
2. Is the assumption that patterns are peripheral rather than essential to the production of English correct?

What is international English like? Cook's article implies that the model for most learners of English should be, not the native speaker, but the speaker who operates comfortably in English in international settings. This very reasonable suggestion raises the question of what 'International English' is like, a question which could be answered by collecting a corpus of international speakers. The aim would be to describe the English of 'inter-national' users, not the range of varieties of English such as might be described as 'New Englishes' (Kachru 1986), which are catered for by the ICE corpora and other national corpora. The 'International English' corpus would not be without its problems. For one thing, given the number and variety of speakers of English as an International Language, it would need to be very large indeed. Questions would need to be answered regarding inclusion: would speakers of English as a second (as opposed to foreign) language be included? how 'comfortably' should a speaker be able to speak English to qualify for inclusion, and who would decide this? It would, however, be perfectly feasible to establish criteria and so to construct the corpus. One of the many advantages in doing so would be to be able to distinguish between the idiosyncratic language behaviour of a single speaker and any regularities that might be established by most speakers.

Assuming that such a corpus existed, then, we might ask: what behaviour, in terms of words and their patterns would we expect to see exhibited? There are (at least) three possibilities:

a. For a given word, the International English corpus might show patterning that was similar to the patterning in a corpus of native speaker English. It is possible, for example, that the verb *decide* would typically be followed by a to-infinitive clause, a that-clause, or a wh-clause, or by a limited selection of prepositions such as *on* and *against*, as it is in the Bank of English.

b. For a given word, the International English corpus might show patterning that was consistently different from the patterning in a corpus of native speaker English. For example, the noun *privilege* might typically or often be followed by a to-infinitive clause, rather than by a prepositional phrase consisting of *of* and an '-ing' clause, as is more frequently the case in the Bank of English. The verb *suggest* might, in addition to its other patterns, be shown to be used frequently with the pattern **V n to-inf** (as in 'He suggested me to go'). The verb *emphasise* might consistently be used with the pattern **V *on* n** and rarely with the pattern **V n**. Such regularities, if observed, would not be treated as 'errors' but would be accepted as patterns in International English.

c. For a given word, the International English corpus might show no consistent patterning. For example, there is a sense of the noun *point*, identifiable in the Bank of English corpus and given as sense 7 in the Collins COBUILD English Dictionary, which means 'a particular time or a particular stage of development' and which is often used in the phrase '*at this point*' or '*at the point where*', that is, following the preposition *at* and with a word, phrase or clause which adds further information. It may be that in our corpus of International English no such regularity would be identifiable, that speakers either did not use this sense of *point*, or that it was used by some speakers with *at*, by other speakers with *in, on* or *with*, or that all speakers used this sense of the noun with any preposition, showing no preference for one over the others.

In other words, the International English corpus might show regularities in patterning, either different from or the same as those found in a native speaker corpus, or it might show no regularities in patterning. Probably, different words would behave in different ways, but if, overall, no regularities in patterning were shown, this would suggest that patterns were essentially unimportant, as communication in English would be taking place satisfactorily without them. (We would be very surprised if this turned out to be the case.) If, on the other hand, regularities were observed, this would suggest that patterning is a necessary feature of language.

As we have stressed before, it would be immaterial to this argument whether the regularities were the same as or different from the native-speaker patterns. If the patterns were different, however, they could be identified in a dictionary or grammar book as 'International English' patterns. Similarly, a pattern that was never or rarely found in the IE corpus could be identified as such, giving the learner a choice of models.

Thus we agree with Cook that a serious attempt to describe International English would be a valuable, though massive, undertaking. Until there is evidence to the contrary, we continue to make the assumption that patterns would be important in that description, as they are in descriptions of native-speaker varieties, though we do not assume that the patterns would be the same.

Are patterns essential or peripheral? In the absence of any evidence to the contrary, then, we continue in our belief that patterns are a necessary feature of language. We need to defend this view against the contrary argument that phraseology is a peripheral aspect of language, and that a language may be used perfectly adequately without adopting the specific phraseologies that native speakers use. This argument in turn depends on an assumption that, within language learning, phraseology is relevant only to accuracy, that is, to conformity to an arbitrary norm. This in turn suggests that what is important in language learning is to learn vocabulary and general grammatical rules. Details such as the preferred phraseologies or pattern behaviour of certain lexical items are a refinement that can be added if the learner is particularly anxious to sound indistinguishable from a native speaker, but they are not essential to communication. Patterns, in short, are peripheral to the main business of language teaching.

This is not our view of patterns, and it is worth explaining why. Firstly, as we have discussed at length in this book, we agree with Sinclair's conclusion that pattern and meaning are associated. It follows from this that most words have no meaning in isolation, or at least are very ambiguous, but have meaning when they occur in a particular phraseology. The phraseology, or pattern, is therefore central to the meaning of the word and cannot be treated as separate from it. From the point of view of reception, we might say that phraseology is a necessary part of the redundancy in language; we can afford to mis-hear some words in a dialogue, for example, because we can reconstruct their meaning from the pattern they are used in.

Secondly, patterns are essential to fluency as well as to accuracy. It is an unfortunate learner who has to think of every next word separately when uttering a sentence. In proposing the idiom principle, Sinclair has suggested that most language is composed of more-or-less prefabricated strings. Patterns, in the sense used in this book, are important contributors to these strings. Learning strings rather than individual words enables the learner to compose lengthy utterances with the minimum of effort.

Thirdly, let us reconsider the question of accuracy. We have discussed the question of the native-speaker model above, but let us assume for the moment that a learner does wish to be able to converse with expert speakers of English of a particular variety (which does not need to be a so-called 'native speaker' variety). If this is indeed the aim, and if that variety is the learner's target, then differences between patterns used by the learner and patterns used in the target variety will constitute 'errors'. As with any error, problems in communication are caused not by one occurrence but by a multiplicity, which deny the interlocutor a baseline from which to interpret the 'wrong' part of the utterance. To put this somewhat crudely, a learner does not need to get all patterns right, but needs to get some patterns right, in order to be understood. This applies both to someone learning a foreign language and to someone learning a different variety of their native language.

9.4 Conclusion

Our aim in this book has been to describe a research project into the patterns of English verbs, nouns and adjectives that was carried out at COBUILD during the 1990s, using the Bank of English corpus. We have tried to argue for the 'pattern' as a useful tool in the description of English both for researchers and for language teachers.

We have considered also the theoretical implications behind our work and work in corpus linguistics in general, arguing along with others that the (relatively) new instrument of the corpus inevitably leads, not only to new observations, but also to new models of language that will take full account of those observations. We have noted that corpus linguistics in general, and pattern grammar in particular, tends to cast doubt upon previous orthodoxies, such as:

a. the distinction between lexis and grammar;
b. word class as a robust system of categorisation;

c. functional grammatical categories such as Object, Adjunct etc;
d. constituency grammar, especially units such as group and clause.

In place of these orthodoxies, we have proposed others:

a. that there is a strong association between meaning and pattern;
b. that grammar and lexis are one and the same thing;
c. that grammar may be interpreted linearly as well as in constituent terms;
d. that a multiplicity of grammars, mapping meaning roles on to lexico-grammatical configurations, might be a useful alternative to a general grammar.

In making these suggestions we follow other researchers, especially Sinclair and Brazil. We have tried to add something to the ongoing search for a consistent language theory that is based on the new observations of language made possible by corpora (following Stubbs), but at the same time we have acknowledged that the new theory of language may be less unifying or explanatory than others have been.

While we must wait for a definitive theory of language based on corpora, we can with greater confidence recommend our findings and our methods to language teachers. Phraseology, we have argued, is a crucial aspect of language as a pedagogic object, and patterns are a valuable way of finding useful generalisations among a mass of information about individual lexical items. Language teachers in training, we suggest, should be encouraged to identify patterns as grammar points for learners to notice. This identification can take place in texts, and/or in concordance lines. We look forward to information about patterns being incorporated in language teaching materials, probably in the form of consciousness-raising exercises.

As for the future, we look forward to the development of an automatic pattern identifier. This would allow many important further studies to be carried out. In particular, we could identify which patterns are most frequent or significant in given sets of texts, for example, in spoken English, in newspaper articles, students' essays, and so on. This would in turn allow us to evaluate coursebooks in terms of the patterns they include. We could also match corpora of learners' English with corpora of native speakers' English to identify key points of difficulty.

Other proposals that we have made could also be investigated further, with or without further computational assistance. We have speculated, for example, (in Hunston and Francis 1998) that speakers might accommodate to each other in terms of the patterns they use. Our suggestions regarding the configurations of patterns and text in different genres could also be tested out. Given large corpora collected over periods of time, our hypothesis that language patterns change over time through analogy could also be tested.

Thus, we believe that patterns have a valuable part to play in language theory, in language pedagogy, and in practical investigations of language use. We look forward to seeing this new view of grammar take its place in the meta-language of linguistics.

References

Aijmer, K. and Altenberg, B. 1991. *English Corpus Linguistics: Studies in Honour of Jan Svartvik*. London: Longman.

Aitchison, J. 1976. *The Articulate Mammal: An Introduction to Psycholinguistics*. London: Hutchinson.

Allen, C. 1999. A local grammar of cause and effect. Unpublished MA dissertation, University of Birmingham.

Arnaud, P. and Bejoint, H. (eds) 1992. *Vocabulary and Applied Linguistics* Basingstoke: Macmillan.

Baker, M., Francis, G. and Tognini-Bonelli, E. (eds) 1993. *Text and Technology: in Honour of John Sinclair*. Amsterdam: Benjamins.

Barnbrook, G. 1996. *Language and Computers*. Edinburgh: Edinburgh University Press.

Barnbrook, G. and Sinclair, J.M. 1995. "Parsing COBUILD entries". In *The Languages of Definition: The Formalisation of Dictionary Definitions for Natural Language Processing,* J.M. Sinclair, M. Hoelter and C. Peters (eds), 13–58. Luxembourg: Office for Official Publications of the European Communities.

Biber, D., Conrad, S. and Reppen, R. 1994. "Corpus-based approaches to issues in applied linguistics". *Applied Linguistics* 15: 169–189.

Bolinger, D. 1975. *Aspects of Language*. 2nd edition. New York: Harcourt Brace Jovanovich.

Brazil, D. 1995. *The Grammar of Speech*. Oxford: OUP.

Briscoe, T. and Carroll, J. 1996. "A probabilistic LS parser of part-of-speech and punctuation labels". In Thomas and Short (eds) 135–150.

Carter, R. 1987. *Vocabulary: Applied Linguistic Perspectives*. London: Allen and Unwin.

Carter, R. and McCarthy, M. (eds) 1988. *Vocabulary and Language Teaching* London: Longman.

Carter, R. and McCarthy, M. 1995. "Grammar and the spoken language". *Applied Linguistics* 16: 141–158.

Clear, J. 1996. "'Grammar and nonsense': or syntax and word senses". In *Words: Proceedings of an International Symposium, Lund, 25–26 August 1995* KVHAA *Konferenser 36*, J. Svartvik (ed). Stockholm.

Clear, J., Fox, G., Francis, G., Krishnamurthy, R. and Moon, R. 1996. "COBUILD: the state of the art". *International Journal of Corpus Linguistics* 1: 303–314.

Conrad, S. and Biber, D. 2000. "Adverbial marking of stance in speech and writing". In *Evaluation in Text: Authorial Stance and the Construction of Discourse*, S. Hunston and G. Thompson (eds), 57–73. Oxford: OUP.

Cook, G. 1998. "The uses of reality: a reply to Ronald Carter". *ELTJ* 52: 57–63.

Coulthard, M. 1994. *Advances in Written Text Analysis*. London: Routledge.

Cowie, A.P. 1988. "Stable and creative aspects of vocabulary use". In Carter and McCarthy (eds),126–139.

Cowie, A.P. 1992. "Multiword lexical units and communicative language teaching". In Arnaud and Bejoint (eds), 1–12.

Downing, A. and Locke, P. 1992. *A University Course in English Grammar*. London: Prentice Hall.

Fillmore, C.J. 1968. "The case for case". In *Universals in Linguistic Theory*, E. Bach and R.T. Harms (eds), 1–88. New York: Holt Rinehart.

Firth, J.R. 1957. "A synopsis of linguistic theory, 1930–1955". *Studies in Linguistic Analysis* Special Volume, Philological Society. 1–32.

Francis, G. 1993. "A corpus-driven approach to grammar — principles, methods and examples". In Baker et al. (eds), 137–156.

Francis, G. 1994. "Labelling discourse: an aspect of nominal-group lexical cohesion". In Coulthard (ed.), 83–101.

Francis, G. 1995. "Corpus-driven grammar and its relevance to the learning of English in a cross-cultural situation". In *English in Education: Multicultural perspectives,* A. Pakir (ed). Singapore: Unipress.

Francis, G. and Sinclair, J.M. 1994. "I bet he drinks Carling Black Label: a riposte to Owen on corpus grammar". *Applied Linguistics* 15: 190–200.

Francis, G., Hunston, S. and Manning, E. 1996. *Collins COBUILD Grammar Patterns 1: Verbs*. London: HarperCollins.

Francis, G., Manning, E. and Hunston, S. 1997. *Verbs: Patterns and Practice*. London: HarperCollins.

Francis, G., Hunston, S. and Manning, E. 1998. *Collins COBUILD Grammar Patterns 2: Nouns and Adjectives*. London: HarperCollins.

Garside, R. 1996. "The robust tagging of unrestricted text: the BNC experience". In Thomas and Short (eds), 167–180.

Garside, R. and Rayson, P. 1997. "Higher-level annotation tools". In Garside et al. (eds), 179–193.

Garside, R., Fligelstone, S. and Botley, S. 1997. "Discourse annotation: anaphoric relations in corpora". In Garside et al. (eds), 66–84.

Garside, R., Leech, G. and McEnery, A. (eds) 1997. *Corpus Annotation: Linguistic Information from Computer Text Corpora*. London: Longman.

Gledhill, C. 1996. Scientific innovation and the phraseology of rhetoric: posture, reformulation and collocation in cancer research articles. Unpublished PhD thesis, University of Aston in Birmingham.

Greenbaum, S., Nelson, G. and Weitzman, M. 1996. "Complement clauses in English". In Thomas and Short (eds), 76–91.

Halliday, M.A.K. 1976. *System and Function in Language* edited by G. Kress. Oxford: OUP.

Halliday, M.A.K. 1978. *Language as Social Semiotic: The Social Interpretation of Language and Meaning*. London: Arnold.

Halliday, M.A.K. 1982. "How is a text like a clause?". In *Text Processing: Proceedings of Nobel Symposium 51*, S. Allen (ed), 209–239. Stockholm: Almquist and Wiksell International.

Halliday, M.A.K. 1993a. "Language and the order of nature". In *Writing Science: Literacy and discursive power*, M.A.K. Halliday and J.R. Martin, 106–123. London: The Falmer Press.

Halliday, M.A.K. 1993b. "Quantitative studies and probabilities in grammar". In *Data, Description, Discourse*, M. Hoey (ed), 1–25. London: HarperCollins.

Halliday, M.A.K. 1994. *An Introduction to Functional Grammar*. 2nd edition. London: Arnold.

Halliday, M.A.K. and Hasan, R. 1985. *Language, Context, and Text: Aspects of Language in a Social-Semiotic Perspective*. Victoria: Deakin University Press.

Halliday, M.A.K. and James, Z.L. 1993. "A quantitative study of polarity and primary tense in the English finite clause". In *Techniques of Description: spoken and written discourse*, J.M. Sinclair, M. Hoey and G. Fox (eds), 32–66. London: Routledge.

Hanks, P. 1987. "Definitions and explanations". In Sinclair (ed.), 116–136.

Hasan, R. 1987/1996. "The grammarian's dream: lexis as most delicate grammar". In *New developments in Systemic Linguistics* Vol. 1: *Theory and Description*, M.A.K. Halliday and R. Fawcett (eds), London: Pinter (1987); and in *Ways of Saying: Ways of Meaning*, R. Hasan (C. Cloran, D. Butt and G. Williams eds), 73–103. London: Cassell.

Hoey, M. 1983. *On the Surface of Discourse*. London: Allen and Unwin.

Hornby, A.S. 1954. *A Guide to Patterns and Usage in English*. London: OUP.

Hunston, S. 1995. "A corpus study of some English verbs of attribution". *Functions of Language* 2: 133–158.

Hunston, S. 1997. "What makes English difficult? (And how to make it easier)". Paper read at the RELC Seminar *Learners and Language Learning*, Singapore, April 1997.

Hunston, S. (ed). 1998. *Language at Work*. Clevedon: BAAL/Multilingual Matters.

Hunston, S. and Francis, G. 1998. "Verbs observed: a corpus-driven pedagogic grammar". *Applied Linguistics* 19: 45–72.

Hunston, S. and Sinclair, J.M. 1999. "A local grammar of evaluation". In *Evaluation in Text: Authorial stance and the construction of discourse*, S. Hunston and G. Thompson (eds), 75–100. Oxford: OUP.

Joseph, J. 1998. "Why isn't translation impossible?". In Hunston (ed), 86–97.

Johns, T. 1995. 'Pedagogic Grammar'. Teaching materials, University of Birmingham.

Kachru, B. 1986. *The Alchemy of English: The spread, functions and models of non-native Englishes*. Oxford: Pergamon.

Kettermann, B. 1997. "Using a corpus to evaluate theories of child language acquisition". In Wichmann et al. (eds), 186–194.

Krashen, S.D. 1981. *Second Language Acquisition and Second Language Learning*. Oxford: Pergamon Press.

Lakoff, G. and Johnson, M. 1980. *Metaphors We Live By*. Chicago: The University of Chicago Press.

Leech, G. 1983. *Principles of Pragmatics*. London: Longman.

Leech, G. 1991. "The state of the art in corpus linguistics". In Aijmer and Alternberg (eds), 8–29.

Levin, B. 1995. *English Verb Classes and Alternations: A Preliminary Investigation*. Chicago: The University of Chicago Press.

Lewis, M. 1993. *The Lexical Approach: The State of ELT and a Way Forward*. Hove: LTP.

Louw, B. 1993. "Irony in the text or insincerity in the writer? — the diagnostic potential of semantic prosodies". In Baker et al. (eds), 157–176.

Louw, B. 1997. "The role of corpora in critical literary appreciation". In Wichmann et al. (eds), 140–251.

Martin, J.R. 1998. "Practice into theory: catalyzing change". In Hunston (ed), 151–167.

McEnery, T. and Wilson, A. 1996. *Corpus Linguistics*. Edinburgh: Edinburgh University Press.

Melčuk, I. 1988. "Semantic description of lexical units in an Explanatory Combinatorial Dictionary: basic principles and heuristic criteria". *International Journal of Lexicography* 1/3: 165–188.

Melčuk, I. 1995. "Phrasemes in language and phraseology in linguistics". In *Idioms: structural and psychological perspectives,* Everaert et al. (eds), 167–232. Hillsdale, New Jersey: Lawrence Erlbaum Associates.

Moon, R. 1992. "Textual aspects of fixed expressions in learners' dictionaries". In Arnaud and Bejoint (eds), 13–27.

Moon, R. 1994. "The analysis of fixed expressions in text". In Coulthard (ed), 117–135.

Moon, R. 1998. *Fixed Expressions and Idioms in English: A Corpus-based Approach.* Oxford: Oxford University Press.

Nattinger, J. 1988. "Some current trends in vocabulary teaching". In Carter and McCarthy (eds), 62–82.

Nattinger, J. and DeCarrico, J. 1989. "Lexical phrases, speech acts and teaching conversation". In *AILA Review 6: Vocabulary Acquisition,* P. Nation and R. Carter (eds), 118–139. Amsterdam: AILA.

Nattinger, J. and DeCarrico, J. 1992. *Lexical Phrases and Language Teaching.* Oxford: OUP.

Owen, C. 1993. "Corpus-based grammar and the Heineken effect: lexico-grammatical description for language learners". *Applied Linguistics* 14: 167–187.

Owen, C. 1996. "Do concordances require to be consulted?" *ELTJ* 50: 219–224.

Pawley, A. and Syder, F.H. 1983. "Two puzzles for linguistic theory: nativelike selection and nativelike fluency". In *Language and Communication,* J.C. Richards and R.W. Schmidt (eds), 191–227. London: Longman.

Peters, A.M. 1983. *The Units of Language Acquisition.* Cambridge: CUP.

Pike, K.L. 1959. "Language as particle, wave and field". *The Texas Quarterly* 2: 37–54.

Prodroumou, L. 1990. "English as cultural action". In *Currents of Change in English Language Teaching,* R. Rossner and R. Bolitho (eds). Oxford: OUP.

Quirk, R., Greenbaum, S., Leech, G. and Swartvik, J. 1972. *A Grammar of Contemporary English.* London: Longman.

Quirk, R., Greenbaum, S., Leech, G. and Swartvik, J. 1985. *A Comprehensive Grammar of the English Language.* London: Longman.

Renouf, A. 1987. "Corpus development". In Sinclair (ed), 1–40.

Rudanko, J. 1996. *Prepositions and Complement Clauses: a Syntactic and Semantic Study of Verbs Governing Prepositions and Complement Clauses in Present-day English.* New York: State University of New York Press.

Schmidt, R. 1990. "The role of consciousness in second language learning". *Applied Linguistics* 11: 17–46.

Searle, J. 1979. *Expression and Meaning: Studies in the Theory of Speech Acts.* Cambridge: CUP.

Short, M., Semino, E. and Culpeper, J. 1996. "Using a corpus for stylistics research: speech and thought representation". In Thomas and Short (eds), 110–131.

Sinclair, J.M. 1987. "Grammar in the dictionary". In Sinclair (ed.), 104–115.

Sinclair, J.M. (ed) 1987. *Looking Up: An Account of the COBUILD Project in Lexical Computing*. London: HarperCollins.

Sinclair, J.M. 1991. *Corpus, Concordance, Collocation*. Oxford: OUP.

Sinclair, J.M. 1994. "A search for meaningful units of language". Paper read at the International Symposium on Phraseology, University of Leeds, April, 1994.

Sinclair, J.M. 1995. "Written discourse structure". In *Techniques of Description*, J.M. Sinclair, M. Hoey and G. Fox (eds), 6–31. London:Routledge.

Sinclair, J.M. 1999. "A way with common words". In *Out of Corpora: studies in Honour of Stig Johansson*, H. Hasselgård and S. Oksefjell (eds). Amsterdam: Rodopi.

Sinclair, J.M. and Coulthard, M. 1975. *Towards an Analysis of Discourse*. Oxford: OUP.

Sinclair, J.M. and Renouf, A. 1991. "Collocational frameworks in English". In Aijmer and Altenberg (eds), 128–144.

Skehan, P. 1989. *Individual Differences in Second-Language Learning*. London: Arnold.

Stubbs, M. 1995. "Collocations and semantic profiles: on the cause of the trouble with quantitative methods". *Functions of Language* 2: 1–33.

Stubbs, M. 1996. *Text and Corpus Analysis*. London: Blackwell.

Swan, M. 1994. "Design criteria for pedagogic language rules". In *Grammar and the Language Teacher*, M. Bygate, A. Tonkyn and E. Williams (eds), 45–55. Hemel Hempstead: Prentice Hall.

Tadros, A. 1994. "Prediction in Text". In Coulthard (ed), 69–82.

Thetela, P. 1997. Evaluation in academic research articles. Unpublished PhD thesis, University of Liverpool.

Thomas, J. and Short, M. 1996. *Using Corpora for Language Research*. London: Longman.

Tognini-Bonelli, E. 1996. The role of corpus evidence in linguistic theory and description. PhD thesis, University of Birmingham. Published as *Corpus Theory and Practice*. Birmingham: twc.

van Ek, J.A. 1975. *The Threshold Level*. Strasbourg: Council of Europe.

Weinert, R. 1995. "The role of formulaic language in second language acquisition". *Applied Linguistics* 16: 180–205.

Wichmann, A. 1997. "The use of annotated speech corpora in the teaching of prosody". In Wichmann et al. (eds), 211–223.

Wichmann, A., Fligelstone, S., McEnery, T. and Knowles, G. (eds) 1997. *Teaching and Language Corpora*. London: Longman.

Wilkins, D.A. 1976. *Notional Syllabuses: A Taxonomy and its Relevance to Foreign Language Curriculum Development*. Oxford: OUP.

Willis, D. 1990. *The Lexical Syllabus: A New Approach to Language Teaching*. London: HarperCollins.

Willis, J. 1997. "Exploring lexical phrases: from research to pedagogic practice". Paper read at the IALS Symposium, *Language in Language Teacher Education: New Directions?*, Edinburgh, November 1997.

Willis, D. and Willis, J. 1996. "Consciousness-raising activities". In Willis and Willis (eds), 63–76.

Willis, J. and Willis, D. (eds) 1996. *Challenge and Change in Language Teaching*. Oxford: Heinemann.

Winter, E. 1977. "A clause relational approach to English texts: a study of some predictive lexical items in written discourse". *Instructional Science* 6: 1–92.

Wray, A. 1999. "Formulaic language in learners and native speakers". *Language Teaching* 32: 213–231.

Wray, A. and Perkins, M.R. 2000. "The functions of formulaic language: an integrated model". *Language and Communication* 20: 1–28.

Texts used as examples

Adams, D. 1979. *The Hitchiker's Guide to the Galaxy*. London: Pan.

Bennett, A. 1994. *Writing Home*. London: Faber and Faber. Page references to QPD edition.

Holmes, J. 1996. *Women Men and Politeness*. London: Longman.

Stubbs, M. 1996. *Text and Corpus Analysis*. London: Blackwell.

Thomas, J. 1995. *Meaning in Interaction*. London: Longman.

Wilson, R.M. 1996. *Eureka Street* London: Secker & Warburg. Page references to QPD edition.

Newspapers and magazines

The Guardian 28th May 1997.
The Guardian 11th June 1997.
New Scientist 18th November 1995.
What's On 31st May-13th June 1997.

Appendix

In June 1999, the Bank of English comprised 329 million words, consisting of the following corpora:

Corpus	Word count	Description
BBC	18.52 million	Transcripts from broadcasts of the BBC World Service, 1990–1991
National Public Radio	22.26 million	Transcripts from broadcasts of National Public Radio, Washington, 1990–1993
British Spoken	20.18 million	Transcriptions of mainly spontaneous, informal conversation from all parts of Britain, recorded post-1990
Economist	12.13 million	Issues of The Economist magazine, published in London, 1991–1995
Guardian	24.26 million	Issues of The Guardian, published in London, 1995
Independent	19.45 million	Issues of The Independent, published in London, 1990 & 1995
New Scientist	6.09 million	Issues of The New Scientist magazine, published in London, 1992–1995
The Sun/News of the World	6 million	Issues of The Sun and The News of the World, published in London, 1998
Times	20.95 million	Issues of The Times and The Sunday Times, published in London, 1995–1996
Today	26.61 million	Issues of Today, published in London, 1991–1995
British Books	42.13 million	Books published in Britain, post-1990, including 384 non-fiction, 188 fiction
British Ephemera	4.72 million	Junk mail, brochures, leaflets, newsletters etc, collected in Britain, post 1990
British Magazines	30.14 million	Issues of 66 different periodicals, general and specialist interests, published in Britain 1992–1993
US Books	32.66 million	Books published in USA, post-1990
US Ephemera	1 million	Junk mail, brochures, leaflets, newsletters etc, collected in USA, post 1995
US News	8.58 million	Issues of The Wall Street Journal, published in New York, 1989; issues of the Palo Alto Weekly, Palo Alto, 1994
Australian News	33.38 million	Issues of the Courier Mail and Sunday Mail, published in Brisbane, 1994–1995

Name Index

Subject Index